The Man with the Black Dog

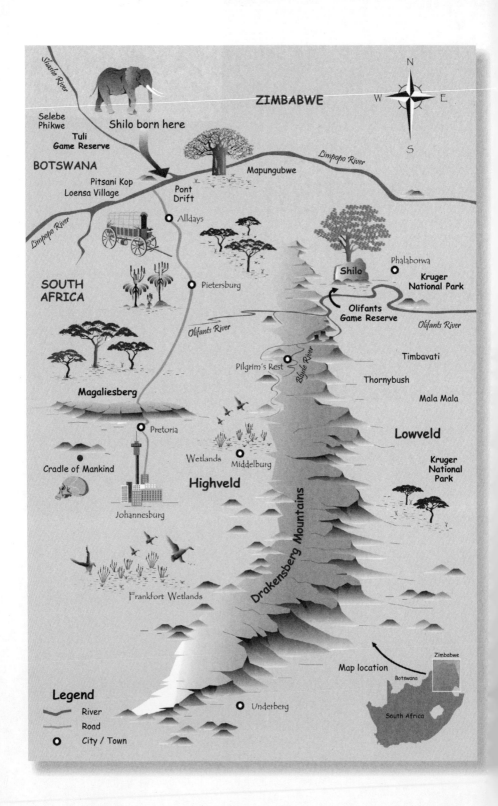

The Man with the Black Dog

Mario Cesare

Jonathan Ball Publishers
Johannesburg and Cape Town

In Memory of Shilo

First published in trade paperback in 2011 by
JONATHAN BALL PUBLISHERS (PTY) LTD
PO Box 33977
Jeppestown
2043

Twitter: www.twitter.com/JonathanBallPub
Facebook: www.facebook.com/pages/Jonathan-Ball-Publishers/298034457992
Blog: http://jonathanball.bookslive.co.za/

ISBN 978 1 86842 462 7

Cover design by Michiel Botha, Cape Town
Map by Cartocom
Typesetting by Triple M Design, Johannesburg
Set in 10.5/14 pt ITC Stone Serif Std
Printed and bound by CTP Book Printers, Cape

CONTENTS

PREFACE

Until one has loved an animal,
A part of one's soul remains unawakened.

ANATOLE FRANCE

Dig deep enough and you will invariably find that everyone has a story to tell. Sadly, however, the vast majority of people never get to tell theirs. Their lifelong learning literally dies with them, and what was once born of flesh and blood becomes constituent of the surrounding dust. As dramatic as this may sound, it's true.

I also believe that the matrix of our environment governs what we become. No living organism is above this law; none of us can escape its influence on us, and no two of us are identical. As individuals we adapt and respond to the various stimuli out there in varying degrees and in various ways. Essentially it is what makes each of us unique, shapes us and moulds our way of thinking from the earliest age, particularly the way we interact with each other and the myriad other creatures with which we share the planet. In my case this has stemmed from a love of animals and the natural environment, which grew into an all-consuming passion and a career in nature conservation.

Many of my childhood escapades, both imaginary and real, were fuelled by what I gleaned from the pages in books. The common element in the character make-up of most of the story books and plays I grew up with was animals, mainly dogs. In some, they played a minor role, but mostly they were integral to the story, the principal characters. In those days children in suburbia knew less about wild animals and the circle of life than they do today, but dogs we could associate with. From the scruffiest little terrier to the largest canine couch potato, they were part of our everyday lives, and almost everything we did, we did together.

* * *

Since primitive man first brought wolf cubs back to his cave, dogs have been one of life's greatest gifts to mankind. This book is largely about the privilege of having shared a part of my life with a very special one of these gifts. I don't wish to hint at being an expert on dogs, far from it; however, of my love for our canine friends in general, and more particularly this one, there can be no question, and for this, there is no measurable qualification necessary.

From my earliest memory, dogs stand out as having played the most important role in bringing me closer to nature. Even while I could not have been more than a clumsy cub to them, the dogs I knew as a child always treated me as a kindred member of their pack, even taking me on forays into the surrounding veld when they went exploring, which pricked my interest and stimulated an awareness of the environment. This was the beginning of an insatiable appetite for adventure and the outdoors.

Next to the classic dog tales of yore – *Old Yeller, White Fang, Lassie* and *Jock of the Bushveld*, to name but a few – Shilo's tale is a comparatively modern account of the life of a game ranger and his dog in the African bush. In fact, the odyssey of Shilo had already become part of my life years before the movie of *Jock of the Bushveld* was made. The revival of this iconic tale on the big screen prompted numerous game rangers and wannabe game rangers to go out and acquire 'Jock' look-alikes. While their Staffies may have resembled Jock in looks, alas, for most that's where the romantic notion and similarity ended.

* * *

This book is more than a nostalgic collection of vignettes on the life and adventures of a game ranger's dog. It is a tribute to the greatest dog I've known, an unfolding journey through life, from my and Shilo's earliest days together, which has inevitably included many exciting interactions with the rich diversity of wildlife we encountered, from elephants in Botswana's Tuli Reserve, to leopards in the Lowveld, and from teal in the wetlands of the Drakensberg, to trout in the frigid streams of the snow-covered highlands near Lesotho. Naturally, along the way, I have included stories of pluck and peril involving other dogs and the valuable lessons learned, while inescapably, attentive readers will find jostling for their attention many more observations and relevant anecdotes arising from a career that now spans decades in wildlife conservation.

This memoir would be incomplete without the people, the dogs and incidents that helped shape my early thinking before Shilo became an integral part of this multifarious way of life.

In the fourteen years we spent together, Shilo was never away from my side for more than a few days at a stretch, and that only happened on two unavoidable occasions. To the locals who didn't know my name, and even to some of those who did, I was 'the man with the black dog'. Shilo was my constant companion in the bush, a brave colleague and one of the finest wildfowl re-trievers I have ever known. Above all, he was the embodiment of unconditional love and devotion.

Many of our wonderful experiences together are liable to emerge from my memory at any time with all the freshness of the day they happened. However, there has been the odd occasion of frustration, when I found myself wanting of more expression with the pen, to capture the emotions and sentiment of the moment. Suffice it to say, I have endeavoured to paint a picture of our life together, to re-live that beautiful relationship as it unfolded, and trust that through the coming pages, you will too.

1

AS FAR BACK AS I CAN REMEMBER

I have often wondered what path my life would have taken if I had been born in the bush, under a mosquito net, in a simple thatch-roofed bush camp on the banks of some remote river. Or in a small town steeped in pioneering history, on the border of a big five game reserve, or on a game farm – or any farm, for that matter.

The Queen Victoria maternity hospital in the city of Johannesburg was about as far away as you could get from that romantic scenario. It was there on an icy cold June morning in 1956 that I took my first breath of Africa's air. Insulated and sterilised as it was within the confines of that first world environment, outside its walls lay the rest of Africa.

Until a couple of years later, I don't remember much at all. We lived in an apartment in the suburbs, and although there's not much about the inside of the flat I'm able to recollect, the outside of the block remains vivid in my mind. I remember a sandy coloured facebrick building that surrounded a concrete courtyard on three sides. On the side that got the most of what little sun shone into the gloomy quadrangle there were rows of washing lines which stretched from one end to the other, and except for those mornings when they were festooned with laundry, the yard was empty and bleak.

All the kids who lived on that block played in this common yard; basically it was the only recreational area we knew at the time. To spice things up occasionally there was the scowling, crook-backed milkman who would chase us away from his delivery van, brandishing a small stick. Our high-pitched squeals, a mixture of fear and excitement, echoed around the hollow courtyard as we ran on chubby little legs that carried us nowhere fast. I suspect that although he was a scary looking character, he was harmless, but we didn't think so then. However, the cranky old milkman was the least of my worries; it wasn't him I was scared of, I dreaded something else, and although I certainly didn't think so at the time, they were much smaller and quite inoffensive.

In the corner of the courtyard near the back entrance was a grey-plastered, windowless room with an enormous padlock on a stout wooden door with a sign of a skull and crossbones fixed firmly in the middle of it. We never did figure out what it was inside that never stopped droning, but imaginations ran wild. Next to this room was a small roofless enclosure where the dustbins were kept ... a place to be avoided. This was where the green-eyed fluffy monsters I feared so much would hang out. They were quick and lithe, I never heard them approach, and never knew they were there until I'd feel the soft ghost-like brush of fur as they sneaked up from behind and painted my legs with their tails. More than anything, it was the serpentine gyrating of those tails and not so much the feel of their fur that I ran screaming from, and there was no rational explanation for this phobia. Although this fear of cats that haunted my little mind more than anything else as a toddler rapidly disappeared as I grew up, it remains the most vivid of my earliest memories. I could never have dreamed then that my future life would inexorably be entwined with some of the biggest cats on earth – wild African felines many times the size of those fluffy monsters.

* * *

My happiest memories were always those of the little adventures I had outdoors. I enjoyed accompanying my father to his ten-acre plot of land near the Klip River valley, about 40 kilometres south of Johannesburg. 'The farm' as he called it, gave him a much-needed respite from the pressures of working in the cacophonous chaos of the five-star hotel kitchen he managed. Although he dabbled a little with intensive livestock farming, and loved to grow heaps of vegetables and herbs, he never made much money from it. He was proud of what he grew, and derived enormous pleasure from supplying friends and family with fresh veggies, as he invariably gave away far more than he ever sold. There were obvious therapeutic benefits simply to getting his hands dirty with the rich red soil.

Driving through the countryside with the wind whistling through the small triangular windows of the car was always exciting. I remember you couldn't hear this sound driving around town, it was only when the car was going relatively fast on long journeys that the wind whistled through. For me it was a most comforting sound, mostly because I associated it with escaping from the concrete courtyard and cats' tails for something far, far more pleasurable.

I loved the farm, particularly the farm animals my father kept there. Although there were those who found the smell of their dung and urine in the barn and the kraal unpleasant, it was never offensive to me. On occasion when my father wasn't watching, I'd sneak into the milking shed to eat some of the cow's dairy meal, which they were given when being milked. I remember that although crunchy and very dry, it tasted good, not unlike some breakfast cereals sold today in supermarkets at ten times the price. The feed shed next door was filled with bales of fodder and farm implements; it was a great place to look for chickens' eggs, and I would treat each search like a treasure hunt. Many of the eggs I'd find were still warm to the touch.

Of course there were cats on the farm, much wilder than those in the suburbs, and besides the odd glimpse of them around the feed shed, they avoided any contact with people, which suited me just fine. These were working cats which, besides the odd saucer of milk, were never fed, apparently they made a good living off the rats and mice they caught, as well as the odd sparrow that wandered too far into the grain store.

The farm dogs were my best, two huge Alsatians – maybe they seemed so big because I was so small. I distinctly remember the black one was called Satan; he was as black as soot with wolf-like eyes and a very red tongue. The other dog, Wolfie, was light brown with silvery grey guard hairs on his back that stood up when he was angry and made him look so much like the wild grey wolves depicted in story books.

Wolfie was less restrained than evil-eyed Satan; he was always the first out to greet me, rushing up to me with his tail wagging so hard it would sometimes knock me over, his muzzle tickling as he sniffed me from head to toe. My mother was never comfortable with the Alsatians around me, but I loved being with them. One day I followed Wolfie barefoot into a paddock where my father's Jersey bull was kept. I remember not being able to get back out because of the devil thorns in my feet, and each attempt at walking only gathered more thorns. I stood there crying helplessly until an uncle of mine, who was only fifteen years old at the time, came to my rescue. He hoisted me up onto his shoulders and carried me out to safety at a run. Jersey bulls are notoriously short tempered and not to be trifled with, but this enormous animal didn't frighten me, it was just a big cow that nobody ever milked ... and I liked cows. Often I'd stay out all day, seldom bored; only hunger would bring me back to the house.

*   *   *

Our first house was a classic old brick and sandstone Victorian-styled home, complete with wooden-framed sash windows and corrugated iron roof. Two tall date palms stood sentinel over the formal, well-established garden which was liberally planted with masses of hydrangeas and roses of every colour and variety. Rockeries with a selection of aloes and other succulents were incorporated into the terraced layout leading up to the entrance. Halfway to the front door was a large triple-tiered fountain filled with lilies and goldfish, the focus of the local hamerkops which (although primarily frog-eaters) found the bright orange fish provided easy pickings. The paved pathway ended at a wide stairway flanked by Roman-style cast concrete pillars and wrought iron lattice work that supported the roof trusses over the red polished floor of the stoep. Inside, the ornate pressed ceilings looked down on spacious rooms with beautifully polished wooden floors and fittings of Oregon pine, oak and teak. There was a fireplace in the lounge, which we never used, and a huge free-standing coal stove in the kitchen, where we spent many cosy winter evenings huddled together, sipping Milo while listening to ghost stories and plays on Springbok Radio. Television was still a dirty word in South Africa in those days.

Set on an acre stand, which even then was considered large by urban standards, our new home opened up exciting possibilities. Most importantly for me, the space meant the family could now own a dog, a big energetic dog if we wanted. With so much room it could run around, dig holes and play with us to its heart's content. Secretly I wanted my own dog, and though I was too young to take on such a responsibility at the time, I remained determined in my quest. On the day we went to choose a dog at our local SPCA I was so excited that I'm sure some of this enthusiasm must have rubbed off on my parents, because we ended up adopting two! Both were fully grown dogs, and although clearly mongrels of some distant Rhodesian ridgeback heritage, they were good-looking dogs. One of them, obviously the older of the two, was heavier set with large jowls. My father wanted to call him Mussolini, but my mother would have none of it, so we named him Frenchie. The younger dog was leaner and boisterous to a fault, he was called Reggie, and though he'd play a little rough at times, my mother was far more relaxed with him than she was with the two Alsatians on the farm.

Besides the loquat trees which grew along one side of the grapevine-shrouded driveway, the back yard had been planted with a variety of fruit trees. There were apricot, peach, pear and plum trees as well as two massive figs from which my mother would make tons of the most delicious whole-fig jam. To this day, although it remains my favourite, I am reluctant to buy any, not because there's nothing commercially available these days

5

that comes close to my mom's fig jam, but because once the jar or tin is opened, I cannot resist, and usually consume the whole lot in a day!

Recently while shopping at Woolworths, I noticed that a single pomegranate, no bigger than a cricket ball, cost R25! I vividly recalled the long row of pomegranate and quince trees that formed a huge hedge between us and the neighbours. I clearly remember that we never enjoyed the fruit, finding that despite patiently peeling away the loose, bitter folds surrounding the sweet pips, we inevitably bit into them and got more bitterness than sweet. Eating this fruit was just not worth the effort, so the ripe ones would simply fall onto the ground and rot. I still believe that pomegranates are rather overrated as a fruit and overpriced as a result. And so it was with most of the quinces, which the older folk seemed to enjoy and preserved, but which as children we found much too tart to eat fresh.

Next to the row of quince trees, up against the fence, was a thick stand of bamboo. Young boys from all over the neighbourhood would often visit us asking to cut a few of the dry stalks, which were then split and used for building lightweight frames to make kites. We also used this versatile material for crude bows and arrows, spears, swords, tomahawks and tepee frames which kept us amused for hours. Needless to say, we spent a lot of time in and around this stand of bamboo. One day while digging up a few roots and corms for a friend who wanted to take some home to plant his own bamboo stand, I discovered gold!

Everyone knew my mother was an avid coin collector, so, as a rule, any unusual-looking or foreign coin found its way to her collection. But nothing brought in from the far-flung corners of the globe that she'd acquired to date would match the one we found ten metres from our own doorstep!

Standing at the back door so as not to muddy up the kitchen, we handed her what we thought was just another common coin; even so, it was always intriguing to see what it was. She took the little mud-covered coin and washed it in the kitchen sink while four grubby kids and two muddy pawed dogs crowded around the doorway. The grime washed off easily, and seconds later my mother held out a gleaming gold coin as immaculate as the day it was minted! I remember she didn't smile immediately; instead her mouth hung open in surprise. Although at the time we couldn't know what it was, my mother did, she knew coins ... she knew that the gold coin that lay glinting in the palm of her hand was one of the legendary Kruger pounds!

'Where did you find this?' she whispered, turning it over slowly in her fingers.

'In the bamboo patch,' I said.

Under my mother's supervision we spent the next two days digging in that spot. The bamboo roots formed an underground lattice of tough corms that proved extremely difficult to penetrate. Nevertheless, we persisted until there was an excavation the size of a small kitchen table and about as deep as a wheelbarrow – nothing!

* * *

To this day I cannot help wondering who the hapless traveller was that dropped that coin from their saddle-bag at the turn of the nineteenth century, and how he or she must have felt at the loss of something so valuable. Or could this have been just one of the thousands of coins reputed to have made up the famous Kruger millions, which have never been found? Just one from such a trove might never have been missed! However, the reality was that at the beginning of the twentieth century the amount of gold used to mint a single Kruger pound equated to a labourer's earnings for a year, or the down-payment for a small farm. Those were also the days when the last remaining hartebeest roamed freely above the rich goldfields of the Witwatersrand and foothills of the Magaliesberg. I later learned that a small herd of sable antelope, the first ever recorded on the South African highveld, were seen where the old Johannesburg stock exchange used to stand. These must have been interesting and exciting times indeed.

Years later, on one of my rare visits to Johannesburg from the

7

bush, I took a trip down memory lane, curious to see what had become of the house I'd grown up in. Not wanting to arrange a formal visit with the new owners, I simply walked up the driveway of the block of flats next door and peeped over the fence. From there I could see that a lot of changes had been made. The palm trees and garden had been replaced by lawn, and most of the fruit trees I remembered were gone; only the bamboo stand was still there, growing thick and strong as if in timeless defiance. I could see the exact spot where I had found the Kruger pound nearly fifty years previously. As I leant reflectively over the fence I remembered the mini 'zoo' I kept in the yard next to the garage. Besides dogs, hamsters, tortoises, rabbits, white rats and a small aquarium of tropical fish, my passion was a huge walk-in aviary that housed small seed-eating birds, including a variety of wild finches, waxbills and quails.

I suspect it may have been here that a certain seed took root. I'd constantly strive to emulate an environment as close to their natural habitat as possible. It was both creative and rewarding. I would get enormous satisfaction when they eagerly inspected the natural materials I regularly selected and brought in for them from the veld close by. The shyer species were particularly fond of the gnarled hollow tree trunks and thatching grass I provided, some of which they would use to build nests with and breed in – and to me a breeding bird was a happy bird. A huge treat on rare occasions was a chunk of termite mound, which I broke into smaller pieces to reveal the termites scurrying about. It brought out the hunting instinct of even the most delicate little seed-eating birds; even those few birds that weren't partial to termites enjoyed 'ant heap time' – perhaps they simply loved being in amongst the frenetic activity with all the other birds.

Today I find myself doing much the same, striving to maintain an environment in which wild animals are happy and are able to coexist inter-dependently with all the natural props and materials they need to thrive ... except that my 'aviary' is now much, much bigger, and largely self-sustaining. So, whether watching a herd of over a hundred elephants enjoying a mud bath at one of the waterholes on the reserve today, or a couple of dozen waxbills and finches splashing around in a freshly filled bird bath in my aviary all those years ago, the deep sense of satisfaction in me would have been the same. It was already clear back then what path I would be taking in life, and although I knew it was not going to be paved with gold in a fiscal sense, I feel my life is richer for having chosen to walk it.

2

GOD'S IMPALA

At a moderate stretch of the imagination the South African high-veld may once have resembled the pampas of Argentina or the prairies of the midwestern United States. Essentially a high-altitude, naturally treeless plateau of undulating fertile grassland, lightly sprinkled with small bushes in those areas with shallower soils, it is not quite the sweeping, umbrella-thorn-studded savanna usually portrayed as typically African in wildlife documentary films.

The highveld we see today has been greatly altered, for the most part thanks to man's progress and greed. Gold and coal mining activities gave rise to rapid urban development and industrial growth, and it is growing still. Pioneer farmers made their contribution by planting cereal crops on the rich soils and establishing unattractive groves and plantations of eucalyptus, pine and wattle trees. Initially intended for windbreaks, shade and timber, these invasive and thirsty aliens have now all but taken over the outlying areas of highveld. It is extremely disconcerting to see drainage lines, wetlands and river ecosystems of the higher lying rural areas so suffocated and deprived of water that they cannot function normally, and how quickly vast tracts of grassland have become a bastardised mix of semi-sterile, austral-alpine-afro habitat as a result.

While it is clear that the 'horse has bolted', a concerted effort at reining this problem in is now under way. A government-sponsored task force known as 'Working for Water' is implementing a rigorous eradication programme targeting established aggressive alien trees, which will then aim at systematically controlling their further spread. This gallant effort is being driven more out of concern for the rapidly diminishing wetlands and subterranean water levels than the degradation of indigenous vegetation itself. Nonetheless, as these are inexorably linked, it is only through the restoration of the natural habitat that the water table will be improved.

* * *

Man's influence on the highveld has not been all bad, however, courtesy of the gardeners of Johannesburg. A combination of favourable climatic conditions and care has allowed their gardens, avenues, green belts and recreational areas to flourish. Collectively this growth has now erupted into a forest of vegetation, evident from satellite images taken in winter which clearly reveal the green island of Johannesburg in a surrounding sea of khaki. Besides the associated endemic fauna and flora, a plethora of smaller indigenous and exotic wildlife is being attracted to this 'jungle', and their numbers grow by the day. I may be going out on a limb when I say that it boasts the richest diversity of plant and animal species of any city in the world. I suppose it could be described as an 'urban semi-evergreen temperate-forest ecosystem' ... and if I'm off the mark, I'm sure it won't be by very much.

On the extreme southern edge of Johannesburg's suburban sprawl, isolated pockets of indigenous bush can still be found. These islands of woody vegetation associated with the conglomerate rock outcrops of the Klipriversberg range intrude into the otherwise featureless grassland. The variety and contrast of this mini-bushveld ecosystem have attracted a host of interesting smaller species of wildlife.

I loved this little patch of wilderness. It was where I began exploring the veld, at times with a friend, but mostly on my own. I learned the habits of some of the more secretive wildlife that

11

occurred there. We never needed to carry water, the Klipriversberg had a number of small streams, which ran so clean and clear that we simply drank from them when we were thirsty. These waterways were also the habitat of crabs, frogs and minnows, and I knew just where and how to collect them when needed for school projects. Needless to say my biology teachers loved me. Not all the creatures within the range were small, nor were they easy to see. Common duikers weighing up to 20 kilograms were the largest wild mammal to occur there. However, these fleet-footed antelope were also extremely wary and used their knowledge of the thickets to evade our clumsy attempts to get a good look at them. We'd hear them more often than we saw them. One morning I was eventually able to touch one ... but it was not as I'd envisioned the encounter was going to be. Strangled to death in a wire snare, the small grey form of a once beautiful little buck now lay stiff and cold. I was horrified, but it was more than the death of the little duiker that shocked me; it was *how* it had died. Suddenly I felt that this piece of bush had been violated, and so did the many others I notified. That day the story made it into *The Star* newspaper.

Though the Klipriversberg area was some consolation for me back in my youth, I always longed for the 'real' bush. If you wanted to visit a 'real' game reserve in the sixties, the Kruger National Park would probably have been the chosen destination. These trips would more often than not include the rest of the family, so you and your siblings would invariably spend the entire trip vying for window space in order to get the best view of the wildlife from the confines of the car. This visual contact through a glass barrier would be the limit of your interaction with that wonderful environment. Although I never visited the Kruger as a child, I tried to imagine what it may have been like from outings with my rather large family to the Lion Park and Krugersdorp Game Reserve. From this I extrapolated an uncomfortably cramped and claustrophobic experience, not quite like going to the drive-in-movies with your girlfriend, but rather like the time you found yourself stuck in a car at the drive-in with a crowd of indifferent people, when all you actually wanted to do was watch the show.

Besides the emerging concept of private game reserves like Thornybush and Mala Mala, in the late sixties there was really nowhere else to go, unless of course you were one of the privileged few who owned or had relatives who owned a piece of land in the Timbavati, Klaserie or Sabi Sand game reserves. Game farms and game lodges as we know them today were virtually non-existent. To get an invitation to a bushveld farm was mostly through someone with relatives or friends who farmed with domestic animals somewhere in the bushveld. These were usually free-range stock farms which shared the habitat with the endemic wildlife. Nobody I knew when I was a youngster knew anyone who actually 'farmed' with game. In the main, wild animals were regarded as direct competition to livestock, so they weren't accorded the conservation status they enjoy these days. For the most part I am pleased to say this has now changed dramatically, due largely to the soaring demand for wilderness and wildlife in order to satisfy the eco-tourism, safari and trophy-hunting industries (ironically enough, particularly the latter). Game reserve properties, particularly those with the 'big five,' have become precious ... and so it should be.

As a youth I regarded the bushveld as hallowed ground, where I was beginning to believe only an ordained few were allowed access. I yearned to be in the bush, to be part of it, to take in the smells, feel the heat and listen to the sounds. I suspect that even then it was much more than simply wanting to hunt an antelope. The highveld abounded with blesbok and springbok, yet I had no real interest in hunting either species. I wanted to be in the particular environment where impala and kudu occurred, the criteria associated with their chosen habitat and the aura of those surroundings mattered more to me than simply shooting a buck.

* * *

Hein Brundyn lived across the street from me. He attended an Afrikaans school, but despite our different home languages, communication was never a problem and we were good friends. I suspect that our common interest in the bush had more than a little to do with transcending this 'barrier'. He often mentioned his uncle's farm situated in the heart of the bushveld near Marken, a tiny village about 110 kilometres northwest of Potgietersrus, now Mogopane. I would hang on his every word when he tried to describe the bushveld to me, even though he didn't know all the English names of the wild animals – Afrikaans was just fine with me. For years I never knew impala by any name other than *rooibok*, directly translated to mean red buck. How descriptive Afrikaans names are.

One day he invited me to join him on a visit to his uncle's farm. This would be my first trip to the bushveld. Although it wasn't the 'big five' lowveld bushveld I'd dreamed about, it had wild animals roaming around in it; to me it was the bushveld in every sense of the word. I was fourteen years old ... it was high time.

Heading north on the train via Pretoria to Potgietersrus, it wasn't long before acacia trees, mostly sweet thorns, began to appear on the rolling grassland vista outside the window. Gradually the sparse thornveld of the Springbok Flats gave way to typical bushveld savanna, as more bushes and umbrella thorn trees began to dominate the hilly landscape. With midday approaching the train began to slow, and we came to a stop at Potgietersrus station. We hurriedly alighted with our bags, then looking around and feeling the relatively warm air, the realisation suddenly hit me, at last I was standing in 'real' bushveld!

A broadly smiling man of about fifty by my juvenile reckoning beckoned us over to his pick-up truck behind the station; it was Hein's uncle, Boet Danie. Apparently there were more than two hours of driving yet to do before we got to the farm, but I didn't care, it was all a new experience for me and I was loving every minute of it.

It was a good thing the rickety old Datsun 1300 wasn't noted for its speed – this allowed my eyes to linger that little bit longer at the scenery. Of course I also scanned the bush for wildlife, but my city eyes, unaccustomed to knowing what to look for, didn't pick up as much as Boet Danie's did. Besides a family of warthogs trailing a troop of nervous baboons that dashed across the road in front of us, a few smaller mammals, and some interesting birds I'd never seen before, we didn't see very much. As the sun began to sink behind a small flat-topped mountain range, and the shadows lengthened, the little truck came to a dusty stop in front of an old dimly lit farmhouse. The smell of paraffin from gently glowing lamps hung in the warm evening air; we had arrived at our destination.

It was immediately obvious that Hein's uncle had fallen on hard times. A succession of poor rainfall years had completely bankrupted him, and as a result he and his wife were living on bare necessities. Having spent part of my youth growing up on the wrong side of the tracks, so to speak, I remembered all too clearly the times my parents struggled to make ends meet. I knew what it was like to be poor ... well, I thought I did, until I met Boet Danie, and real adversity stared me in the face. Nothing I'd experienced was quite in the same league as the conditions that Hein's uncle and aunt were living under. Despite this, these God-fearing people were inherently hospitable and far too proud to say no to two young boys with bottomless pits for stomachs wanting to visit them. Moreover, their warm welcome was humbling and their faith resolute: God would provide, they insisted.

All things considered, He must have done. We had a clean warm bed at night and we didn't want for food; nearly everything we ate came off the farm. The evening meals would invariably consist of a basic mutton stew, maize porridge, pumpkin, rice or potatoes, followed by home-baked bread with thick cream for butter and home-made chunky peach jam. Breakfast was always maize porridge, milk and sugar or fried eggs, followed by bread, cream and jam. During the day we were out most of the time, so we would simply help ourselves to bread, cream, jam and oranges whenever we came back to the house. I remember there were always plenty of oranges.

We didn't eat badly at all; what we lacked in selection we made up with volume, and although we never went hungry, a little more variety would have been nice. Mutton was the only

15

meat we ate, except on the one Sunday when we had chicken, and it soon became apparent why. The day before our arrival, Boet Danie had slaughtered one of the eleven fat-tailed sheep he owned. The carcass was then hung in a small dark rondavel that served as a cool-room-cum-pantry. Muslin was placed over it to keep the flies off until the air had dried the outer skin and sealed the carcass. Needless to say, the objective was to cook and eat as much of the sheep as possible before it got too high, common practice in the days before refrigeration.

* * *

Hein and I spent every day in the bush with Petrus, one of the farm labourers' sons, who was about the same age as we were. Not only was he good company, he also knew the bush like the back of his hand. Unfortunately, besides his native Sotho, Petrus could speak only limited Afrikaans, so I found it extremely frustrating not being able to tap into his encyclopaedia of bush knowledge. Nevertheless, I found the bush was all that I'd dreamed about and more; it was much thicker than I'd imagined, and moving through it quietly wasn't as easy as I'd thought it would be. The trees appeared a lot bigger when you actually walked amongst them, and the more prominent ones made useful reference points, particularly the gargantuan baobabs. These awesome old relics epitomised a time dimension that I knew little about, but could certainly feel. Two ancient specimens that grew on the farm were thought to be the biggest and oldest in the area, both trees predated the names and dates carved on their trunks by at least a thousand years. If only they could speak, I thought, what a fascinating account we'd have of what they'd seen pass under those branches!

The well-worn sandy trails that wound through the bush revealed the tracks of a number of different wild animals that inhabited the area. Some we knew, others Petrus helped us identify. Among the more common hoofed spoor, we came across warthog, common duiker and steenbok, but we had yet to see a track or sign of impala. Then, near a grove of buffalo thorn trees one morning, we saw the spoor of much larger antelope – kudu, Petrus announced. This was the first time I'd ever laid eyes on their tracks; at least four kudu had passed through a few days previously. I tried to form a mental image of these iconic antelope browsing where I was standing now, and remember how small it made me feel. We heard the occasional duiker when they noisily broke cover well ahead of us as we walked, easily evading our clumsy attempts at hunting them. The baboons made a mockery of us, barking from the mountain cliffs, warning everything of our presence. Between these sharp-eyed primates, the 'go-away' birds and our amateurish approach, we'd have starved to death had we to survive on what we managed to shoot.

Undaunted, we persisted … still, there was no sign of impala.

* * *

Evenings back at the farmhouse were much shorter than we city boys were used to. There wasn't much to do after supper except talk about the day, wash the dishes and clean the old guns; sometimes we'd listen to the radio or play checkers until it was time to go to bed. The paraffin lamps and candles didn't produce much light, so reading wasn't really an option. One evening, after a few unsuccessful days in the bush, we got around to discussing the possible reasons for not being able to 'bring home the bacon'.

Boet Danie was not a great hunter, but he knew the habits of the local wildlife, particularly those that occurred on his farm. Smoking an after-dinner pipe on the stoep, he shared his experiences as we sat wide-eyed and all ears to hear what he had to say. One of our problems was that traditional cattle fences, which were only about a metre high, offered no major obstacle to antelope such as kudu and impala, which simply leaped over them and went pretty much where they wanted to. The other was that game on farmland was hunted and had become extremely wary. Some diurnal species adapted to the hunting pressure by becom-

17

ing crepuscular feeders; yet others, under extreme pressure, became nocturnal.

Warthogs and bush pigs were regular pests in the fields, Boet Danie said, taking a pull on his pipe. Then, looking out into the darkness, he spoke again, this time with less contempt. Kudu, on the other hand, were great wanderers, and unless there was a crop of tomatoes or a field of lucerne to visit at night, you'd never see them; they'd leave as quietly as they had arrived, without a sign.

You could tell Boet Danie had great admiration for kudu. Later in life I'd know why. Impala were more predictable, he said, and not nearly as wary; they stayed close to surface water and were less nomadic, not moving around as frequently as the kudu did. This was the reason why we had not seen them or their spoor anywhere, though they were not as a rule difficult to find. The impala were simply not there; they could be on the farm next door or miles away. He looked solemnly at me: 'If either of you come across impala, it is a sure sign God has sent them to you, treat them like manna from heaven; don't hesitate to take one.'

It was essential to leave as early in the morning as possible. By getting out at least a couple of hours before any breeze picked up we would greatly improve our chances. 'Use only the footpaths and tracks,' Boet Danie said. 'Walk quietly but not stealthily; avoid walking through thick bush if you can help it. Game gets used to seeing people walking on these paths, so don't change your pace if you see anything, walk on past without making eye contact if possible, then, when you're some way off, strategise and begin your stalk.' Boet Danie yawned, then, looking at our eager faces, he smiled, knocked his pipe out against the outside wall and said goodnight.

* * *

That night I found it difficult to fall asleep. Instead of counting sheep as I should have, my mind was focused on impala and what Boet Danie had said. It was still dark when I shook Hein awake, but he groaned that it was too early for him and that he'd catch up with me later. I got dressed, picked up the shotgun and my shoulder satchel, which I filled with a handful of home-made rusks and a few oranges from the kitchen, opened the back door and stepped into the yard. A smiling Petrus, his white teeth gleaming in the half light of dawn, was already there waiting for me. He had brought nothing except a stick, so I gave him the satchel to carry as this had proved to be a cumbersome piece of kit when 'leopard crawling'.

By the time the sun began to show itself we had covered quite some distance in the bush – unannounced. Boet Danie was right; we were able to move relatively quickly and quietly along the farm tracks. The baboons hadn't yet wiped the sleep out of their eyes, and the go-away birds were more concerned with finding breakfast than with shouting at us. In the early morning light we could clearly make out the spoor of a number of small nocturnal creatures like porcupines, scrub hares and common duikers on the open strips of road on either side of the dew-soaked *middel-mannetjie*, but, still there was no sign of impala.

I was about to suggest to Petrus that we try to bag a couple of guineafowl for the pot instead, when his left hand went up, halt-ing me in mid-stride, his right-hand index finger pressed over his lips. 'Shhhh,' he said. Bending over slightly he pointed to the road, and I could see the unmistakable tracks of larger antelope. 'The impala are back!' he whispered. According to Petrus there were approximately five of them, only a few minutes ahead of us. I looked up at the sky, remembering Boet Danie's words, then promptly exchanged the birdshot for a buckshot cartridge and loaded the old single-barrelled Harrington and Richardson.

The tracks showed that the impala had followed the road for a short distance and then turned off, following a faint game trail that headed into a patch of thick bush. On my stom-ach now, I leopard-crawled for a few metres then paused and looked up, repeating the procedure again a few times until I saw a slight movement up ahead. I was so focused on the objec-tive that it hadn't occurred to me I was sopping wet from the morning dew. Through a saucer-sized opening in the bush, a tail flicked, white in contrast to the background patch of ochre red and the two small vertical black bars characteristic of the rear end of this antelope. Although it was enough to enable me to make out one of the impala, I knew that in order to use the shotgun effectively, I had to get much closer. I needed to be within 25 metres of the impala to make the shot. Although making up those last few metres was painstakingly slow, the effort paid off; the small herd of impala was still totally unaware of me. With my heart thumping in my ears, I pulled the hammer back and steadied myself, then, taking careful aim, squeezed the trigger.

When my eyes had stopped jangling in their sockets, and I was able to focus after the shoulder-numbing recoil, a *rooibok* lay dead in the yellow grass.

Petrus, who had kept a discreet distance behind me while I was crawling through the grass, wasted no time rushing to the scene. He whooped for joy, dancing around the impala like you see Red Indians do with captive cowboys in the movies, and then hugged me, rattling off something in exuberant Sotho.

My reactions were somewhat mixed. I shook from the surge of adrenaline; it was the first antelope I'd ever killed. Sure I was happy, happy that we had succeeded in putting meat on a needy table, and that I had pulled off a clean shot doing so. However, now able to get close to the impala, being able to touch it and marvel at its beauty and perfection was an incredibly humbling experience. Lying there, it seemed so big, no doubt enhanced by the early morning sun on its glossy coat which accentuated the vivid contrast to its surroundings. Closer examination revealed that except for a few small ticks at the root of its tail, the impala was spotlessly clean and free of any blemish. I also remember the feeling of regret and sadness that came over me when I saw its glazed eyes staring up at the heavens. I could have sworn a hint of doleful acceptance lingered ... or, was I just wishing there was?

* * *

I have never forgotten that impala God 'sent me'. However, I rather suspect it was sacrificed in answer to a prayer from Boet Danie, whose needs at the time were much greater than mine. To this day I have a tremendous empathy for these beautiful 'red buck', and little respect for those in the conservation world who treat them with disdain and regard them simply as 'goats of the bush' deserving nothing but indiscriminate reduction of their numbers. In my career as a wildlife conservationist it has been my duty from time to time to cull impala in the course of herbivore population management, but I have done, and still do so, most reluctantly.

3

THE CALL OF THE WILD

Ever since I can remember I aspired to become a game ranger. I knew it wasn't going to be easy; particularly back in the mid-1970s when the prospect of a career in one of the more popular national parks was fraught with even more obstacles than it is today. To add to the challenge, game ranging was usually a lifetime's dedication, a job that was taken and stuck to until retirement, so vacancies were almost never advertised – in fact, they were often filled through nepotism before they were empty. At one stage I was told there was a seven-year waiting list … whatever that meant.

Besides a couple of private game reserves in the lowveld, career opportunities were limited to the national parks or the provincial conservation bodies. I exhausted every avenue to get a foot in the door, offering to do the most menial tasks. I made proposals that fell only just short of selling my dignity to prove to them I was passionately committed and dedicated to a life in conservation, that I was more than willing to start right at the bottom and work my way up … all to no avail.

My passion knew no bounds; it was also fraught with a degree of idealistic expectation and determination that clouded reasoning. When I was fifteen years old an aunt submitted an application to Mala Mala Game Reserve on my behalf; not surprisingly I never received a reply. However, to their credit, I was later to find that they kept it on file for years.

Having heard nothing positive from any prospective employers, I obtained a passport, bought a train ticket and journeyed up to Rhodesia, now Zimbabwe. I'd heard the prospects of becoming a game ranger or tsetse fly control officer were more promising 'up north'. Whatever the outcome was going to be, I knew this was something I just had to do; I needed to put my mind at rest, to know I wasn't wasting my time pursuing a pipe dream.

Although I found their cadet ranger training programme most promising, it would have meant emigrating from South Africa. This was the only time I was sternly warned – emigrating wasn't an option; my parents were dead against that idea. Despondently I returned to the classroom, buried my nose in my books and focused on finishing school. I then planned to study further in order to try and get a bigger veldskoen in the door, so to speak. But this was interrupted by the South African border war, and compulsory military commitments in Namibia and Angola, an interruption that would steal nearly two years of my life.

The odds of being accepted in one of the most sought-after careers in the country were stacked heavily against me. I was only nineteen years old, had no tertiary education yet, or any family employed in conservation. To add to this, English was my first language, I was single, inexperienced, city-born, and had a strange foreign-sounding name that Afrikaans-speaking people would always pronounce 'Kessarrie'. You could hardly blame the old regime for sending me the employment world's version of carefully worded 'Dear Johnnie' replies each time I applied.

* * *

Knowing that I would be desperately unhappy working in an urban environment, I refused to allow these setbacks to swallow my soul; as far as I was concerned it was merely a question of time and persistence. In the meantime, I needed to consider the alternatives. Although I hadn't given up trying to become a game ranger, I still needed to earn a crust, so I looked for a job that would at least take me outdoors and fund the odd weekend excursion into the 'wild'. I considered working on a cattle farm in the bush: there appeared to be an increasing interest in keeping game on cattle farms, which was a cause for optimism. However, although the seed was planted in some minds, nothing had really got off the ground.

Eventually I applied to Eskom, though the vision I had of standing in a hard hat working on massive power lines in the middle of the wilderness while wildebeest grazed in the background turned out to be anything but. After a couple of months I still found myself toiling away in dirty workshops with dingy offices whose grimy walls were festooned with calendar-girl pinups. Most of my time was spent running around doing the most menial tasks, helping to repair oily transformers, sorting nuts and bolts for rigging, cleaning and polishing things. I was told this was part of the training and that I'd be at it for a while. I was able to retain my sanity by spending every spare day getting as far away from Johannesburg as possible. This respite was facilitated in no small measure by a Zundapp 50cc motorcycle which my father had given me for my sixteenth birthday. This incredibly reliable piece of German engineering took me thousands of trouble-free kilometres around the country, particularly remote parts of the country. There was a modicum of comfort in knowing that I could simply pack a saddle bag, fill the tank and head out into the country any time I wanted to.

The aviary I started when I was ten was still my chief hobby, and when I was not collecting eggs, capturing and breeding wild birds for my aviary, I was ringing raptors with researcher Desmond Prout Jones, who was not only a respected authority on raptors, having published a number of papers and a book on fish eagles, but also an honorary nature conservator for the Transvaal division of Nature Conservation, and was one of only eleven people in the country at the time with a bird-ringing permit. However, though all this was most impressive for a young protégé, to me, none of these attributes were as important as the fact that he had time for me. Recognising my interest in the natural world, he would involve me at every level of his part-time work for the department, particularly on raptors. Des took me in under his wing, and pretty soon I'd gained enough knowledge to be of some assistance to him – well, at least he always told me so. Whether the praise was deserved or not was insignificant, it gave me heaps of encouragement and made me feel I was doing something important. A couple of years later, Des happily wrote my very first reference.

Understandably, there will be those who find it incomprehensible that 'stealing' birds' eggs for a hobby, trapping birds for captive breeding, using mice or doves as bait to catch raptors in order to place rings on their legs, and shooting game birds for the pot, could possibly be done by someone with compassion for wildlife and a desire to conserve nature. However, it needs to be said that this is how many conservationists have developed their relationship with nature. Any good hunter will closely study the animal he intends to hunt, as getting to know their habits will improve his chances of success. Inevitably, this close study also reveals intimate aspects of the life of the quarry, and the accumulation of this knowledge invariably culminates in an admiration for the hunted by the hunter, at times paradoxically expanding to love and respect.

By way of extreme example, the San Bushmen have worshipped the eland for aeons, and many still do, regarding them with a god-like reverence. These huge, majestic antelope were as central to their culture and spiritual beliefs as the bison were to the Sioux Indians in North America, yet they also hunted, killed and ate them. When they were not hunting them, they dreamt about them and decorated the walls and ceilings of their homes with beautifully painted images of them. These illustrations capture their subjects in such fine detail that they can only be interpreted as an expression of the artists' passion. Thankfully many fine examples of these illustrations survive to this day. As do both the American bison and the African eland.

For another personal, somewhat less dramatic example of the respect inherent in this relationship, I am reminded of an incident that occurred during my military service. More often than not, the training of infantry riflemen, whether for conventional or bush warfare, took place in rugged, naturally beautiful areas of the country. For the most part these areas were remote, and, except for a few training exercises, were otherwise left relatively undisturbed, so there was usually some game about. One day while on manoeuvres near Bloemfontein, I was leading a platoon up a steep rocky hillside that rose from a sea of relatively flat grassland. Nearing the crest, I came across an enormous bird sitting on a large clutch of eggs and recognised it immediately as a spurwing goose. To my surprise only a very few of my fellow soldiers knew what the huge bird was, and two of them were maize farmers' sons. They knew about geese – all grain farmers know about wild geese and the effect these birds have on crop yields.

A few years previously I had hunted spurwing geese that inhabited the wetlands of the northern Free State. This would take place out of breeding season, during the two coldest winter months of the year, where temperatures fell as low as minus 13 degrees Celsius at times. There, among nearly a hundred species of other wetland birds, thousands of spurwing geese would congregate during maize harvest time. Naturally I had studied the ecology of the spurwing, and as I was the only one of the regiment of soldiers there that had, I also knew that these geese typically breed miles away from water, often on dry hillsides where one would normally expect to find mountain reedbuck and rock hyraxes, and often did! It didn't take too much convincing to make the commanding officer realise that my plea was heartfelt and backed by a thorough knowledge of these birds and their ecology. He immediately suspended all manoeuvres and training exercises in that area for two months, ensuring that this bird and many others that had chosen the training area to nest in would be allowed to breed in peace that season.

I wasn't conscious of the fact at the time, but while pursuing these hobbies and activities, a rudimentary understanding was being accumulated in regard to certain birds and their habitats. These bits of information were being placed in the grey filing cabinet of my subconscious and securely stored, to be retrieved and processed as and when needed. Later in my quest for work, I found that this practical knowledge would stand me in good stead.

Private funding for tertiary education was beyond my parents' means, so unless I could get a bursary or qualify for a student loan, this avenue would stay closed for me. I soon realised that I needed to save now and study later, which I did, but in the meantime, life simply had to carry on.

At that stage I still lived with my parents. One afternoon as I returned home from work, my mother handed me a small piece of newspaper: 'Next-door saw this in the newspaper, son. She thought you might want to give it a try.'

Opening the folded piece of newspaper that had been neatly cut out of the smalls section, I read: *Game Ranger wanted. Must be single, bilingual, between 18 and 25 years of age, have a driver's licence, and sound knowledge of wildlife. Mechanical knowledge and a third language will be an advantage. Interviews of short listed applicants will be conducted on the reserve, No chancers please!* ...

Game ranger wanted! I had never seen an advertisement for a game ranger before, anywhere. There was no address to post a CV off to, only a name and phone number. I dialled immediately and was put through to a Mr Wyndham-Quin, who explained that he had recently leased a private game reserve in the lowveld and needed to train young rangers/guides to conduct safaris with international clients. The more he described the job, the more I knew I could do it. After patiently listening to my excited babble in response, he promised to call me back the following day.

There was no way I would have been able to concentrate on working in the dingy workshops at Eskom, so the next day I phoned in, made some excuse and booked myself off. Making myself comfortable with a book on the larger mammals of the lowveld, I hogged the phone, cutting all conversations on incoming calls brutally short. By the time the phone rang just before midday, I had managed to wade through an impressive number of facts about the better-known African mammals. It is amazing how much you can absorb when you need to. The caller was Mr Wyndham-Quin himself to say they had short-listed me and another chap named Andy who had recently moved down to South Africa from Rhodesia. He gave me Andy's telephone number and suggested I arrange to meet up with him that Friday afternoon in Johannesburg, from where we would be driven up to the reserve for the long weekend.

Andy was a thoroughly pleasant chap, and besides looking the part, he had few years on me; he also had a couple of years' experience in conservation under his belt, and was a helicopter pilot to boot. I stood as much chance against him as that poor chicken did at one of Alice Cooper's 'music' concerts. What the hell, I thought; at least I'd get to spend a couple of days in the bush.

Leaving Johannesburg at about 5.30pm, we drove straight through, arriving at Thornybush main camp close to midnight. Andy and I were shown to our respective thatched rondavels and told to be down for breakfast at 7.30 the following morning. I wasn't tired; in fact, I was so excited I couldn't fall asleep for a while. Somebody thoughtful had placed a plate of sandwiches and a couple of small bar-sized cokes under the bedside lamp. Next to the cokes, on one of those old flat candle holders, propped up with a box of matches, was a small card that simply read 'Welcome to Thornybush'. The sandwiches were delicious and most welcome, but I have never been partial to Coca-Cola, so only managed half a bottle before brushing my teeth, setting my alarm clock and going to bed.

The next morning I was up with the first raucous cackle of the Natal francolin, long before the alarm clock. Wasting no time, I had a quick shower, got dressed and walked across the lawn to the lodge. I made my way through the lounge and found myself standing on the patio overlooking the partially dry Monwane River, where it made a huge bend in front of the camp. This was the 'real' bushveld I'd always dreamed about. It was awesome.

For a while I stood there deep in thought and anxious anticipation of what the day held in store for me. The solitude wasn't long lived, the squeak of rubber soles on the highly polished patio floor, mingled with a more subtle click, click of dogs' claws made me turn around. A suntanned middle-aged man dressed in khaki came walking up to me; he was closely followed by three dogs which I recognised immediately as English pointers. The man stuck out his hand and introduced himself simply as Frank. However, it didn't take long for me to realise he was the manager.

'I'm glad to see there's one Joburg lightie that doesn't mind getting up early,' he said. 'Mario … are you Portuguese?'

'No, I'm half-Italian,' I said, 'My father is Italian.' Babbling enthusiastically, I insisted that the Portuguese make bicycles, and that Italians make Ferraris.

Frank laughed: 'And Alfa Romeos – I used to race Alfas in Mozambique.' Then without elaborating, he abruptly cut the train of the conversation. 'But that's enough about fast cars; I want to find out why you want to work in the bush.'

At that point I was on one knee stroking the dogs, which were really enjoying the attention, I love all dogs, but gun dogs ... well, they're especially special, so I may have lingered a bit before standing up. Before I could start selling myself, Andy came through and introduced himself. A few minutes of small talk followed, interrupted by the beating of a drum that reverberated through the lodge. Breakfast was being announced, African style.

The smell of grilled bacon and percolated coffee made my mouth water. At the table we met Frank's beautiful wife Dawn tucking into a wedge of fresh papaya. Dawn was responsible for the catering and administration of the lodge. It was now clear who the caring somebody was that had left those delicious sandwiches and welcome note.

* * *

As the morning wore on it became increasingly apparent that there was going to be no formal interview, and that our evaluation was going to be based on a series of impromptu practical tests. This included demonstrations of communication and people skills, combined with bush know-how and knowledge of the local fauna and flora.

One of our first tasks was to go fishing. Frank explained that the river was drying up and he needed to move fish that were stranded in the rapidly drying pools to the safety of deeper pools in the river. Nets had to be made to catch the fish and containers sourced to transport them. This problem was quickly solved by using shade cloth borrowed from the vegetable garden, and a couple of cool boxes which we took from the bar, their tight-fitting lids would prevent water spillage on the bumpy roads.

Using the shade cloth to great effect, we soon filled the containers with hundreds of beleaguered fish, and transported them to the deeper pools. Next, Frank made us take turns driving the old Series 2 Land Rover. This particular model had a pre-synchromesh gearbox, one of those that required a little double clutch in order to change gears smoothly. He also had us position the vehicle for photography, and pick our way off road through the bush. As we drove he casually questioned us at random about wildlife, mainly from a tourist's perspective, while also throwing the odd curved ball at us testing our knowledge of current politics. Carefully worded questions were posed, questions that from experience he knew we'd be asked from time to time by tourists from overseas, so of course, he needed to hear how we responded to them.

Naturally I was expecting to be asked about some of the larger mammals that occurred in the area; instead, to my surprise, Frank concentrated his questions on birds and bird identification. My thorough knowledge of waterfowl, which I had learned from wing shooting, and the experience gained helping to capture and ring raptors, helped me with the identification of the more common birds of prey at a distance. It would be fair to say that even at that stage my knowledge of birds was above average, which appeared to impress Frank. My aviary hobby had also proved to be a tremendous help, particularly with the identification of the smaller seed-eating birds such as waxbills, finches, weavers, and canaries.

My fascination with egg collecting helped with the identification of those species which were not aviary birds, but some of whose eggs I'd collected. Finding a bird is so much easier than finding its nest, so the more about its ecology I knew the better chance I had of collecting their eggs. It was most important to know how many eggs each species normally lays as this was vital in determining how many eggs, if any, I could safely remove without adversely affecting their breeding ... So I learned.

Weapon handling skills, the test of our practical shooting ability … it had to come. After ensuring the rifle was sighted in, we were given the opportunity to shoot an impala. Given the circumstances, however, this was really no test of hunting skill, rather to assess our familiarity with a weapon. Through casual conversation Frank became aware that I was a keen wing shooter, something he also enjoyed and which his dogs were bred for. Frank's pointers had bloodlines going back hundreds of years. Using this excuse to put them to the work they lived for, we used the 12 bore shotgun to good effect: needless to say the dogs did him proud, and soon we had bagged enough crested francolin to make a delicious casserole. Dawn prepared it, of course. What an excellent caterer she was, particularly with game: nothing was too challenging for her, and I still believe she could turn boot leather into schnitzels if she had to.

That evening we went out on an interesting spotlight night drive, returning to a boma dinner, where more of the expected interaction with international guests was emulated. Although I had made the most of it and enjoyed myself, in my heart I knew the next day would be my last in this beautiful place, and although I put on a brave face, I feared my sombre mood wouldn't go unnoticed.

The next morning, long before the francolin even thought about squawking, I was up and about. It was still dark when I walked down to the patio and slumped in one of the cane loungers; the strong musky smell of waterbuck which had spent the night on the lawn hung thick in the still morning air. In melancholy contemplation I gazed out onto the dry riverbed, my eyes fixing on nothing in particular. I listened to the sounds of the African bush as it slowly woke and greeted what I thought would be my last day in paradise. The millions of stars that earlier lit up the night sky slowly faded, and above the riverine trees it began to get light, intensifying as the heavens glowed a faint peachy pink – dawn was breaking. As the sun rose there appeared to be an eager impatience by the bush inhabitants to start the day. On the clearing opposite the camp an impala ram was blowing his harsh rutting call as he herded his harem of nearly fifty ewes into a tighter group. Lions called miles away, I guessed somewhere near the Timbavati boundary, and suddenly I felt my spirits begin to lift a little.

*   *   *

If pointers were able to talk, I would have known a minute earlier. They came rushing down to greet me, tails wagging hard and their cold wet noses against my bare legs. I could now hear Frank's veldskoens squeaking on the polished screed floor following closely behind. Cutting the greeting short and glancing around to see that we were alone, he said: 'You know you have the job if you want it, don't you?'

This was something I had honestly not expected, and I was understandably stuck for an answer. But even before I could collect my thoughts and respond, he added: 'How soon can you load your belongings and get back here?'

And so my career in nature conservation began. I was earning R150 per month, over and above free board and food; I was also given four days' leave for every four weeks worked, and two free guest nights per month. What more could I possibly wish for? I was where I'd always wanted to be; I was in paradise.

Taking walking trails or game-viewing safaris in open 4x4 vehicles for tourists is not strictly game ranging; rather it is a combination of being a ranger and a safari tour guide – a 'jeep jockey', as some say. I must emphasise, however, that these guys spend more time in the bush observing wildlife than most game rangers in the National Parks do ... Fact! The state could never afford to have their conservation personnel spending up to eight hours a day behind the wheel of a fuel-hungry 4x4, merely driving around, observing and photographing nature, unless of course it was part of an endorsed research project. So, by getting a foot in the door in wildlife tourism, I now had an excellent opportunity to spend time in the bush observing wildlife in their natural habitat, thereby helping to prepare a solid grounding for my future in conservation. Ironically though, it would be the 'people' and communication skills that I learned and developed in this facet of the industry that would be the key to my future. It was not so much the ability to rattle off pages of facts on wildlife, or to disseminate pre-digested scientific names of fauna and flora; rather it had to do with the response of total strangers to your message of conservation, propped up by those facts you enthusiastically imparted. By imparting a basic knowledge of wildlife with enough passion, I found you could hold just about anyone in the palm of your hand, no matter the profile of the audience.

I have known brilliant conservation scientists who have quietly withdrawn into themselves, or simply faded away into a world of academic obscurity, rather than have to deal with hordes of people. Many of them preferred to have papers published in recognition of their dedication and academic prowess, rather than to communicate their knowledge in an interactive way to a broader audience, stoically lacking the desire to market their 'product', with murmurings that it would be tantamount to prostitution of knowledge. However, I believe it is a great pity that many scientific journals and papers never get to the masses, and often it is only those people in similar fields of interest who take the trouble to pull them from their dusty filing cabinets to read or research them.

Being a game ranger today is a multifaceted occupation, and although many would like to believe that it is strictly about environmental conservation science, it is not that simple. Nor is it being a practical, jack-of-all-trades MacGyver type, or a former big game hunter turned ambassadorial exemplar of protecting beleaguered wildlife and wilderness. However, I think it is safe to say, somewhere in amongst all these criteria, are the elemental building blocks for a definition.

* * *

Looking back on the time I spent at Thornybush, there could not have been a better kick-start to my career. Much of what I learned was new: what an interesting learning curve it was for me! Most of my days were filled with excitement and pleasure, I was in 'big five' country guiding tourists nearly every day for hours on end, and I was getting paid for it!

In amongst all this I made time to spend with Frank's pointers, Lola, Ranger and Gina, and grew to understand dogs in a way I'd never have been able to had I been living in a suburban environment. In the bush they could be themselves and show off their remarkable abilities. I was impressed by them, and have to admit that those three pointers had a profound effect on me. As time went by I realised that there was a lot more to dog ownership than meets the eye, especially keeping a dog in a bushveld environment, more particularly a commercial safari lodge. I also learned that I would be limiting my employment prospects anywhere else if I came with a dog in tow.

So, as hard as it was to resist the temptation, I made the decision to give it a year or so before venturing down that road, which, as it happened, turned out to be a good decision at the time.

4

MAGNA FAUNA SAFARIS

At twenty, I desperately wanted to live some of those moments portrayed by the legendary hunters and game rangers of yore, and I hung on to every word the old legends had to say in the bar. Despite my sober observation over time, which led me to realise how many of those stories were embellished with egotistical bullshit, the underlying romance and intrigue never wore off. Getting to work for a reputable hunting outfit usually meant filling dead men's shoes, so when I was offered an apprenticeship with Magna Fauna Safaris, I immediately seized the opportunity. As a young ranger, I doubt my time could have been spent any more gainfully than it was at Thornybush Game Reserve. It was a gradual immersion into the shallow end of an enormous pool of all-round bush knowledge and practical experience. Although I had been happy working as a ranger and guide, I realised that in order to broaden my horizons and obtain experience with big game, I needed to move on – I knew there was nothing in the photographic safari industry at that stage that would take me quite as close to the 'edge' as hunting would.

* * *

There can be no denying that the era of the 'white hunter', with all its controversy, was a rich part of this continent's history. Back in the nineteenth century, as European settlers spread throughout South Africa, a hunting free-for-all ensued. With the discovery of incredible mineral wealth, it seemed that everything was up for grabs. The resultant influx of people took a terrible toll on the natural environment, and the huge herds of wild animals that roamed the veld were the first to go. At first, game was shot and utilised by prospectors and settlers, at times on a scale of wanton slaughter. Yielding good meat and hides, these animals were hunted mainly for these subsistence benefits. However, as the hinterland began to be settled, there was a concerted effort made by farmers to eradicate wild animals perceived to threaten agriculture or to be competing with domestic stock for resources. Effectively, except for ivory, game had no real monetary value, and no status. By the time big game trophy hunting became a lucrative business, so much wildlife had already been decimated in South Africa that the country could not be seriously considered a big game safari destination. In fact, up until the late 1970s, big game safaris or trophy-hunting safaris were conducted primarily north of our borders.

Fences shrunk the wilder areas of our country, boxing them into parcels of agricultural land and unviable bushveld farms. The rapid decline of what little remained of our big game areas was inevitable, and soon we had much less to offer than our neighbours, many of whom still boasted huge areas of unfenced virgin Africa, while most of our country's wilderness areas suffered ecological rape and its wildlife quietly diminished daily. There was so much more available north of the Limpopo River in which to offer a true African big game safari, it was not surprising that there was very little demand for what were sometimes referred to as 'bacon-and-egg safaris' or 'ranch hunts' down south.

The halcyon days of the 'white hunter' with millions of acres of open Africa at his disposal were long gone by my time. The violent tribal conflict and in some cases civil war that followed the euphoric delirium of 'Uhuru' had led to lawlessness and anarchy in already marginalised economies. People who were forced into survival mode naturally turned to living off the relatively abundant wildlife resources. However, the benefits from uncontrolled harvesting and indiscriminate hunting were short-lived, and had far-reaching detrimental effects on the environment. When that was depleted, game reserves and wildlife sanctuaries were penetrated, eventually with the same prognosis.

Instead of utilising the abundant natural resources in these hunting concessions and game reserves on a sustainable basis, the plundering and uncontrolled slaughter of wild animals that ensued was so brutal and devastating that most of these areas have never fully recovered. In many countries, running a safari business was no longer viable. Consequently the trophy-hunting industry in southern Africa, notably that of Botswana, began to take root and flourish.

Back then the concept of professional hunting in this country was a relatively new one. There was no formal schooling or academic course, nor was there any recognised examination for which to study – basically you were on your own. Most aspiring young hunters wanting to make a career in trophy hunting depended largely on a mentor who was prepared to take them on as apprentices and teach them the ropes. Not all good hunting outfitters were good teachers, so invariably you became Q.B.E. (Qualified by Experience), which proved to be the best method of learning. There could never be a better grounding in this profession than the practical one-on-one with clients and dangerous game in the field; experience of real-life situations is something no university on earth can prepare you for.

Adding to the limitations, reputable big game hunting safari outfitters were few and far between, many comprising father-to-son legacies which were confined to the remote concessions in Zambia, Zimbabwe and Botswana. In number those early outfitters were a mere shadow of the huge industry we know today. Naturally then, opportunities for someone 'unconnected' to become proficient and earn a reputation for being able to hunt the big five in tight situations, or safely conduct walking trails with confidence in big game reserves, were extremely limited in South Africa. However, Rhodesia provided more opportunities, and recognised that a few years' apprenticeship under a reputable professional hunting outfitter was sufficient training to be let loose.

Prior to the ban on trophy hunting in Kenya and Tanzania,

these countries were the bastions of big game hunting safaris; this was where the term 'white hunter' was born. The romance and allure associated with this prestigious title was good for business, attracting the rich and famous, and setting a high standard of exclusivity and hunting ethics at the same time. The larger firms, some sporting triple-barrelled names, were built on solid reputations and became synonymous with service par excellence in the industry.

On the other hand, the majority of South Africans entering the field were dismissive of tradition, which was thought to be fraught with the pomp and ritual commonly associated with Englishmen and their approach to field sports. Nonetheless, this became accepted practice, and over time, intrinsic to the activity. Everyone knows that a worm skewered on a bent pin will catch trout anywhere in the world, so why then are there thousands of elaborate fly patterns in use, and well over four hundred books written on how to catch trout? Many people observing these practices have sought an explanation, in particular, of why one is expected to wear a tweed jacket and tie when fly-fishing for salmon, or shooting grouse? And the answer that unhesitatingly pops back on the return serve each time, by anyone remotely familiar with the ethics and tradition of sports afield, is simply this: 'It is to show respect for the quarry, old chap!'

This summed up the traditions and attitude that built the reputation of sportsmanlike conduct in the field, extending from the art of fly fishing using a Tonkin cane rod with silk and horsehair line to delicately present a tiny artificial rendition of a mayfly to a fastidious trout, through to the way the largest African elephant was hunted, using purpose-built guns firing bullets the size of cigars. However, not everyone aspiring to hunt professionally took this as seriously as they should have. Many South Africans, particularly those in the farming community who had access to game, were misguided into thinking that all the paying clients expected from you as a 'big white hunter' was that you were able to shoot a rifle accurately, tell a trophy animal from a representative of the species, grunt occasionally when spoken to, and be able to consume vast amounts of liquor. How horribly wrong they were. The expectations of people paying the kind of money that trophy hunting generates go far beyond that, as many farmers and their sons who tried taking foreign clients into the bush on the back of their Isuzu pick-ups found out ... the hard way.

* * *

Rob Mann had recently packed up his worldly goods and moved down south from Rhodesia. The country he loved was in the midst of a bush war, and when his clients began to get caught up in the fray, he realised it was time to go. Leaving the landmine-infested hunting concessions of his war-torn country wasn't easy for him. Most of what he had built up in his involvement with Diamond T Safaris had to be left behind. However, Rob didn't arrive cap-in-wringing-hands while giving the 'when we' lament; rather, he brought with him the old ways of tradition, etiquette and professionalism.

After much procedural red tape, Rob finally pioneered the means to secure a hunting concession in South Africa. By managing to obtain an annually renewable lease from the then Gazankulu government for a respectable chunk of African wilderness, he set the benchmark for sustainable trophy hunting. This was the first deal of its kind in the lowveld – in South Africa for that matter.

The area known as Letaba Ranch comprised a 20 000 hectare big five game reserve bordering the Kruger National Park. Situated between the Groot and the Klein Letaba Rivers, this strategically sensitive and spectacularly beautiful area was also big game country in every sense of the word. Prior to this it had been earmarked to become farmland. By leasing the concession for strictly controlled big game hunting safaris, Rob's hunting deal had ironically saved thousands of wild animals from wholesale slaughter and prevented the destruction of a vast area of pristine bushveld. Interestingly, prior to Rob's lease, a tender to shoot all the game in the area in a culling-type eradication programme to clear the area for domestic stock was put out, and the highest of-fer submitted to do the shooting was R25 000! Thank goodness this option wasn't considered! Instead, Rob's proposal was, and 'Magna Fauna Safaris' was established.

Although this happened over thirty-five years ago, Letaba Ranch is still used primarily for trophy hunting, and its environ-ment remains relatively unspoilt. Big game still thrives in this wilderness area, so much so that to this day it is regularly put out on tender and leased on a renewable basis as a safari hunt-ing concession. Most importantly, the selective trophy hunting of certain animals has proved to be sustainable, and the long-term outlook is promising. Members of the local community are reaping greater financial rewards from this type of land use than they would have had it been ploughed up to plant maize or to be grazed to a dustbowl by a few scrawny cattle. So, as strong as the arguments against hunting as a sustainable use of natural resources are, this example, although not squeaky clean on all counts, takes a helluva lot of beating.

*   *   *

The local Shangaans named Rob 'Ingwe', the name for leopard almost throughout Africa. He was a small man, about the size of a steeplechase jockey, and to say he had a point to prove would be an understatement. He strove to do everything as well as, or better than the next man, something that may have been at-tributable in part to the fact that he was just over five feet tall. However, I suspect it had more to do with his professional ap-proach to what he did, and his fastidious attention to detail. The only sign of acknowledgement of compensation for his stature was that he had 10 centimetres cut off the stock of his .458 mag-num rifle, so it would fit into his shoulder properly. Also, having come up through the ranks himself, he had learned the hard way; he knew through practical experience what worked and what didn't. I believe that was the hallmark – the essence, if you like, of his success. From the get go, he made it clear how he wanted things done; it was simply 'his way or the highway', and I accepted that it wasn't going to be easy being his apprentice.

Looking back, I guess I have to say that I was indeed fortunate to have had Rob as my hunting guru. Having said this, there was another side to him. Besides his dedication to the safari business and flying his Piper Aztec, Rob nurtured another passion not many people knew about, one quite disparate from his established way of life: he would have preferred to be a wildlife veterinarian. So, in between hunting, he would use his dart gun at every opportunity to rescue wild animals in distress, all at his own cost of course. In those days the laws regarding the use of immobilising drugs were less stringent, so availability was not a problem.

Letaba Ranch was surrounded on three sides by fences – nothing like the effective barriers they are today. The eight-strand rusted excuse for a veterinary cordon fence that separated the Kruger National Park from Letaba Ranch was broken by elephant almost every night, and would lie in a state of disrepair sometimes for days on end. Most of the escapees and migrants were tolerated; indeed some were welcomed by farmers, but unfortunately there were those that posed a real threat to crops or livestock, and from time to time the lives of local community members were at risk. It was in these situations that Rob was able to put his dart gun to good use, and as I said, given the choice, he always preferred to use a dart rather than a bullet. By nature Rob was a hunter, not a killer – and I was learning to differentiate.

*   *   *

When pursued by incoming dominant males in a territorial takeover, young lions will sometimes be forced to flee the sanctity of protected nature reserves and hunting concessions. More often than not, they are pushed out of their old territory into neighbouring farmland. In order to survive, they quickly adjust to their new environment by killing livestock. These sluggish and tasty prey make easy pickings, but this apparent good fortune comes at a terrible price: the tables are turned, and the hunters become the hunted. The 'outlaws' now need to learn how to survive the most deadly threat to their lives ... man. This is not a gradual evolutionary adaptation, it has to be learned quickly, and only the shrewdest will live long enough to teach others. Not surprisingly, second-generation cattle killers become less predictable and more elusive than their reserve-dwelling counterparts.

One morning Rob and I were called out to former Springbok rugby player Sakkie Sauermann's farm, which bordered Letaba Ranch. Sakkie was a huge man, with a heart to match. To watch as he and Rob stood on the edge of cropland having a chat was like watching David and Goliath squaring up for their legendary conflict. But this was no imminent duel to the death; in fact Sakkie admired Rob and what he had done with Letaba Ranch. He also knew how much Rob loved to play 'animal doctor', so whenever unwanted or 'problem' animals strayed onto his farm, he would give Rob the opportunity to capture them. To date we had darted a few bushbuck and waterbuck that were damaging his crops and released them on Letaba Ranch. This time, however, there was urgency in Sakkie's voice, and I knew this situation was going to be a little more complicated.

Five lions had recently moved onto his farm and killed three of his cattle in two weeks. We needed to get them off before they killed again, he told us, failing which, he would have no choice but to shoot them. Needless to say, Rob was up for it.

I was tasked with building the blind, which needed to be strategically positioned overlooking the remnants of the cow that the lions had recently killed. We were sure they were lying up close by and would return that evening.

*　*　*

It took well over an hour to construct the blind according to the method Rob had taught me. As the sun sank lower and the shadows grew longer, it began to look decidedly welcoming and cosy. Then, just as it became time to settle in for the night, Rob arrived with an enormous, light-grey, doe-eyed donkey. Staring open-mouthed, I silently took the rope halter that was held out to me, trying hard not to look into the poor animal's eyes.

Rob anticipated my question: 'I collected it from the abattoir in Phalaborwa. It will be our back-up if the cow is finished before all the lions are darted; we may need to give the lions something to keep them within range, and lions are partial to donkeys,' he said.

I led the donkey away and tethered it to one of the vehicles we had parked about 200 metres away, upwind from the blind. I couldn't hide my feelings, and again, Rob read my thoughts.

'I know how you feel, pal, and although it doesn't make it any easier, try to think of it like this – it's the donkey or the lions.'

I couldn't argue with that.

Rob knew that he couldn't start darting the lions until 11pm, preferably later, as the immobilising effects of the drug would last a little over six hours. We calculated that by 5am it would be light enough to locate the slowly recovering lions and administer a further top-up dose in order to transport them safely in the open Land Cruisers back to Letaba Ranch.

Making ourselves as comfortable as possible, we settled down in the blind just as the sun was setting. The stench coming from what remained of the cow's putrid flesh was quite overwhelming, compounded by the fact it was the time of day when smells seemed so much more perceptible in the still air; the same time of day when the air in the lower-lying areas of the bush hangs thick with the pungent smell of the potato bush. Anyway, we had purposely positioned ourselves downwind from the carcass, which meant we had to live with the reek. Fortunately we didn't have to wait long.

At first a single lioness silently appeared as if from nowhere, and without suspicion began to feed. Aha, I thought, Rob will be pleased that the lion hasn't noticed the blind, a tribute to its meticulous construction no doubt. Although I knew he'd never tell me, his silence was all the praise I needed.

A couple of minutes later she was followed by another lioness trailing three small cubs of about four months old. Soon all five lions were feeding on what was left of the carcass. The sound of tougher gristle being chewed by the lions' scissor-like carnassial teeth, punctuated now and then by mushy chewing sounds as they ate the softer rotten flesh, was all that we could hear. Occasionally there was a soft 'eeaaow' protest from the cubs when one of them was elbowed out of the way. Otherwise they ate in virtual silence. The competition for space was a sure sign that the there was not much left of the carcass to go around.

For the best part of an hour the lions fed without interruption on the scant remains and tougher bits; it was clearly evident they had reached the finger-lickin' stage of their meal. It was then that Rob turned to me and whispered what I knew was coming, but had been dreading to hear: 'They're going to finish what's left of the cow before we can start with the darting ... sorry pal; we're going to have to use the donkey.'

As quietly as we could, Rob and I snuck out the back of the blind. I carried the .22 rifle fitted with a silencer, and Rob his .458. Needless to say, the lions heard us, grunted and ran into the bush.

'Don't worry,' Rob said confidently. 'They'll be back.'

We made our way up to the vehicles where the donkey was tethered. The frightened animal was straining on its halter; ironically it wasn't Rob and me it was frightened of. Instead it stared past us, its nostrils flared, still filled with the scent of the lions it had been able to smell for over an hour. Of course, I looked at Rob, but there was going to be no reprieve; instead, with a nod he gave the rookie the shitty job of having to put the donkey down.

I have never forgotten what that felt like, and despite it being rather insignificant in the context of what was expected of an aspiring hunter, I fought hard with myself, trying hard not to show how much I hated doing it. The only consoling factor was that I knew the poor animal needn't live in fear anymore, and its end would be swift and painless ... which it was.

Overcome with curiosity, I surreptitiously looked into the donkey's mouth, which revealed an extremely worn set of teeth – the animal had lived a full life, and its fate had already been sealed

... Neither made what I'd had to do sit any easier with me. I remember thinking about the situation at the abattoir, where this is routine. How do those people destroy hundreds of animals like this one, animals which they have eyeball-to-eyeball contact with? How did they do this day in and day out, without it having some negative psychological effect on them? The answer ... somebody has to.

The deed duly done, we loaded the donkey and drove down to where the remains of the cow carcass lay. The noise of the vehicle moving through the bush was in harsh contrast to all the trouble we had taken earlier to be stealthy and unobtrusive. I wondered why the donkey hadn't been put out before the lions arrived that evening ... but in my defence, I knew little of these things at the time – I was only a student, and eager to learn as much as I could.

Securing the donkey right next to the cow's remains, we opened the abdomen of the still warm carcass, hoping to attract the lions back with the smell of fresh meat. Lions cannot resist donkey ... right?

Back at the blind, Rob and I once again settled down, making ourselves as comfortable as possible, waiting for the lions to return. The luminous dots on my wristwatch told me it was only 9pm. I could feel this was going to be a long night.

Ages went by without a sound. Then, just as I began to doubt Rob's experience, a small grunt broke the silence, followed by the unmistakable crunch as powerful teeth sheared through small bones and gristle. Turning on the low-power spotlight, I could see that the lions had indeed returned, and they'd resumed feeding on the rotten cow! Though the donkey carcass lay right next to them as they fed, not a single lion touched it. Initially all they did was give it a sniff, after which they appeared to lose all interest; in fact, they lay in the body fluids and stomach contents of the donkey while feeding on the cow carcass! Incredible as this was, Rob knew that if they didn't start feeding on the donkey soon, he'd have to start darting before they'd finished what little remained of the cow... It was nearly 10.30pm.

Shortly before 11pm Rob darted the first lion with a perfectly placed dart. The lioness grunted and ran off, quickly swallowed up by the surrounding bush. Then systematically all three cubs were darted. By the sound of things Rob guessed they hadn't gone too far. We could hear them as they moved about the bush, stumbling clumsily as the drug began to take effect. At a little after midnight the remaining lioness was darted, and a while later an eerie stillness fell.

Satisfied she had gone down, we went up to inspect the donkey carcass. Rob was totally perplexed at their behaviour, he had never seen anything like it in his life – despite there being virtually nothing left of the cow, the donkey hadn't been touched! Other than that, he was happy and somewhat relieved that all the lions had been successfully darted, particularly both the adults. Having a lion that was not drugged hanging around while you tried to kidnap her cubs might prove problematic.

Rob had done what he could. Now all we needed to do was settle in and wait for the first francolin to call, heralding the pre-dawn light that would help us locate the lions. As it turned out, we found them easily enough and didn't need to do much tracking. All five lions were loaded into the one vehicle without a problem; however, one of the lionesses was starting to show signs of coming round, lifting her head and growling when anyone moved suddenly. This unnecessary stress was alleviated by covering her eyes with a hand towel secured with insulation tape.

We arrived at the hide on the edge of Badarukwe Pan, one of Letaba Ranch's permanent waterholes, just as the sun rose over the treetops. We wasted no time unloading the lions and pulling them into the shade a safe distance from the water. Rob removed the blindfold from the lioness, then quietly retreated to join me some 30 metres away to monitor their progress from the safety of the vehicle. Not having fully recovered from the immobilising drug, they lay sprawled like a heap of drunkards struggling to regain their composure after a serious binge. In this state the lions were extremely vulnerable, and would remain so for a little while, but we weren't about to leave them just yet.

Not much made Rob break into a grin, but on this occasion I saw a huge smile on the small man's face. He told me he was relieved that everything had gone so smoothly technically, and that he was particularly happy he had saved five lions from be-ing shot. In celebration he brought out his thermos and shared the tepid dregs of his customary tea with me ... actually it didn't taste that bad at all.

* * *

I spent a year at Letaba Ranch, often at the coalface, in adrena-line-charged situations, stalking dangerous game cheek-by-jowl with seasoned professionals. I didn't know it then, but the ex-perience and knowledge I was gaining would save my life on a number of occasions later in my career. However, the most im-portant lesson I learned during this time was that professional hunting wasn't for me. I realised that although there was a place for controlled trophy hunting in the broader conservation sense, it was merely one cog in the wheel that drove it. I did not want to kill animals for a living. So, having completed the season with Rob, I took the first opportunity when things quietened down, and reapplied for a post as a ranger at Mala Mala Game Reserve. This time my application met with more success.

5

SHILO'S BEGINNINGS

Life happens ... sometimes it creeps up on you gradually, in a progressive, evolutionary way; you hardly notice as you adapt and adjust to its twists and turns. Then, quite suddenly and without warning, the wheel turns abruptly; your plans go awry, and the journey you've meticulously mapped out for yourself changes direction from one moment to the next – for ever. Although I was enjoying what I considered the most carefree lifestyle imaginable, there were times when I felt something was missing. I had always suspected that freedom in its basic, uncluttered form teetered on a knife edge, somewhere between altruistic responsibility and selfishness. I believed that you could not enjoy real independence if you had something or someone you dreaded losing. I now believe freedom is relative, and we are not all architects of our own future.

Head hunted from Mala Mala, I was lured away by the promise of a management position running another game lodge in the Sabi Sand Reserve. The prospects looked good at the time, a juicy looking carrot indeed. After only a couple of months, however, the owner's lack of commitment became evident and an inevitable cul-de-sac loomed. I decided to move on.

* * *

It was mid-October 1981, and I had just turned twenty-five.

Having spent the best part of the last six years in lowveld reserves, the intrigue of more remote parts of Africa took on a pioneering, romantic vision. I became mildly obsessed; I yearned to investigate and become part of the bush beyond South Africa's boundaries. So, when the opportunity to work in a relatively remote area presented itself, I leaped at it, and was appointed manager of a game reserve in the northeastern corner of an enormous wilderness area in Botswana known as the Tuli Block.

The Tuli Block is located just above the tropic of Capricorn, at the point where Zimbabwe, South Africa and Botswana meet, and a more rugged tract of bushveld you'd be hard pressed to find. Though home to many species of Africa's big game, it is famous for its great elephant herds, which have been largely responsible for shaping this habitat as we see it today. It is a harsh landscape of open, grassless plains – vast expanses dotted with small evergreen shepherd's trees and endless stands of stunted mopane scrub.

The undulating terrain of sparse scrubland is punctuated here and there by huge baobab trees, scarred and resolute, corpulent sentinels over a dying breed of giants. The destruction by elephants of their seedlings and the younger trees that stood in line to reign is now complete. For the 'upside-down tree' of Tuli, there is no hope of succession.

Moving towards the lower-lying areas of the reserve, the shallow stony soils begin to taper off and merge with the deep alluvial deposits of the river floodplains. Enormous trees along the river courses break the monotony of the scrubland in a transformation that is naturally wild and dramatically beautiful.

Though prone to brief periods of volatile flooding in the rainy season, after spate the rivers recede rapidly, and for the most part they barely flow at all. Legend has it that the floodplain's upper reaches were last covered in water when the ox-wagons carrying Cecil John Rhodes and his entourage got bogged down on their way to discover Rhodesia ... or was it when Frederick Selous brought his ivory back through Mashonaland? None of the local tribal elders were sure. According to some of the older farmers across the river on the South African side, there were a couple of times in more recent memory – in the days of the rinderpest, perhaps, or just before the Second World War. At any rate, the level of flooding necessary to replenish the floodplains was a rare event.

*   *   *

The Tuli Game Reserve lies confined in strategic geographical neatness between three rivers, which collectively comprise the major arteries supplying the life blood to this otherwise arid and inhospitable environment. To the north is the Shashe River, with its beach-like sandy river bed, up to 500 metres wide in places. Besides the odd hippo-crammed pool, this river course lies dry for most of the year, its width belying the volume of water it carries on rare occasions to the Limpopo River. At the southwestern extreme of Tuli lies the smallest of the three, the Matloutsi River, which runs through an enormous basalt dyke known as Solomon's Wall, cutting through it so cleanly you would think it was sectioned for this purpose with a gigantic cleaver. On top of this wide wall, on the northern bank, are the ruins of a prehistoric stone-walled village, and there as if planted among the detritus of an ancient people, a number of gigantic old baobab trees. Viewed from the lowlands of the valley floor, they stand starkly silhouetted against the sky line, surreally beautiful. Baboons, partial to the cream of tartar fruit, may have inadvertently deposited the seeds when they roosted there thousands of years ago; their descendants still roost here, propagating baobabs to this very day.

Lastly, to the south lies the great, grey, green, greasy – and now, due to soil erosion, gritty – Limpopo River, which is by far the largest of the three. Like a huge glistening python it slithers along a sandy course flanked by a narrow belt of huge riparian trees that grow in vivid contrast to the surrounding sea of semi-desert scrub. Here in dramatic splendour it demarcates the reserve's southern limit, which in turn forms the northern boundary of South Africa with Botswana and Zimbabwe, as it flows ever more sluggishly eastward through Mozambique and into the Indian Ocean. Steeped in folklore, the Limpopo River is as mysterious and dangerous as it is beautiful and nurturing.

It is here, in the cool shade of a huge nyala tree, on this legendary river's southern bank, that Shilo was born, nearly thirty years ago, and his odyssey began.

* * *

More often than not, a rewarding and successful relationship between people depends on the degree of commitment and effort they put into it, so why should it be any different when it involves a dog? There are many well known accounts of the extraordinary companionship between people and their dogs, a special bond of friendship.

They say a man has only one dog in his lifetime, just one with which he will share that special bond. Like the soul mate one may find in a human relationship – which, I also believe, you will have only once in your lifetime – it cannot be bought or planned for; the chemistry is either there or it isn't. However, having said this, nothing is ever quite that simple. Even with the right mix of chemicals, it doesn't happen automatically; both scenarios require a certain degree of commitment and sacrifice in order to achieve the desired state of happiness. These are unlikely to be 50/50 affairs; invariably one gives or receives more than the other – and like a good many human beings, dogs can be moody and temperamental, they too have good days and bad days. However, that is where the similarities end. A dog's emotional swings do not have any effect on the degree or intensity of its love for you. Free of reason or judgment, which affect even the strongest of human relationships, a dog will always be loyal to its master; its love is never measured, always given unconditionally.

There are many people who, for fear of making the wrong choice, or having to face the inevitable loss and subsequent emotional pain, never venture down this road, but then again, they will never know the rewards and fulfilment of such a relationship either. The classic cliché, 'It is better to have loved and lost, than never to have loved at all,' could not be more applicable.

Although I never had a true one-on-one 'boy-dog' relationship as a youth, we had family dogs like many families do. But like most youngsters, I'd always hankered for my very own dog, a dog devoted to me more than anyone else, without quite realising the degree of commitment necessary for that to happen. Later I was to find out that dogs have hearts and souls, and that they are capable of experiencing a wider range of emotions than we fully understand. Owning a dog is a huge responsibility, not to be taken lightly; they cannot be treated as a fad or a quick trial run, and they are entirely dependent on you, often to the point where their proper care and upkeep will tie you down at times. Understandably, for a young person this can be a daunting prospect. If things don't work out you cannot meet a dog for lunch and break it off, or send them a 'Dear Johnny' SMS, so, unless you have an alternative home, you don't simply dump a dog. It should be a relationship entered into for better or worse, and this is never, ever interpreted to mean euphoria or euthanasia!

* * *

I was based at Tuli Safari Lodge, approximately six kilometres upstream from the Pont Drift border control post, right in the heart of the Tuli Reserve. The lodge itself lay partially hidden, shrouded among the most magnificent indigenous trees on the edge of the Limpopo's expansive floodplain – a more beautiful setting for a luxury safari camp would be hard to imagine. The thatched cottage I lived in was discreetly tucked away at the bottom of an enormous well-established garden, a couple of hundred metres from the main lodge. Meticulously tended beds of exotic bulbous plants and shrubs were grown under the shielding canopy of nyala, jackal-berry and ana trees. Generous twice-weekly irrigation had resulted in a mini-jungle of lush vegetation which seemed to erupt with growth, creating a veritable oasis in the semi-arid bushveld. A small, manicured lawn about the size of a tennis court led up to the steps of the spacious gauze-enclosed verandah, where even on hot days the air moving freely through the screens kept the house relatively cool and comfortable.

Not having accumulated much in the way of furniture at that stage of my life, I had rather a lot of space in my cottage. Some might have described the decor as minimalist, even Spartan, but I preferred functional and uncomplicated. Living in those surrounds, conventional trappings were not essential; I didn't need much more to be comfortable.

Due to the relatively remote location of the operation, logistics were problematic; we were obliged to access South Africa frequently for communications and supplies. This meant having to cross the Limpopo each time and go through the formalities at the border posts on both sides. Owing to the security threat and the consequent military presence on our borders at the time, the South African border control post at Pont Drift was manned by members of the South African Police Force, who performed the function of immigration as well as customs and excise. Naturally, as we used this point of entry and exit almost on a daily basis, we became well acquainted with the officials on both sides of the river. Ockert Brits, 'Ockie' as everyone called him, was one of the customs officials on the South African side. He was a pleasant young man who was keen on the bush, and we had built up a good rapport.

One afternoon on my return from a monthly shopping trip in Pietersburg, now Polokwane, Ockie called me aside, a huge grin spread across his face. This time it wasn't to show off the newest set of magnesium wheels on his little bakkie, or a new fishing outfit; rather, it was to proudly inform me that his dog had given birth to five puppies a few days earlier. Unable to contain his excitement, he asked if I would like to take a quick look at them – then, with a note of paternal concern, added that they were still very small. I guess this was a subtle way of asking me to be gentle when I handled them.

It was a particularly warm day, but then again, very few days in this neck of the woods aren't, so I knew the truckload of fresh supplies I'd bought in Pietersburg that morning would spoil if left too long in the heat. However, even though owning a dog at that point was the furthest thing from my mind, I was naturally curious ... who doesn't love a puppy?

'Okay,' I said, relenting: 'A quick look.'

Parking the truck in the shadiest spot I could find, I made my way back through the gate to his house where he stood waiting for me. As I approached he turned and beckoned me to follow him. With that I was ushered through his house to the bottom of the spacious yard that overlooked the river.

The pups' mother was a fawn-coloured Labrador cross, whose relatively short hair and lean build hinted at some distant Rhodesian ridgeback or possibly even pit bull terrier lineage. I had often admired her beautiful proportions and the inquiring intelligence in her eyes. This was her first litter, yet, lying at the entrance of a 44-gallon drum which served as her kennel and nursery, she appeared to know exactly what was expected of her as a mother. The nursery was in a cool spot in the shade of a huge nyala tree, where she enjoyed the added comfort of a gentle breeze over the hollow she had dug for herself. Later I would learn that dogs have an in-built thermometer for always finding the coolest spot in any location. Lying there flat on her side in the relatively cool sand, she thumped her tail softly on the ground in response to our approach, showing that she was both happy to see her master and comfortable with my visiting her. She looked weary; it was also apparent from her still glistening teats that she had only recently suckled the pups. Even though I had seen her previously on numerous occasions when I'd gone through the border post, I'd never made any contact with her. Other than knowing she was devoted to Ockie and he to her, I hardly knew her, and am deeply embarrassed to admit that I cannot remember her name.

The sun shone bright and brassy, causing the dingy interior of the drum to appear even darker in contrast. I never wore sunglasses in those days, for fear my eyes would become too accustomed to them. I had been led to believe that should the glasses ever get damaged or lost I'd be handicapped, so I stupidly toughed it out until years later when I started fly-fishing, for which Polaroids are an essential piece of kit. Peering blindly into the shadows at the back of the drum, there was nothing to focus on; I couldn't make out an individual form to aim for.

Too impatient to wait for my eyes to adjust to the light, I presented the back of my hand to the pup's mother, who cautiously threw quick furtive glances in the direction of her brood, a natural protective response. Ears flat, she lowered her head and cautiously licked my hand, which I then slowly slid past her and into the back of the drum, her wet nose gently pressed against the underside of my upper arm, as if to let me know she was watching me.

Feeling around gently, I located the bundle of sleepy puppies. They were soft and warm, and although it was difficult to feel their individual forms, collectively they made a limp, lumpy softness, like a handful of fresh marshmallows. Managing to get my hand under one of their relatively hot, hairless tummies, I gently scooped one of the tiny pups out of the drum. Looking down at the little bundle, which resembled a big black mole, I carefully turned it onto its back and could see it was a male. The loose skin around his eyes was screwed up in a wrinkled frown, as even through tightly closed lids, they responded reflexively to the sudden exposure to sunlight.

I showed mom, who had been nudging my elbow ever so gently, that I meant her baby no harm, and as if in acknowledgement, she licked her son's face, and this time her tail thumped the ground with much more vigour. A minute later, I bent down slowly and put him back with his siblings. Much as I wanted to linger and look at the rest of them, my mind was also on those supplies standing in the sun on the back of the truck.

We left the mother peering into the drum, and headed back to the border post.

'That's the only black one,' Ockie said, trying to prick my interest, 'The only one that looks like his father.'

* * *

An onslaught of unwelcome thunder storms over the next few

weeks took us into the start of the wet season. Although any rain in the arid Tuli region was welcomed, I couldn't help thinking of how much more the veld would have benefited from a gradual build-up, rather than the hard falls that pelted the parched earth, resulting in massive topsoil runoff, which in turn invariably precipitated flash floods that seemed to do more harm than good.

The rain-swollen Limpopo made it impossible to cross the low-level causeway at Pont Drift for days on end. At times we were compelled to use a rickety cable car which had a habit of breaking down, leaving you precariously perched centimetres above the crocodile-infested river, until, in fits and starts, the operator got it running again. We were so busy trying to run the Lodge in the face of these logistical challenges, that time simply flew by unnoticed. By the time the river receded and things got back to a semblance of normality, it was over a month since I'd held the little black pup for the first time. They were nearly five weeks old now; no wonder Ockie was on a mission to find good homes for them, I thought.

My girlfriend, Vee, had already spent a few months working with me in Botswana. City born and bred, like me, she had been lured by the magic of the bushveld to Londolozi Game Reserve, where as a founder staff member, she'd been swept along and caught up in their heady passion for conservation. It was here that we met a couple of years later, while I was working next door at Mala Mala. After an on-and-off relationship that had undulated through peaks and troughs of indecision for a couple of years, it appeared as if she was finally ready to settle down in Tuli. Vee was clearly happier in the bush environment than the city.

Having crossed the border post umpteen times since her arrival, she had naturally got to be on familiar terms with the customs and immigration officials on both sides of the Limpopo. Ockie cornered her as she was about to go through to Pietersburg one day – and although Vee tried telling him neither of us was overly keen to own a dog at this stage, he persisted. Later she confessed that the looking part was the easiest to resist, but that once she'd held them and they had licked her face with their little pink tongues and puppy breath, well, of course, she didn't want one, she wanted all of them!

Owning a dog was still the farthest thing from my mind. Besides, we weren't allowed to have dogs at the lodge. But that wasn't the only reason. I valued being a free spirit; my independence meant a lot to me, and though I loved dogs, I didn't want the responsibility and encumbrance of owning one at that stage of my life. Perhaps this was selfish, but I have to admit that my reluctance was also largely based on what I had experienced of other people's dogs, particularly dogs which were untrained and unruly in the bush.

Although our employers had yet to be consulted for approval, the bug had bitten deep. Vee was determined to get a dog first and ask for consent later, figuring that once they had seen how cute the pup was, the lodge owners' hearts would melt, and then with only a little convincing they would relent.

A couple of days before she went through to collect her dog, I decided to go and visit the pups for myself – more out of curiosity than anything else, you understand. They were developing fast, and as with lion cubs, appeared to be growing into their disproportionately huge paws. Their folds of soft skin hung loose and supple, waiting to be stuffed taut with powerful muscles, and of course there were still traces of that unmistakable puppy breath that would linger for a couple of weeks yet. As they approached six weeks of age and their individual personalities began to show, it was clear that no two were the same.

I still had no intention of owning a dog at that stage of my life ... even the little black pup, which I felt curiously drawn to. I didn't want Vee to bring him home, because despite my doubts, I knew that if she did, there'd be no return ... for me the shy black pup was a keeper. I still don't know why, or what it was that attracted me to him. I was inexplicably torn – I didn't really want that dog, yet strangely, neither did I want anyone else to have him. I told Vee I'd been to check the dogs out, and that they were all in great shape; however, remembering how the black pup cowered at the back of the 'kennel' while his siblings lavished me with boisterous welcome licks, I advised her not to get too hung up on him, mumbling something about being worried that he was the least forthcoming of the litter.

At mid-morning the following day Vee returned from the border post. I remember that moment vividly. A billowing dust cloud enveloped the doorless Land Cruiser as it ground to a halt in the lodge's parking lot. There was a brief moment of awkwardness as an otherwise agile Vee, now unable to hang onto anything and climb out with dignity, simply swung her legs off the high seat and slid out onto the ground. She stood there for a moment clutching a pup under each arm, waiting for my reaction. What a sight! Wild, windblown hair, long brown legs, a huge grin and two little puppies ... One of them was the black pup. Now it was my turn to smile. Vee had read me like a book.

We decided to name the bitch Shammy, because her coat was lighter than her mother's, a buckskin tone of chamois leather, and just as soft and supple to the touch. Within a few days it had become apparent how dissimilar the two pups were; besides the colour contrast, they had distinctly different personalities. Shammy was adorable, affectionate and boisterous to a fault; there was so much of her mother's Labrador lineage evident in her nature. The black pup was more attentive than boisterous. He also appeared sensitive to the point of being a little nervy, which I assumed was due to the Doberman in him. However, despite their different natures they were good company for each other, and I remember entertaining the notion of keeping both of them, one for me and one for Vee. Well ... the thought remained just that, because two weeks later she dumped me with the pups, crossed the Limpopo River and walked out of my life.

* * *

Finding myself suddenly alone wasn't easy; I guess I was shocked at the unexpected and abrupt emptiness of it all; it left me with a hollow feeling in the pit of my stomach, a feeling teetering somewhere between butterflies and nausea. Yes, in case you were wondering, even supposedly tough, rugged game rangers can and do suffer from broken hearts! This was clearly a job for distance and time, and although it was difficult in the beginning, I found that by immersing myself in a disciplined work routine, I had less time to get melancholy ... I was able to cope. The days were relatively easy to get through, as there was always so much to do that for most of the time my thoughts were completely focused on my work. This was helped in no small measure by the most beautiful environment that surrounded me, which was always stimulating and uplifting. Whenever I slid into the quagmire of self-pity, I would go out into the bush where the myriad wonderful distractions would winch me up and out onto solid ground in no time.

Moreover, I found myself confronted with two cheerful little faces, two beautiful puppies that looked to me for their needs. I realised I now had two lives depending on me being strong; I guess I was being looked upon as their pack leader. There was no way I could wimp out on them. It soon dawned on me that providing the proper care and training for one dog in the bush was going to be responsibility enough, so I found a home for Shammy. Located in the Honeydew countryside near Johannesburg, on a ten-acre smallholding, it was perfect. I was particularly pleased that there were other dogs on the estate, which would suit her gregarious nature. I walked away leaving Shammy playing with them as if they'd known each other for ages, and although my heart was heavy, I knew she was going to be happy.

Back in Botswana, the nights were the most depressing time for me. By getting absorbed in field projects, a lot of them physically demanding, I found that when bedtime came around, I was exhausted and slept deeply. But, when I woke, I was ... well, not quite so alone any more. Almost imperceptibly, the black pup began filling the void; he gave me a sense of purpose, and became my rock. He could not have entered my life at a better time.

* * *

The gangly little pup and I became inseparable. Wherever I went there was sure to be a little black shadow, all paws, floppy ears and eagerness, following closely behind. We did everything together, and he continued to grow on me: something I couldn't quite put my finger on was beginning to develop between us. Each day he grew bolder and more confident. Most significantly, he now had an identity; he was no longer referred to as 'the black pup' – he had a name.

I called him 'Shilo', pronounced 'shy low'. I had unintentionally dropped the 'h' off the end of the correct spelling of Shiloh, which is the Hebrew word meaning peaceful or tranquil. It is also the name of a small whitewashed church in the United States of America, where a bloody civil war battle, known as the battle of Shiloh, was waged – and, in a somewhat less dramatic vein, the title of one of my favourite Neil Diamond songs ... but, for none of the above did I choose this name. I knew long before I left school that if ever I owned a dog, there would be no question in my mind as to what his or her name would be, for practical reasons as well as the poetry of it.

As a young lad I'd seen a movie about fur trappers and bounty hunters in Alaska's Yukon Territory. I forget the title now, but it left a lasting impression on me, not so much for its story line, but for the dog that starred in it. One particularly memorable scene depicts a blinding blizzard, so harsh that the trappers and their faithful dog get separated for the night. The next day dawns, calm and clear, the crisp snow crunches softly underfoot as they plod through it in their snow shoes ... this is the only sound the men make as they begin the search for their beloved dog. Stopping every now and again they cup their hands to their mouths and call out his name across the snow-covered valleys and mountains. 'Shi—lo.' The echoing of that dog's name resonated so beautifully and clearly, it resounded and stuck with me like a catchy song you find yourself singing over and over again. I couldn't get the name out of my head – in fact, forty years have passed, and I can still hear those men tramping through those mountains calling that dog.

What really impressed me, cinematographic enhancements

and sound engineering skill aside, was how far the call of the name appeared to carry. In my situation this was particularly significant, because as a dog owner I was seriously handicapped – I couldn't whistle! I needed a name with two syllables that could be projected some distance – and as an added bonus, the Shhh part of his name was very effective for low-tone stealth communication.

*   *   *

From day one Shilo went to work in the bush with me. With hindsight, perhaps I should have waited a couple of weeks or so until he'd grown a little bigger. Most puppies have large stores of energy; however, in high ambient temperatures they tire quickly. On the odd occasion when Shilo couldn't keep up, he'd sit on the pathway and give a little yelp; I would then simply pick him up and carry him. Shilo simply loved being with me and I wanted to be with him. Even those times when we weren't out in the bush together, he'd shadow me. He enjoyed following me around the camp grounds, particularly when there were no guests in residence, and I busied myself with routine camp maintenance. It was the same when I pottered around the workshop repairing vehicles, Shilo would be there, close to me. He'd more often than not position himself a discreet distance from the din, strategically picking a spot from where he could watch me the whole time, just in case I dared move somewhere without him. I recall him being confident and independent from an early age; Shilo gave me the impression he wanted to be with me, and it had little to do with security. Even as a pup, he appeared to be secure in himself and didn't appear to need the constant physical contact I've known other dogs to demand. We shared my double bed, so there was plenty of room for the two of us to stretch out when it got too warm. Not one for climbing into the bed, he preferred to curl up at my feet or next to me on top of the covers. During the heat of the day, the cool concrete screed floor of the verandah was his favoured spot.

The concessionary deviation from the owners' hard-line policy of strictly no dogs was honourable, and to show my appreciation I intended to keep my end of the bargain. Having promised them that the dog would be trained and would not become a nuisance to the guests, I was committed. I also knew that our being together and staying together depended on my ability to teach him, and how he responded to the training.

With no idea of how to go about it or where to begin, I made a list of priorities – taking into consideration that pretty much everything was new to him. With his health and safety at the top of the list, mindful of the fact that the nearest veterinary care was nearly four hours' drive away, I began to school Shilo. He needed to be taught about the dangers of living in the bush, and if possible how to avoid injury or death. The rest, I hoped, would follow instinctively.

My initial reservations about Shilo had been based on my immediate impression of his reticent nature. However, as he became more settled and familiar with me, I had the opportunity to see his true spirit emerging. I realised how presumptuous I'd been, how poorly I'd assessed him, and how little I knew about dogs. What I initially took for nervousness and shyness was in fact sensitivity and intelligence, and my nose was pleasantly rubbed into this fact when Shilo turned out to be a remarkably responsive and acutely clever pupil.

* * *

One of the first things I did was to get him vaccinated. Knowing we'd be driving a good distance over rough roads, I made him as comfortable as possible in a basket on the seat next to me. Several gruelling hours later we reached the town of Selebi Phikwe, where the resident veterinarian was recently qualified and fresh out from England. Although he dealt primarily with livestock, I found him to be most enthusiastic and obliging, and soon Shilo had his own medical file registered, and all the necessary jabs administered.

I suspect the volume of medication may have had some effect on Shilo, because despite the bumpy ride he slept most of the way back. Occasionally he would wake up, briefly look up at me, then swallowing lazily he'd tuck his muzzle back into the folds and drift off again. I, on the other hand, was kept alert and attentive by the non-taxpaying road users of rural Botswana. It required concentration and some degree of skill to avoid colliding with the myriad goats, fat-tailed sheep, and cattle – not to mention the ever-present donkey carts, also known as Kalahari Ferraris – which used the sandy tracks and roads outside the reserve.

Closer to home, the sun was just beginning to set behind us as we crossed the distinctive grey sand of the dry Majali River. Climbing out on the far bank, we stopped to watch a breeding herd of more than fifty elephants crossing the road, kicking up a soft dust cloud as the young calves were ushered across by the older cows, much like a teacher does with schoolchildren at a busy intersection. There was no dilly-dallying or posturing, as is often the case with adolescent bulls. When the last of their grey wrinkly backsides had disappeared into the croton thicket, we squeezed past quickly and drove on. An ear-splitting trumpet followed my change to second gear, telling me off for being so impatient.

Shilo lay in his basket through it all, and didn't move until we reached the lodge. As we stopped he lifted a drowsy head to look around at the now familiar surroundings and his little tail began thumping; he was happy to be home, and if I had had a tail it would have been thumping too.

6

WARTHOGS CAN BE REAL PIGS

Rewinding to Thornybush …

I have always had a soft spot for gun dogs, particularly pointers. I had the privilege of living and working in the bush with three just such dogs for over a year, and some of what I learned from them proved invaluable later on. The following account is of a particularly harrowing experience these dogs had while out in the bush one morning, which had a profound and lasting effect on me. Years later, when I began to train Shilo, the knowledge I gained from this unpleasant incident helped me to ensure that he was better prepared for the reality of life in the African bushveld.

* * *

When they weren't pointing on coveys of francolins, or out in the Land Rover driving around the reserve with their owner, Frank, the three English pointers, Gina, Lola and Ranger, were utterly devoted house pets. They were the personification of soppy dogs, and if they'd been small enough, they would most certainly have become lap dogs, particularly Gina, who was the most sensitive of the three, and totally committed to Frank's wife Dawn. Lola and Ranger's allegiance was a more fickle affair, shifting to whoever was carrying a shotgun or heading out into the bush with the Land Rover at the time.

Although I found these pointers to be extremely intelligent and loving animals, there were times when they were restless and somewhat distracted. This single-mindedness would reach fever pitch in the hunting season. Pointers are unable to resist their genetic programming, a trait passed down a bloodline that goes back centuries, which predisposes them to actively course the countryside sniffing out coveys of game birds. Once the birds have been located, the dog freezes and assumes the classic rock-steady pose they have become so famous for. One of the front paws is held up, the tail, straight, often in line with their back, and their head craned forward with eyes firmly fixed on the birds. This posture is known as the point. Their concentration is all-consuming: some dogs will quiver ever so slightly with tension; others will remain as resolute as a statue until given the command to flush the birds. This is their life.

This activity is confined to the winter months, when the birds aren't breeding. In southern Africa this period starts around April/May through to the onset of the rainy season in September/ October, which not surprisingly also seems to be the time gun dogs became most restless. As human beings, despite our relatively poor sense of smell, we are also able to detect the approach of this special time. Unfortunately for some, it manifests itself in hayfever, colds and flu; in a select few, shotguns will be taken out of storage, pointed around a bit, wiped down and then put away again for no reason. Yet others will start tying heaps of trout flies, even though their fly boxes are already stuffed full.

It is most noticeable with the change of season, particularly as the long languid days of summer give way to autumn, and the first subtle nip in the air signifies the imminent onset of winter; the days begin getting shorter, the leaves on the trees turn, and the air fills with the nutty scent of ripe grass seeds. For grain farmers this time of the year also signifies harvest time, a time of expectation and an anticipation of good yields from a promising summer's growth. It is the same with game birds; a good summer usually means that coveys have swelled to more than double their previous size, and the birds are plump and healthy. The air is now filled with the message of their presence and abundance –

naturally gun dogs become restless: this is what they were bred for; this is their season and they cannot help themselves. Under control, a trained pointer coursing a field on the scent of ground birds is something to behold; on the other hand, an uncontrolled dog that chases game at every opportunity is a liability to its owner and itself, especially in Africa's game-filled bushveld.

* * *

I remember that cool May morning like it was yesterday. There were no guests in camp for the first time in weeks, and Frank had decided it was the perfect opportunity to go out and harvest a few 'bush bantams', better known as crested francolins. Finding the back seat of his short-wheel-based Land Rover already occupied by three eager dogs, he carefully placed his favourite 12 bore shotgun, an old British-made CG Bonehill, between the front seats. The pointers knew the shotgun meant birds, and since it would be the first shoot of the season, they were completely hyped up. Before setting off, Frank patted the passenger seat and Lola jumped over to sit beside him. She had obviously done this before. There was no scramble for the seat; Lola was his favourite – she knew it, and the others knew it too. Then with a smug smile and a wave over his shoulder, Frank drove out of camp.

I couldn't go with them that morning because there was something I needed to do, and although I can't recall exactly what it was, it must have been something I was unable to put off for a couple of hours. More than likely it was a problematic water pump motor supplying one of the waterholes or a burst in the pipeline supplying Top Pan, the largest of the water points on the reserve. Otherwise there was no question about it, I would have joined Frank.

Later that morning on my return from the bush I drove into camp via the airstrip and was surprised to see a plane belonging to our veterinarian, Blackie Swart, parked there. Frank came rushing out to meet me. His clothes were covered in dried blood, which although quite shocking, was also rather puzzling. That was when I became aware of the huge tumbler in his hand, which was half-filled with whisky. This was not in itself unusual for Frank, except it was a little earlier in the day than when he usually poured himself a scotch. This time, however, it looked as though he really needed it: his eyes were filled with tears and he was shaking with emotion. I had never seen Frank in such a state before.

'What happened to you, Frank?' I gasped.

Without a word he pointed over my shoulder behind me. I turned around to look across the lawn at one of the guest chalets on the far side of the camp, where I saw a number of people engrossed around what appeared to be a long table. I recognised one of them immediately, though he stood with his back to me. Nobody but Blackie wore sleeveless light blue overalls in the bush.

'It's not me, I'm fine, it's the dogs – they've been ripped up by pig!' he spluttered. 'Ranger's not too bad, but Lola and Gina are in a bad way, I just can't bring myself to look, Gina might not make it.'

I knew Frank had hunted most his life, and that he was no stranger to blood and gore, yet, this 'big white hunter' couldn't watch a veterinarian operate on his beloved dogs? I could only surmise from the state he was in that it must be quite a bad scenario. Naturally I needed to go over and see for myself.

Blackie and his assistant were huddled around what was obviously a makeshift operating table. The location had been well chosen, there was plenty of natural light, and it was relatively cool and airy under the thatch of the chalet's open-ended carport. Blackie stood with his back to me, bent over a large blood-stained table; he hadn't heard me approach on the lawn. As I moved around to one side I could see two dogs on the table, and recognised them immediately as Lola and Gina. Blackie seemed to be concentrating on Gina; his assistant was monitoring vital signs and adjusting the drips of both dogs. One of our staff was mopping up, while another brought on buckets of water.

Ranger lay on the cool cement screed floor, it appeared from the thumping wag of his tail that he recognised me; he seemed to be okay. He was panting a little, having been mildly sedated; later I found out that this was to keep him from running around until they could attend to his wounds. Dawn was nowhere to be seen; apparently she had broken down completely. Gina was her dog. I guessed she had gone over to Frank's mother, who lived in a cottage close to the main lodge. Approaching the table I soon saw why. The wounds were horrific and the smell of blood mingled with wet dog hair hung heavy in the still warm air.

Blackie looked up and greeted me, as cheerfully as he could under the circumstances, but I knew him well enough to know that he was very concerned. I'd seen that face before when we had lost a cheetah a couple of months before. As Frank had suspected, Gina, being the youngest and least experienced of the three dogs, had taken the worst of the warthog's vicious attack, and was indeed the worst off. Besides inflicting numerous gashes and lacerations around her chest and lower neck area, one of the warthog's lower tusks had gone in under Gina's 'armpit', where an upward rip of its incredibly powerful neck had almost severed the right front leg from her body. This appeared to be the area on her body that Blackie was concentrating on when I approached the table. Lola, the oldest and wisest of the three, hadn't fared much better; she lay there completely anaesthetised, while the assistant began preparing her massive wounds for repair. Later Blackie told me that the volume of blood loss had been his biggest concern. Had he not been able to fly in as quickly as he did, Lola and Gina would have simply bled to death.

After the dogs had been sewed up and stabilised, there wasn't much more Blackie and his assistant could do. More loving care than they would get being nursed at home by Frank and Dawn was not possible. Knowing this, the exhausted vet dumped a pile of medicines in a box, mumbled a few instructions then handed the responsibility of the dogs' convalescence over to us. Before leaving, I saw Blackie gently take a tearful Dawn aside and reassure her that Gina had a very good chance of making a full recovery ... At that point it was what Dawn needed to hear.

*   *   *

Later that evening in the bar, Frank was able to go into more detail and told me what had happened to the dogs that morning. Apparently he'd seen a covey of six crested francolins run across a small clearing to find cover. Parking a discreet distance away, he got out with the dogs and brought them up to where the birds had disappeared into the bush. Noses to the ground, they immediately took up the fresh scent trail. It wasn't long before they found the birds: all three dogs stood dead still, Ranger and Gina honouring the more experienced Lola's point and holding back. This trait of respect among bird dogs is fascinating to watch, and good pointers will always do this – even when working with strange dogs, the dominant dog's point will be respected.

Huddled together, the francolins held tight under a thick raisin bush which grew on the side of an old termite mound. Knowing that bushveld ground birds were reluctant flyers most of the time, preferring to run, Frank knew he'd need to use the dogs to get them up into the air. Sitting shoulder to shoulder against the base of the multi-stemmed bush, the mottled francolins blended in perfectly against the autumn-coloured leaf litter surrounding them, and although alert, appeared confident they were safe. They did not want to move, let alone fly … well, that was until Frank decided to send the dogs in to flush them.

Three sniffing wet noses being thrust at them through the spindly stems was just too much to take. As one, all six francolins exploded into the air like feathered rockets, and as they separated, curling up and away, Frank fired both barrels, hoping for a classic left and right, but only succeeded in bagging one bird. Then he mentally marked the spot where it fell, in order to retrieve it before the dogs did – pointers can be a little rough, particularly with the first bird of the season. In the meantime, the noise of the shooting and the commotion from the dogs must have awoken what Frank described as the father of all warthogs.

The old aardvark burrow on the other side of the same termite mound was relatively warm and comfy: it being an overcast cool morning, the old boar had hoped to sleep in a bit. But nothing, not even a lazy old pig, could sleep through the screech of the francolins as they flew into the air, followed by the sound of a double-barrelled shotgun going off and the excited barking of the pointers. The rudely awakened warthog came bursting out of its burrow in a cloud of grey dust, then blinking quickly in the light, turned away at full speed as it ran off into the bush with all three dogs in hot pursuit. They may have thought this was an added bonus to that morning's hunt – nipping at that big fat bum disappearing into the bush promised to be much more fun than retrieving little birds.

According to Frank, the dogs had simply disobeyed him when he called them back. He was certain they had heard him, but in the excitement of the moment ignored his desperate shouts and screams for them not to chase the warthog. He prayed that the warthog would outpace the dogs, but unfortunately, though it could have, it didn't. Frank said that by the time the warthog had turned to face the dogs, he was too far away to have been able to limit the damage anyway; then, when he heard the first scream-ing yelp, he knew the shit had hit the fan. By the time he got to the scene a couple of minutes later, the pig was long gone; only the violent aftermath of what an angry warthog's lower tusks can do was evident.

Warthogs have long enamel lower tusks whose edges are kept razor sharp as they grind against the relatively soft ivory of the upper tusks with each chewing motion. A more perfectly de-signed, failsafe sharpener for the life of these formidable weap-ons would be hard to find. It was a terrible sight that confronted Frank: blood-spattered yellow grass lay flattened and trampled like a shredded coir mattress. The pig's trotters had dug deeply into the soil along the game path it had taken when it left the scene. The well-spaced, even spoor indicated that the warthog had escaped unscathed; also there wasn't a single drop of blood leading away along the path it took. Frank knew enough about tracking to make the assumption that all the blood that had been spilled at the scene belonged to the dogs.

The three dogs were in a bad way: Lola and Ranger were pant-ing heavily, their rasping breath coming in short, rapid gasps. Gina lay there hardly able to move, whimpering each time her mouth closed momentarily. Frank picked her up in his arms, holding her against his chest, he could feel her warm blood soaking the front of his shirt and through to his skin. She lifted her head and feebly licked his face a couple of times as he carried her back to the Land Rover. Lola and Ranger were only just able to keep up, following along behind him.

All things considered, Gina and Lola would not have survived were it not for some fortunate circumstances that came together. That is to say, if Blackie hadn't been on call that morning, if he wasn't able to fly, if the phones were down, and if the incident had taken place further away from the lodge ... The most important 'if' that I took away with me from what I saw on that table was, IF only those dogs could have been trained not to chase warthogs in the first place ...

*   *   *

I have often reflected on that incident between the three pointers and the warthog and still do, so, understandably I was never as surprised as some of my colleagues were, at the tenacity of warthogs. Even large predators like cheetah and leopard would sometimes abort a warthog hunt, particularly on those occasions when challenged by a determined pig. While tourists looked on with mouths agape, I was not taken aback or surprised; I knew what warthogs were capable of, as no doubt those powerful predators instinctively did too.

7

DANGERS IN THE BUSH

It is a most comforting feeling when a dog snuggles up next to you while you sleep. On the other hand, overprotective dogs that bark at every perceived threat can make for distinctly undesirable bedfellows. I didn't want Shilo to sleep anywhere else; besides, I had no need for a barking dog to warn me of intruders. Nor, more importantly, did the lodge's paying guests want to hear a domestic dog barking in the middle of the wilds of Africa. It was bad enough having to put up with the odd rooster we'd occasionally purchase from a nearby village, and which unknowingly would herald its last sunrise with a few 'cock-a-doodle-doos', shortly thereafter being consigned to the pot.

The problem, not surprisingly, was that there were always wild animals attracted into the lodge's grounds. During the day it was mainly baboons, vervet monkeys and warthogs; then under the cover of darkness, everything from cane rats to elephants would move in to eat the lush garden plants. Our trusty night watchman had hell's own time keeping the damage down. Sometimes his frustration would boil over, as happened one night when I was obliged to challenge him on the serious matter of having killed a bushbuck. The poor man was in quite a state, not having intended to kill the animal when he threw his knobkerrie at it in the darkness. However, the ball of the stick struck the bushbuck squarely behind the head, killing it instantly. It was frustrating policing these wary little antelope; not only were they too clever for him, he said, but they were also the stealthiest of the garden raiders. As he cracked his whip to chase them out of one side of the garden, there would be others sneaking in on the far side. I sympathised, but told him that no further animals were to be killed or injured – no garden plants were worth the life of a bush-buck.

Due to their sheer size and power, elephants were by far the most destructive. A herd in Tuli's manicured garden would wreak havoc. At times they did more than target the exotic well-watered plants, pulling up underground plastic water pipes and leaving them festooned on the shrubbery, kinked and useless. Huge trees were easily pushed over due to the soft wet soil, and left virtually uneaten; however, this destructive and wasteful feeding behaviour was usually the work of the bull herds, which although usually numbering fewer individuals, caused infinitely more havoc than the numerically superior breeding herds. The latter, comprising mainly cows and calves, were a great deal more delicate in their feeding habits. However, their weight caused other problems for us. Deep, dinner-plate-sized indentations left by their huge feet on the soft lawn would take months to fill in and smooth out.

Despite their potential for mayhem, elephants are highly intelligent, so would usually respond well to being moved along. Like naughty kids caught stealing fruit, they'd offer no resistance or confrontation; once told off and chased out, they would not return for days. Elephants disliked the crack of the whip, which sounded like a rifle shot, a noise they knew from crop-raiding forays in South Africa, and they knew what guns meant. Hippos, on the other hand, were the most belligerent and dangerous, often returning numerous times in one night, each time becoming less responsive to the cracking whip.

Protecting the delectable plants from drought-stricken animals coming in from the surrounding bushveld was especially difficult in the winter months. Driven by hunger, they persisted in feeding in the lodge grounds where they drew the attention of more than our night watchman. Inevitably the concentration of smaller prey animals would attract predators which quickly began adapting their hunting techniques to suit. Using the dense

cover provided by the garden plants for stalking and concealment, they frequently hunted in the lodge grounds at night.

Shilo's ears missed nothing. Being able to hear the creatures
of the night but not see them was intimidating for the young
puppy, and I suspect he may even have been able to smell them
on occasion. Sometimes I would feel his little heart thumping
away, especially if he heard something near the cottage. When
he barked I would tell him: 'Uh-uh!' – dog-speak for 'No, no!'
Unable to contain himself, he would growl; when he growled I
praised him. Occasionally the growl would involuntarily break
into a 'yip!' and if left unchecked, he would try to bark again. A
few lessons later, even the 'yip!' disappeared.

Soon, with a good measure of reassurance, I had Shilo growling
instead of barking at night sounds. With only one or two excep-
tions, there was nothing for him to bark at during the day either,
so visitors to the lodge never heard a barking dog. Thanks to
Shilo, I was able to keep to my end of the bargain. Fresh roosters
were still on the menu from time to time, however.

*   *   *

Very few dogs that live in Africa's big game country will die of old
age, and invariably it is the bravest of them that will die young.
Add disobedience to the equation, and the dog won't reach its
first birthday without mishap. Most bush dogs are killed or injured when whatever they are chasing suddenly turns on them.
Others are bitten by snakes or taken by crocodiles and other
predators. The list of perils is endless.

Dogs are descended from wolves, and wolves chase their prey
down in much the same way as the unrelated African wild dogs
do. Dogs' natural instinct is to chase things – whether it's a rat,
a cat or a ten-ton truck: if it runs away they will pursue it. In
my world this includes anything from tree squirrels to African
elephants, and nearly anything else in between. Even the most
dangerous of wild animals will usually run from the smallest
plucky dog. By way of example, try to imagine how pumped a

tiny Maltese terrier cross must have felt when a bull giraffe, an animal it had never seen in its life, and weighing nearly 1 500 kilograms, galloped away from it. I witnessed this event, and although I found it hilarious at the time, what I remember most was the expression on the dog's face when it eventually returned, clearly saying: 'Sorry pal, I just couldn't resist that!' Incidentally, I don't know of any Jack Russell terriers that have been successfully trained not to chase things ... There's more about these incredible little guys later.

It was no different with Shilo, except that he was trained when, what and where to chase, or not to chase. In the bush there's no time to dilly dally, so training in this vital aspect of his conduct with wild animals began when he was a little over four months old. Once a dog takes off after something it shouldn't be chasing, there are only a few seconds in which to change the course of action before it is too late. With increased speed, the wind flowing past its flattened ears all but drowns out peripheral noise, particularly any instruction from behind. This is exacerbated exponentially as the distance between you and the dog increases, until the point is reached when there's no turning back. Therefore, the response to your command has to be virtually instantaneous. So, I knew that early training was crucial. The tone of my voice was the key, and before long Shilo could determine the degree of danger by the level of urgency in my voice.

*   *   *

From puppyhood I made every effort to take Shilo out into the bush, which meant he spent a lot of time in the vehicle with me. He loved the open Toyota Land Cruiser and never missed an opportunity to take command of the passenger seat. Standing with his back legs on the edge of the seat and front paws on the dashboard, he'd dance from one foot to the other to maintain balance. He loved to lean into the direction we were travelling, craning his head forward in keen anticipation while chewing at the wind as it blew through his mouth, sometimes making his lips flutter.

Those late-seventies model Land Cruiser pick-ups had no air-conditioning option, so the doors had been removed for added air flow and comfort. However, this also allowed Shilo to alight easily whenever I stopped. Sometimes, he'd run off and chase game before I could grab hold of him and physically restrain him. Many animals recognised that he was little more than a baby, and knowing that there was no real threat from him, treated his clumsy attempts with disdain, often standing their ground and staring him down, or turning and chasing him back to the vehicle. Despite this, whenever a relatively large animal ran from him, it was too tantalising; it provoked his natural instincts to chase. Although these forays were tentative, half-hearted pursuits of short duration and distance, I knew this was my cue – it was time to begin the lessons.

I needed to find a method of teaching Shilo to abort a chase immediately on command, and this had to be accomplished without hurting him in any way. I agonised over the possible scenarios and conventional techniques, none of which sat well with me. I wasn't dealing with a huge wild mustang that needed his spirit broken, or worse! I was dealing with a sensitive young puppy, an animal I loved and which trusted and loved me in return.

Given the limited resources at my disposal, this problem had me stumped. Advice from different sources varied widely, from techniques I was sure were used by Stone Age man to train semi-tame wolves, to the most gentle and progressive of methods advocated by Barbara Woodhouse aficionados. Unfortunately the brilliance of the Dog Whisperer, Cesar Millan, hadn't emerged yet. Nothing conventional was remotely appropriate to my situation. I soon realised I was on my own and needed to adapt the training method to the circumstances.

I was racking my brain for inspiration when something sparked a memory of when, as a teenager, I helped falconer Desmond Prout Jones safely capture and ring large raptors. One of the traps we used to capture small to medium-sized raptors is known as a bellchattery. This simple but effective device employs short lengths of strong nylon fishing line tied into nooses and attached to the top of a small wire mesh tunnel, which in turn was secured to a stable but lightweight base (one side of a commercial barbecue grid was found to be perfect for this). Two live mice, one white and one black, were then placed in the tunnel. The contrasting colour accentuated by their movement would attract the raptor's attention from hundreds of metres away; it was too much for them, they were unable to resist. Predatory instincts would override any suspicion, and the bird would swoop down and try to clamp its talons on the mice. Protected by the wire mesh, the rodents remained completely unharmed, but the raptor's talons would get entangled and ensnared by one or more of the nooses. Tied onto the handle of the base of the trap – it was this feature of the trap's mechanism that I was interested in – was a thin strip of tyre inner tube, approximately a metre long. Onto the other end of the strip, a weight of a few ounces was attached. This effectively broke the shock of the pull or jerk when the raptor tried to fly away. The weight could be balanced and was easily adjusted according to the size of the particular raptor we were targeting or likely to capture. It was just heavy enough for the inertia to slow the captive bird down and prevent it from injuring itself or flying away with the trap. Larger, more powerful raptors were captured using a toothless, well-padded gin trap, but these also needed to use the inertia control principle whereby the inner tube took up most of the shock caused by the sudden jerk as the bird tried to fly away. This was basically the same anti-shock principle that was employed when using the bellchattery. So I simply expanded on the principle and modified the mechanics to use as an aid in training Shilo.

* * *

On the southern edge of the mopane belt, some 60 kilometres south of Pont Drift on the road to Pietersburg, is the small village of Alldays. It was little more than a farming outpost in the late seventies, and I suspect not much has changed since. The community of Alldays and surrounds comprised mainly down-to-earth folk, the kind of people who have largely contributed to South Africans being known the world over for their warm hospitality.

I recall the time I lay ill in bed for a few days in a small clinic there run by Die Vroue Federasie (The Women's Federation). The room I lay in had French doors that opened onto a small stoep, which was flush with an immaculately kept lawn. It was here, on this stoep, not two metres from my bed, that they allowed Shilo to stay. Not only that, but because I was too weak to walk around, they also took it upon themselves to feed and water my dog. Needless to say, he was spoiled rotten. Except for raw bones, which they drew the line at, the food brought to him regularly was obviously tastier than he was getting at home. Shilo didn't lick the bowl clean to be polite, which says something about the hospital food here.

Although the little town was too small to supply the bulk of our needs for running the reserve, what couldn't be found at Wessells' general dealer would probably be on the shelves of the well-stocked farmer's co-operative. Here you could purchase everything essential for survival, from pop rivets to *potjiekos* pots, and from bullets to *bloudraad*. It also happened to have exactly what I needed to make up a training lead for Shilo – a strong leather dog collar, similar to those with pointed studs worn by those mean-looking bulldogs depicted in cartoon sketches, and a length of thin nylon ski rope.

Back at the lodge, I went to the workshop scrapheap, where I found the last item needed in the form of an old tractor inner tube, from which I cut a couple of strips of rubber of varying widths. Cutting a two-metre length of the nylon ski rope, I fixed it to the collar; the other end was then tied onto a strip of inner tube which had been pre-tested for resilience and stretch, which in turn was connected to the remaining eight metres of ski rope. All the while I was watched intently by Shilo, his head cocked to one side in bemused curiosity.

'This is all because I love you, my boy,' I said.

I placed my arm through the looped dog collar and held it in the crook of my arm, and then tested the strip of inner tube, trimming it progressively until I was able to run against the resistance, albeit with some difficulty. I was particularly attentive to the increased resistance felt as the inertia strain was taken up, which had to be smooth but firm. Although my arm got chafed in the testing process, the results were worth it. Most importantly, I was satisfied Shilo wouldn't get hurt by this training method.

Early the next morning Shilo jumped into the vehicle and as usual assumed the position, raring to go. With his mind on other things, he took absolutely no notice as I leaned across and placed the collar on him. It was as if he knew this was going to be a temporary discomfort – as it happened, this would be the only time Shilo would feel a collar around his neck for the rest of his life. I then secured the loose end of the lead to a seat strut and drove out to the airstrip, where I knew impala and wildebeest were likely to have spent the evening. Sure enough, although the wildebeest had left by the time we got there, the impala were still milling around near the windsock.

I managed to get really close to them, then realised why – their attention was fixed on two black-backed jackals lying in the bush close by. Edging closer, we were almost in amongst the herd when I could see Shilo starting to tremble with excitement, so I stopped the vehicle and switched off. As I did so he jumped out and began to run after the now fleeing impala. At the same moment I shouted harshly after him: 'Uh-uh!' Almost simultaneously with the command he was yanked to an involuntary stop. The lead had played out until the inner tube stretched to a point and no further, stopping him so assertively that his front legs were momentarily lifted off the ground, causing him to lose his balance and fall onto his side. There was a mixture of surprise and possibly even embarrassment in his eyes when he ran back to the Cruiser. To add to his dejection, the impala bounded away half-heartedly, as if teasing him with their classic rocking-horse gait. The jackals, masters of subterfuge that they are, had simply disappeared.

After lavishly praising Shilo and letting him know how much I loved him, it was back to class. On the Limpopo River floodplain, where the soil was more yielding, we went through the same routine. This time a murmur of more than thirty banded mongoose obliged by bursting out of a thick stand of reeds where they had been foraging and running across the track in front of us. Their undulating gait over the soft sand was reminiscent of a school of porpoises moving through the waves. Slightly bunched up now, they were slower than usual; this was too much to resist. Again Shilo chased, and again the next thing he knew after hearing 'Uh-uh!' was being stopped abruptly and yanked to the ground.

Later that morning, on the way back, I stopped the Cruiser for a small herd of impala crossing the road. Not surprisingly, all I had to say was 'Uh-uh!' and he stayed put. But this was not the end of it: the next day I went through the routine one more time, just to be sure, and needless to say he passed with an A-plus, as I knew he would. Only now could I move on to the next phase, where Shilo had also to learn when it was okay to give chase on command – after all, he was a bush dog. Assisting with hunting and tracking of wounded animals would need to become part of his life, but there was a protocol to follow and he needed to understand that.

'Teksit!' was a word I concocted that combined 'takes' and 'it'. It was short and sharp, and could be hissed quietly when necessary. It was the only command I ever used permitting Shilo to chase, and it worked well for us. He learned to wait for it, totally focused on the quarry. Adrenaline coursing through his bloodstream would cause him to tremble like a sprinter pressed against the starting blocks at the start of the 100-metre dash, his muscles tensed, ready for explosive flight.

* * *

Though three years had passed since the 'day of the warthog', I would never forget what I'd seen that morning lying on that makeshift operating table at Thornybush. Although the dogs' scars healed quickly, and Gina had only a slight limp to show for her ordeal, I was sure this near tragedy could have been prevented. As far as I was concerned, the most crucial part of Shilo's bush school curriculum had been learnt, and throughout his life in the bush, my fastidious preoccupation with this aspect of his training proved to be worth every moment we spent on it.

We were expecting a chartered aircraft with guests at noon one day, and as usual I went out beforehand to check the surface condition of the airstrip. Back then it was still a dirt strip, and invariably there were one or two depressions gouged out by dust-bathing wildebeest, or there'd be a porcupine excavation that needed some filling in. As I left the run-up pad and drove down the middle, Shilo nudged my ear with his icy cold wet nose. He knew this was impossible for me to ignore – it was his way of saying he'd like to race the Land Cruiser. He loved to run, and unless we limited the amount, he'd literally run the pads off his feet on the rough quartz that made up much of the substrate of the Tuli Reserve. The airstrip was built on a gently sloping gradient from west to east, and I knew the bottom half was sandy and softer than the stony top half, so I let him out just before the wind sock, about half way down. As usual he hit the ground running, kicking up small stones high into the air as he ran. Shilo was about a year old at the time, superbly fit and lean, his narrow waist accentuated by a deep chest indicative of his Doberman heritage.

Nearing the bottom end of the airstrip, I accelerated to close the gap. I wanted to stay within audible range of Shilo. The runway narrows at this point, tapering off and ending in some relatively thick vegetation. Run-off from the rains is channelled to this area, giving rise to vegetation that stays green just that little bit longer than the surrounding area. The game know this and love to feed there, particularly in winter. As Shilo began to slow down, a family of four warthogs that had been foraging in the thicket broke cover and ran across in front of him. Their heads held high and tails erect in typical fashion they trotted across the airstrip, arrogantly showing off their huge dirty white tusks, which appeared so much more formidable against the contrast of their dark grey snouts.

Images of Gina's torn body lying on that bloody table flashed vividly across my mind as I pulled the vehicle next to him. We must have been doing nearly 50 kilometres per hour when I screamed, as loud as I could: 'Uh-uh! Shilo!'

Shilo responded by pulling up and stopping so quickly that he tore the two main pads on his front feet ... but I didn't care! The pads would heal in a few days, and he had passed a big test; in fact, he had graduated ... summa cum laude.

* * *

Unaccustomed to the report of a high-powered rifle, or its association with hunting, Shilo had yet to learn about weapons, the noise they made and the purpose for which they were used in the field. This stage of his training was the ideal time to teach him about firearms. With his mind intent on the game in front of him, Shilo wasn't easily distracted. If the outing depended on me carrying a rifle, I hoped that he would associate the weapon with enjoyment and adventure rather than trepidation. The hard part was going to be getting him accustomed to the noise it made and what it meant. He needed to learn to live for that noise, not in fear of it. Apprehensive doesn't begin to describe how I felt about this part of his training – this was 'make or break' time.

Most dogs are naturally gun-shy – or more accurately, they are averse to sudden loud noises or explosions – and although this is understandable, a dog that runs away in fright at gunshots can be a liability in the bush. One has only to witness the abject terror and confusion that most suburban dogs and cats go through each year on the fifth of November, that one stupid day when fireworks are purposely exploded everywhere by small-minded, inconsiderate people celebrating 'Guy Fawkes'. The plight of a terrified dog fleeing into the bush could in some ways be equated to that of dogs in cities and towns, terror-stricken runaways that could end up dying in some hidey hole, confused and alone, never to be seen again.

Shilo quickly learned to associate my rifle with excursions into the bush. Whether we went out on foot or in the vehicle, he didn't appear to differentiate; either way he bounced around in anticipated joy – it was always exciting for him.

Lessons began slowly. Starting with a small air rifle, I then progressed to a .22 calibre, and finally to a centre fire weapon. To help keep him focused on the target rather than the rifle, I would always give him the command 'Teksit!' immediately before pulling the trigger. When I was satisfied that the noise of the rifle no longer bothered him, I became more assertive with the negative instruction 'Uh-uh!' as well. Very soon Shilo became completely comfortable around guns and shooting, and at the tender age of six months he was allowed to accompany me – as an 'observer' only – when I went out to shoot antelope, mainly impala, for the pot.

Though Shilo was a natural in the bush, I somehow always suspected that deep down in his core beat the heart of an animal with a gentle nature and a soft mouth when required. However, almost two years would pass before I found the particular category of hunting he was predisposed to. Shilo would naturally and without much prompting, reveal the hallmark of these physical attributes, which confirmed my long-held suspicions ...

In the meantime, Shilo would learn to associate various activities with the different type of weapon used for each. The 12 bore shotgun invariably meant the exciting prospect of icy cold wetlands and wildfowling, or high-altitude grassland habitat with exploding coveys of francolins, and even when I took it out for a quick clean or to hand-rub a little linseed oil on its walnut stock, Shilo would lie next to the vehicle in anticipation. The scoped .223 and 30/06 rifles meant riding in the Land Cruiser to look for fresh meat, so he'd jump on before I could say 'on the bakkie'. The big bore rifle was mostly used on game drives and walks with paying guests when it was required for protection and backup, so understandably there was very little response from Shilo when I picked it up, as this often meant he had to stay at home. How he knew which was for what by merely looking at them, I cannot say, as I used the same solvents and oils to clean and care for all of them, so it could not have been their smell alone. I suspect it may have been a combination of the associated paraphernalia, my mannerisms, and details of the different construction and shapes of the various weapons that triggered the association.

8

SHILO GETS 'BLOODED'

Though hundreds of elephants emanating from Botswana's Tuli Reserve on crop-raiding forays managed to wade through the Limpopo and make generous dung deposits on the South African side, tourists caught trying to take a single Christmas pudding-sized dung ball home as a souvenir had them summarily confiscated at the border post. The confiscated-items room at Pont Drift was filled with dried elephant poop, each piece individually tagged, shelved and catalogued. It has to be said that Botswana's customs and excise regulations may have been a tad rigid on this issue; frankly I thought they stank!

Among the plethora of other seemingly inappropriate restrictions, Botswana's customs regulations did not allow the importation of fresh red meat products from South Africa. Veterinary law was strictly enforced due to the risk of foot and mouth disease, and the threat that an outbreak would pose to the huge Botswana cattle industry. This despite the fact that cattle, sheep and goats from Botswana ranged freely across the Limpopo and Shashe Rivers, into and out of South Africa and Zimbabwe. Nevertheless, in the face of logic we were compelled to procure all our red meat in Botswana. However, the logistics of having to buy from the nearest supermarket, which was a bone-jarring four hours' drive away, in ambient temperatures of well over 40 degrees Celsius at times, precluded this financially crippling option, so we were obliged to make do. In order to meet the bulk of our fresh meat requirements we found ourselves compelled to live off the land, so to speak.

Besides the odd fat-tailed sheep, also known as Dorpers, which we bought from a small Zionist village about 30 kilometres away, there was little else to supplement the variety of meat needed to provide for our paying guests. We were left with no alternative but to augment this supply by shooting fresh game meat. However, what was essentially a relatively simple exercise was hampered by Botswana's draconian firearm regulations, which stipulated that you were only permitted 100 rounds of ammunition per weapon, per year. This was not too onerous if you were a reasonable shot shooting for private consumption, but extremely limiting when supplying a commercial game lodge, as the culinary department was largely dependent on a regular, reliable supply of fresh meat.

Shooting for the pot was taken very seriously, and to say that every shot had to count was an understatement. It was not hunting in the classic sense; rather, it was like going shopping for meat in huge open-air butcheries, the main difference being that the meat was so fresh it was still alive. For me this was always an unenviable and unavoidable duty, however, there was some consolation about this harvesting method that helped me live with myself. It was the knowledge that the animals usually died instantly and with no premonition of their impending fate, unlike domestic stock that go through the abattoir process before ending up neatly packaged on the shelves of your local supermarket butchery. Not to mention the ritual slaughter to produce kosher or halal meat – this, in my opinion, is an unnecessarily slow and cruel death. To understand what I mean, simply ask yourself which of the two methods you would choose, if you had to ... an unexpected bullet to the brain, which is instantaneous, or being trussed up and your throat slit where, if all goes well, you may bleed out in about four minutes? Of course, I thought so, it's a no brainer ... pun intended.

There was no shortage of game in the Tuli Block, in fact quite the contrary. The semi-arid environment was subject to periods of drought from time to time, during which hundreds of the more susceptible animals would die. Being part of a relatively large open system meant the reserve's management policy did not include culling; however, a number of animals were permitted to be hunted for the pot each year. Although this had virtually no effect on the overall numbers of animals, or the species allocated, I always took it upon myself to be extremely selective in terms of which animals I'd shoot, and where on the reserve I'd shoot them. For example I would never shoot within 500 metres of a waterhole, on a popular game viewing drive area, out of a breeding herd, or take an animal that was clearly a territorial ram or bull. I chose instead to select from small bachelor herds preferably in thick bush, where the fallen animal would be obscured from his pals; this way the rest of them would run off, never quite sure what had happened. This has proved to be the best option throughout my career, unless non-selective culling was required.

* * *

Shilo lay on the stoep, with his front paws dangling over the top step, gazing out through the open screen doorway. He was casually eyeing a troop of vervet monkeys playing on the newly mown lawn in front of the cottage. These bushveld acrobats can keep an audience fascinated for hours with their antics and agility, but Shilo was past being impressed. He remembered all too well the days when he was a pup, and how the larger male monkeys taunted him, often with aggressive intent. Fortunately, as Shilo grew and his fangs outmatched theirs, so did their cautious respect for him.

Suddenly Shilo lifted his head, holding it in that characteristic half cocked attitude, his ears pricked, and then his tail began thumping gently on the cool cement screed floor. I looked up from the book I was reading to see Julia, our head chef, walking up the pathway to the house, shooing the monkeys as she approached the cottage. These wily little thieves regularly stole from her kitchen; they were not her favourites, though I had seen her show pity when one of them was crushed to death and swallowed by a python behind the kitchen a couple of weeks earlier. I will never forget how the power of that python's constricting coils caused one of the monkey's ribs to break and burst through its skin ... But pythons also needed to eat.

Julia was wearing her apron and chef's hat, which other than in the kitchen itself she never walked around in; this usually meant she needed to speak to me about some major kitchen appliance that was playing up, or to ask me to get meat for the cool room – most of the time, it was the latter. Otherwise, Julia never bothered me, she took every challenge the kitchen threw at her in her stride, and nobody, not even my father, could prepare game like she could. Knowing I didn't like 'going to the butcher' she'd put off asking as long as possible, and then her requests were always somewhat tentative.

'I need some impala please, we're nearly out of fresh meat,' she said.

'No problem, Julia, I'm planning to go out this morning anyway.' I said. Then as she walked back up the pathway I called after her. 'Please keep two raw leg bones for Shilo.'

Shilo wagged his tail at the sound of his name; he knew we were talking about him. Julia glanced back over her shoulder: 'Okaaay,' she said, smiling and waving in acknowledgement.

*   *   *

Picking up my rifle I squinted through the scope, gave it a wipe and then checked that the magazine clip was full. Slipping it back into the padded gun bag I zipped it closed and turned to Shilo, who had been watching me with more than casual interest. Patting him softly on the head, I told him something I somehow suspect he already knew.

'Today's the day, my boy,' I said. This was going to be his first time on a 'hunt'. How he sensed there was something different about that day, I don't know, but he bounded up to the doorway then back again, his tail whipping from side to side, and grinning so hard he sneezed repeatedly. This time, I'm sure it had nothing to do with the promise of a juicy bone or two, but more about what we were going to have to do to get those bones ...

Leaving the rifle in its bag, mainly to protect the telescopic sight's lenses from dust, I placed it in its holder just above the dashboard. Shilo needed no invitation: he'd already leaped up into position, uttering an almost imperceptible whine of excited impatience. I climbed into the Land Cruiser and we drove out into the bush, leaving the gardens of the lodge behind us in a hazy cloud of dust.

I never became complacent about Tuli's rugged beauty, and never more so than with the onset of the winter. As the days shortened and the nights lingered, the surrounding arid landscape would present a strikingly beautiful tapestry of khaki browns and rusty spotted yellows, audaciously peppered with rare flecks of green. It had been a good summer, and much of the lower lying areas that were still covered with foliage were only now beginning to turn. Most noticeably, and as if in defiance of the long dry winter that lay just around the corner, the claret hue of the pods on the plum-coloured *Terminalia* seemed to linger the longest.

Around midday, warm, lip-cracking dry winds would blow across the grassless plains. These often blew up small dust devils, which gave a visual emphasis to the prevailing conditions. Completing the autumn days were spectacular dust-filtered sunsets of shimmering, sharp-edged orange balls that quickly sank away on the western horizon.

Game movement becomes more predictable in the dry season, particularly with regard to water-dependent species such as impala. As surface water became ever scarcer, I knew we were likely to find impala resting up within a radius of less than a couple of kilometres from water. I began by concentrating my search on the shaded slopes of the gently undulating terrain, paying particular attention to the cool pockets of shade provided by isolated shepherd's trees at this time of the year. Lower down, I scanned the thickets of ever-resilient stunted mopane trees, which appeared to grow in defiance of the adverse climate and the relentless attention of elephants. Here they thrived, still daring to transpire scarce, life-giving water through their butterfly-shaped leaves and into the parched air. What would Tuli be without the mopane?

The seven impala rams were easy to pick out against the mottled background of the mopane scrub, their rusty-red coats in the bright sunlight gave them away at a glance. Unconcerned at our approach, they allowed us to get within 50 metres of them before slowly starting to move away, when all but one slowly melted away into the bush. A young ram stopped and turned around to have one more curious look at us … it was his last. Shilo was so tense his muscles started to quiver, but not so that I couldn't shoot. At the shot the impala dropped, and turning to Shilo, I hissed: 'Teksit!' With that, he leaped out of the vehicle so fast that his front legs gave way as he hit the ground, causing him to fall on to his nose. I suspect he'd been so focused on the impala that when he jumped down he didn't make the necessary calculation needed to absorb the impact and land without falling. Undeterred, he was back on his feet in an instant and at the dead impala's side in seconds, where he immediately started worrying and tugging at the lifeless carcass. I heard him squeal and yelp with excitement; the sound he made was reminiscent of the high-pitched vocalisation I've heard when African wild dogs make a kill. Involuntary nerve impulses caused the dead impala to kick a few times, whereupon Shilo instinctively latched on to the side of its neck, as in the rare event of a badly placed shot, his job would be to prevent a wounded animal running off to die miserably if not found. How he ever thought those little puppy teeth could hold an animal five times heavier than he was, I don't know, but he wouldn't let go until the kicking had ceased. I was intrigued to see that at no time had he gone for its throat; there was no attempt made to kill it, he merely held on, tugging at it as if he feared it would get up and run away. Although I gave this no further thought at the time, it went into my memory bank, and was something I'd relate to in the future.

Using my index fingertip, I took a little blood from the bullet wound and made a symbolic cross on the small light brown patch on Shilo's chest – he was blooded. A meaningless ritual to him, perhaps, but it meant so much to me that he now knew what was expected of him.

A while later, after allowing Shilo to worry the carcass to his heart's content, I loaded it and drove back to the lodge with the 'spoils of war' from Shilo's campaign safely in the back of the Cruiser. Up until a couple of hundred metres before the lodge Shilo would turn repeatedly to check that the impala was still on the vehicle. Satisfied now that it wasn't going anywhere, he stood on the passenger seat next to me as he usually did, only this time when we drove into the lodge he stood proudly, his ears back and his nose in the air. There was an unmistakable look of accomplishment in his posture, a look I can best describe as one I've seen depicted by a Roman legionnaire returning from a successful campaign as he rides his chariot along the Via Appia into Rome.

There was no lap of honour for Shilo, no one cheering him on as we drove unceremoniously to the back of the lodge ... but in his chest beat the proudest heart.

The high temperatures of the Tuli bushveld were always a concern when providing fresh meat. All carcasses destined for lodge consumption needed to be processed as quickly and hygienically as possible; therefore the skinning and butchering was done in a fly screen gauze-enclosed structure that had been built in the shade of a huge nyala berry tree close to the kitchen. The tradition of hanging game is not appropriate for most African conditions; in fact, any unsalted fresh meat hung in the bushveld, particularly in summer, would spoil within hours.

Shilo didn't understand any of what was going on; all that concerned him was that someone had summarily removed 'his' impala, so he promptly lay down outside the butchery door and waited. This was one of only a few rare occasions that Shilo didn't shadow me. An hour later, even though the carcass had already been taken to the kitchen's cool room through an inter-leading door, he still hung around waiting for his impala. Eventually, using a juicy lower leg bone of the impala, I managed to persuade him to come home with me ... but I knew it wasn't about the bone.

* * *

This was the first of many similar routine trips to the 'outdoor butchery' with Shilo, and although I could happily have lived my whole life never having to 'buy' from this meat market, he loved every excursion. Admittedly, the shooting aspect aside, each day that we spent out in the bush together was a learning experience for both of us. Every outing had something different in store; you never knew what was around the next curve in the road or in the bush over the next ridge. As Shilo matured, so his experience grew, and I found myself beginning to rely on him more and more in the bush. Essentially our relationship had grown from when I would take him along for fun and companionship, to when I was also glad to have him along for his help. I somehow suspected there were going to be times ahead when I was going to need him and depend on his extraordinary senses.

9

BABOONS – GANG FIGHTERS OF NOTE

As supposedly civilised human beings, we struggle to get our minds around the barbaric concept of devouring our own kind, even in situations where survival means having to resort to cannibalism. The question is, are we in a position to judge those who have been so close to death by starvation that the unthinkable is overwhelmed by the desire to live? This degree of desperation in adverse circumstances brings out survival instincts long dormant in our DNA. The most publicised example of this scenario in recent times was when an aircraft crashed in the Andes Mountains in the late seventies. Perfectly normal, affluent people, some of whom I later met in 1979 when I worked at Mala Mala, were reduced to cannibalism in order to survive. In case you were wondering, no, we didn't discuss their ordeal, in fact we never came remotely close to broaching the subject, and nor did they volunteer to discuss it. My understanding of Spanish at that time was such that it didn't allow me to pick up on any subtle innuendos either. However, young rangers being what we were, I admit that a few tasteless jokes were bantered around the staff table at meal times. With hindsight, the language barrier may have been a good thing.

When intelligent primates, under apparently normal conditions and not driven by resource stress, resort to eating their own kind, we are equally repulsed. This macabre act touches a nerve deep in our subconscious, I suspect because we tend to regard large intelligent primates as 'family'. Pet hamsters, rats and mice routinely consume their young, as do many fish species, and some wild animal species are known to resort to cannibalism in certain circumstances, but this is the exception rather than the rule. Taking an objective scientific approach doesn't really make it any easier, and although we may reluctantly accept it as part of nature, it is particularly disturbing when it occurs among those species known to be gregarious and socially tightly knit animals.

To actually witness this horrible act can turn even the strongest stomach, as it did to those of some otherwise strong men when a large male baboon was seen to systematically chase, capture and kill three young baboons in the space of a morning. They were grabbed from their screaming mothers' clutches, ripped apart, partially eaten and discarded. Another mother cleverly shoved her baby deep into the tangle of some driftwood tree roots, where the murderous male could not reach it. This gory rampage, which lasted over two hours, was witnessed by a number of construction workers and their supervisor while working on one of the lodges on the reserve.

Cannibalism is not typical of social behaviour relating to hierarchy changes or take-over scenarios among chacma baboons. The male in question was obviously fit enough to chase his hapless victims around for hours, an activity which burns calories, so he was not acting out of hunger brought on by resource stress; he was apparently well nourished and fit. So why are there so many incidents that are so out of character for these primates occurring in a relatively small area?

Baboons are chiefly vegetarians; nonetheless, they are known to consume a fair amount of animal matter to supplement their diets, and depending on availability of easy prey, some individuals go to the point of becoming active predators. It is well documented that antelope such as bushbuck, duiker, nyala, klipspringer, steenbok and other small mammals that habitually hide their young fall prey to these primates. Although it is deemed normal feeding behaviour, I have intervened on three separate occasions to rescue young nyala antelope from the clutches of large male baboons which were intent on devouring them. Normally I'd have allowed nature to take its course;

however, nyala are relatively large antelope, and are sometimes left only partially eaten and still alive. Recently, I have become increasingly concerned that baboons in unnaturally high numbers could have a detrimental effect on the population of some of those smaller antelope species. Therefore I believe baboons should be factored into the game management equation as predators in their own right, and managed accordingly. This is apart from their negative impact on ground nesting birds, any nests and birds' eggs, for that matter, all of which they are known to actively seek out and eat.

In light of these concerns, we need to question the advisability of boosting already high baboon numbers by artificially sustaining them through the dry season with supplementary feeding. However, there are situations beyond our control, such as agriculture within range of their foraging spread and beyond. Farmers of nourishing crops inadvertently, and most reluctantly, provide sustenance to these primates during lean periods. These periods of drought are particularly important for population control among baboons. It is during dry cycles that, through natural selection, only the fittest survive, populations are kept in check and the balance between supply and demand is maintained.

When times are good, the baboons of Tuli – particularly those troops that live along the Limpopo – have a natural protected refuge and food resources aplenty. Unfortunately, they are also able to unnaturally augment their winter supply by raiding the irrigated crops across the river. Inevitably, the resulting competition for food spills over into brazen aggression among overlapping troops and conflict between baboon and man.

Unless fortified with effective physical barriers such as electric fences and barbed wire, geopolitical boundaries demarcated by cut line roads and fluctuating river levels offer no hindrance to wildlife. They cross from one country to another at will, usually following ancient game paths and migration routes as they have always done, as nature decreed prior to the whims of man. On the rare occasion when the Limpopo River is in spate and flowing bank to bank, it presents a natural obstacle to game movement. However, for most of the time it runs shallow enough to allow wildlife and other animals, including dogs, to cross from one country to the other.

Besides drought, disease and insects, an African crop farmer's greatest natural enemy is baboons. Nowhere was there more evidence of this ongoing battle than on the farms across the river from Tuli Lodge. Crop-raiding baboons consciously used the reserve as a refuge; it was the perfect retreat after raiding the farmers' crops on the South African side of the river. Even 'South African' baboons would be given asylum. Their hit-and-run tactics worked well because their human pursuers weren't allowed to follow them into Botswana without going through the time-consuming formalities at the border post. Once in, there was nothing they could do about these fugitives anyway, and I'm absolutely sure the baboons were well aware of this. Their taunting barks and squabbling in between mouthfuls of stolen citrus fruit could be heard miles away. To make matters worse, they'd often sit just out of reach on the Botswana side, in full view of the frustrated farmers whose fruit they sat and ate, while subordinate troop members fought over the discarded scraps.

Out of sheer desperation, the farmers resorted to using dogs to chase the marauding gangs out of their crops, and as the dry season wore on, the situation became progressively more desperate. It was just too much temptation, the irrigated citrus orchards, as well as the winter wheat and mealie fields beckoned the drought-stricken primates to cross the river and face the wrath of the farmers and their dogs. It was only a matter of time before the inevitable conflict and confrontation exploded into death and destruction.

* * *

Shilo lay on his back at my feet while I sat watching a rugby match on my little black-and-white portable television set. He seemed to be enjoying having his tummy and chest rubbed with my bare foot. The game had only just started when we heard baboons kicking up an awful racket along the river close by.

Through the roar of the crowd at Loftus and the din the baboons were kicking up, something else came through that made Shilo spin around onto his chest in an instant. His ears pricked, and his head cocked to one side, I knew he'd picked up something unusual, something other than the normal raucous squabble of baboons, which he had grown accustomed to and largely ignored. I reached forward and turned the volume on the set right down.

Our cottage was only about 100 metres away from the river, so the noise was impossible to ignore, however, this time I could distinctly hear what Shilo had heard moments earlier. Standing outside on the lawn I was able to make out the faint sound of a dog barking in amongst the baboons' screeching and distinctive guttural barks. That's what Shilo had keyed into, and it was coming from our side of the river. I grabbed my rifle, put on a pair of boots and climbed into the vehicle. Shilo had already assumed his customary position, back feet on the passenger seat and front paws on the top of the dashboard. Craning his neck forward, his tail held as stiff as a rod, he moved his nose from side to side, testing the air, and his body language told me he had sensed something unusual was happening. Despite the wind rushing past my ears as we headed out, I could still clearly hear the relentless screams and barking of the baboons above the roar of the engine.

The river road traversed numerous erosion gullies that ran at right angles to the road, so it was relatively slow going. Formed by storm water rushing into the river, some of these ditches cut deep into the floodplain, forming miniature box canyons. It was in one of these steep-sided dongas that we found the gang of baboons, and all of them were enormous males. From what I could tell they'd lured a couple of the farmer's dogs to where they had the home ground advantage and were numerically superior; which had proved to be a deadly combination. Besides the flattened grass and trampled soil, I could clearly see some of the lighter leaf litter splattered with copious amounts of blood. There was no doubt; I knew this was the killing field. To confirm this, the motionless body of a large dog lay in the road about ten metres in front of the vehicle, it looked as though it might have been a cross Irish wolfhound/German shepherd. A quick glance at the way it lay sprawled and its torn throat told me it was dead. Looking up the narrow steep-walled gully where all the commotion was coming from I saw three large baboons which had cornered what looked like a bull terrier. The dog was being attacked and bitten from all sides, and although it was outnumbered and dwarfed by the primates, it was far from giving up the fight. Only small patches of white which identified the dog's colour could be seen through its blood-covered coat. I knew it would only be only a matter of time before they'd kill this plucky dog as well. It stood no chance.

Large male baboons have canines that can reach well over 70 millimetres in length. The fronts of these huge teeth are rounded, tapering to a sharp cutting edge at the back. Using their hands to grip whatever they're biting, they sink these fangs in deep, and then push away, pulling back with their heads at the same time, thus inflicting the most horrific wounds imaginable.

'Uh-uh! Shilo ... sit!' I hissed, grabbing his back leg at the hock with my left hand ... just in case. This was one gang fight I really didn't want him embroiled in. Reflexively I removed the rifle from its holder, then using it one-handed, I took aim, making sure that the dog wasn't in the line of fire, and shot the baboon that appeared to be doing the most damage.

At the shot, the other two baboons ran away without uttering a sound. The bull terrier, unaware of the rifle shot, must have thought he'd killed his adversary, which had suddenly fallen limp in front of him. He immediately fell upon the dead baboon, and couldn't seem to get enough of biting and worrying it. Now thoroughly exhausted, he lifted his head to take a breather. His bloodied tongue hung out of the side of his wide, panting mouth, and his stick of a tail was wagging in short stiff wags as he turned to look back at us over his bloody torn shoulder. Seemingly oblivious to the extent of his injuries, he'd turn back every now and again and nip at the lifeless baboon. It appeared as if the terrier hadn't had enough and was trying to provoke the baboon into another fight, each time glancing back at us again, as if to say. 'Did you see that, huh, did you?'

Leaving the bull terrier with the dead baboon, I climbed out of the vehicle and walked directly over to where the other dog was lying motionless in the road. Without needing to examine it physically, I was able to confirm that it was dead. After a minute or so, the bull terrier left the baboon and trotted up to his dead companion, where he stood panting for a while. After a thorough sniffing and nudging of his fallen comrade, he too must have realised there was nothing he could do for him and came over to where I stood next to the Land Cruiser. At this point, and as both dogs were in neutral territory, so to speak, I let Shilo jump down to meet him. Shilo had never seen this dog before, and given the prevailing mood and circumstances, the greeting between them was quite relaxed. It was a rather brief, mere formality of the usual greeting ritual. Though the terrier was smaller than Shilo, there appeared to be recognition of mutual respect for each other, though I'm sure I detected a hint of admiration in Shilo's eyes for this wounded fighter.

While focused on the greeting ritual, the full extent of the damage inflicted by the baboons on the bull terrier was now evident. His left eye appeared to be missing, it had either been punctured or pushed into the recess, or it had been ripped out completely. It was difficult to be sure, bull terriers have such small eyes as it is, nevertheless I wasn't about to stick my finger into the bloody eye socket and confirm the whereabouts of his eyeball. A small flap of his scalp just above the eye was peeled open, and his powerful chest and shoulders were covered in deep bloody wounds that stood out clearly against the white coat

Shilo went over to where the dead dog lay, cautiously lifting his feet, tiptoeing as if he didn't want to wake it. Closer now, he tentatively craned his neck and sniffed at the blood-soaked wounds. This fallen fighter was the first dead dog Shilo had ever seen. Although I detected an element of foreboding, similar to when I had seen him smell lion urine, I couldn't help wondering if he understood what had happened and why. This was one of the very few times in our relationship when I wished Shilo was human, just for a moment, so that I could explain that this was why I trained him; this was what I never wanted to have happen to him … because I loved him. Well, I thought, at least he knew that I loved him, and he didn't need to be human to know that, not even for a second.

Worried that Shilo would wander over to the dead baboon out of curiosity, and that the bull terrier might get possessive over the carcass, I told him to get back on the vehicle and stay. Making my way to the front of the Land Cruiser, I retrieved the two canvas water bags that always hung on the bull bar. These simple bags are able to keep water cool on the warmest day. Taking the fuller of the two, I slowly emptied the contents over the bull terrier, gently cleaning some of the blood and dirt off the wounds, revealing just how deep some of them were. There was nothing else I could do; it was clear that many of the lacerations were going to need stitches. I took Shilo's water bowl from behind the seat, poured the remaining water into it and gave it to the terrier to drink; he lapped it up in no time.

Using the drier of the two bags, I emptied it completely then wrote a message on it, briefly describing what had happened, and addressed the note to the closest farmer, who presumably either owned the dog, or knew who did. Using the carrier rope attached, I hung the bag over the dog's neck and sent him back across the river. Initially he appeared very reluctant to leave, and I couldn't help wondering why it was that he didn't want to leave us and get home. Was it his dead companion or his dead 'trophy', or was it possibly because he and Shilo had begun to hit it off? I'll never know.

* * *

Floodplain soil is soft, a little like fine beach sand, so in less than half an hour I had dug a hole that was deep enough to bury both the dog and the baboon. How ironic, I thought, as I shovelled soil back into the grave over the two adversaries – two former enemies in life, they now lay in a macabre embrace side by side in death. It was almost dark when I patted the mound of soil with the back of my small camping spade. I'd never expected to dig a grave with this tool; rather it was kept behind my seat for those unavoidable excursions into the bush when rudimentary toilet facilities were called for.

It was nearly dark when I dusted myself off and climbed back into the vehicle. Shilo lay curled up on the passenger seat, and I suspected that, like me, he was ready to call it a day. In the distance I could hear the baboons squabbling over the best branch space as they settled in the trees they had chosen to sleep in ... However, that night one of their troop wouldn't be coming home to roost, and I was reasonably sure they would know that too.

For a while I reflected on that afternoon with mixed feelings. Should I have allowed the baboons to kill the bull terrier? After all, they were defending themselves. Did I live with myself having shot the baboon and saved the dog's life, or should I console myself with the pragmatic view, and see it as being a life for a life, in the context of an eye for an eye, which could be regarded as a fair outcome by some? ... Okay, but what about the eye, didn't the baboons still owe the bull terrier one?

A few weeks later I received a note left at the border post by the dog's owner. Although he thanked me for saving his dog's life, it was clear I'd simply saved the dog to fight another day. Apparently the one-eyed bull terrier was back on duty in the citrus orchards about a week after his close shave with the baboons, seemingly more determined than ever. I somehow suspect he wanted more than to simply chase these marauding primates from his master's crops. Perhaps he was on a relentless mission or vendetta to find that particular baboon that had taken his eye.

10

LOVE ME – LOVE MY DOG

At a little over twelve months of age, Shilo began to teach me a thing or two about 'dog culture'. It wasn't all one-way teaching and learning; I was beginning to absorb a little about those behaviours inherent in his lupine ancestry, traits which set dogs apart from cats, for example. One of the most important is that all dogs are inherently pack animals; they need to know they belong; they want to know their place in any given situation. At the time Shilo and I were more of a coalition than a pack. Nevertheless, an alliance such as ours boasted strong qualities inherent in pack order, in that there was a pecking order of sorts, and we were happy with things as they were. Though we welcomed temporary recruitment on occasion, if and when circumstances allowed, it was never allowed to interfere with the status quo. Dogs get used to a routine; they are team players and need to know where on the field they are to be positioned; for example, we all know there's no place for two hookers on a rugby team. I learned not to mess with this aspect too much, as apparently it disrupts things and confuses them.

As far as I was concerned, emotionally I was smarting from an old wound, and though nine moons had waxed and waned, the scar was still sensitive to the touch. For a while I skirted every potential relationship which even hinted at heading for the next level. I remained as wary as a wounded leopard; I wasn't going to be lured to the bait again quite so soon. But don't get me wrong, I didn't turn my cottage into a bastion of celibacy, nor did I dwell on what used to be and become a long-haired, bearded recluse. I was getting on with my life in the bush.

* * *

The busy routine of running an international game lodge waits for nobody: there's no time out given for personal issues, life must go on, and busy is good. Crossing at the border post one morning on our way to do some shopping, I let Shilo out to go and say hi to his mother as usual. It was always heart-warming to watch as mother and son greeted each other muzzle-to-muzzle through the diamond mesh security fence. I left him with her as I was sure they had a lot of catching up to do, and climbed the highly polished steps to the passport counter.

'Morning,' I called through the bars.

Ockie looked up and smiled. Getting up halfway out of his chair, he motioned me around to the side door of the building and through into his office. As I reached his desk he leaned forward to hand me a small note. It was simply a message for me to phone Edward Engela; the telephone number had been scribbled down underneath the name. Ockie pointed to the phone on his desk, turned it around and pushed it toward me.

'Be my guest,' he said.

This was the only real phone we could use, and even though it was a party line, which meant that several farmers and the operator could listen in, it was a far better option than the radio telephone back at the lodge – which was a joke, unless of course you didn't mind waiting a day to make a call, and then having the whole of Botswana listen in on your conversation.

Edward Engela – Uncle Ed, as I called him – was not only an old friend; he had been like a father to me for most of my teen years. We shared a passion for fishing and wildfowling, and at one point he had almost become my father-in-law. I suspect he had looked forward to having our relationship upgraded to son and father-in-law as much as I did at the time, so I was really pleased we'd made contact again after so many years. Naturally I invited him to come up and spend a few days with me. Of course, I asked after his daughter, too.

'Bernice is very well, thank you' he replied. 'In fact she wants to come up to the bush with me, if that's okay with you.'

I paused momentarily. It was going to be a little uncomfortable having the woman I nearly married sitting across the dinner table from me for a week, let alone having to politely shoot the breeze with her boyfriend, whom I assumed she would have wanted to bring along. However, as if he had read my mind, Uncle Ed shot back: 'There's no one in her life at the moment, it will just be Bernice and me.'

I couldn't explain why, but at that moment, it was what I wanted to hear. The thought of seeing her again brought a sudden twinge of excited anticipation to the pit of my stomach. Never mind the years that had passed, I couldn't ignore the fact that I'd once loved her enough to want to marry her. Nor could I ignore the wounded leopard in me which circled restlessly, cautiously keeping my senses on full alert to incoming emotional vibrations.

The two weeks flew by, and before I knew it, Shilo and I were on our way to Pont Drift to collect Uncle Ed and Bernice, who had driven up from Johannesburg that morning. The timing was almost perfect; I had only waited about fifteen minutes when their car pulled up to the parking lot at the border post. With Shilo at my heels I walked up to the passenger side door, but before I'd reached it, Bernice had already climbed out of the car. She straightened up, threw back her shoulder-length blonde hair and kissed me.

'It's good to see you again,' she said, smiling.

Bernice was even more beautiful than I remembered. Father time had lovingly smiled on her: in order to stop myself gawking, I needed to look away. Turning to Uncle Ed, I could see he had aged a little: his bushy moustache was now grey, not the salt and pepper that I remembered, though his lean frame was still limber and sprightly. The first thing he did after shaking my hand was to bend down and make a fuss of Shilo, who took to him immediately. Later, when Shilo sniffed his car's tyres and proceeded to pee on each one, Uncle Ed didn't mind at all; having owned English pointers all his life, he understood dogs.

In the office, a beaming Ockie quickly went through the formalities at his desk instead of at the counter, the huge grin on his face widening each time he caught my eye. Ockie knew all about Bernice, because in a 'small community syndrome' sort of way, he just had to know the 'buzz', so prior to their arrival, I had been thoroughly interrogated and tortured into confessing. Needless to say I was glad when we had loaded their luggage into the Land Cruiser and were heading across the Limpopo ... the customs officials weren't nearly as nosey on the Botswana side.

Naturally Bernice had climbed into the passenger seat of the open Cruiser ... Shilo's seat. Confused at the new arrangement, Shilo stood outside the vehicle looking up at me with that cocked-head quizzical look of his, so I got out and let him jump up from my side. I was sure he'd be able to stand in between Bernice and me, which he did. After clearing customs on the Botswana side, Shilo was once again obliged to climb into the vehicle from my side and stand on the seat next to Bernice.

About halfway back to the lodge, I noticed Shilo had shifted himself over, and was now in his usual position, while Bernice was perched right on the edge of the seat, hanging on to the handrail just above the glove compartment. Perhaps she had moved over voluntarily, not wanting to get splattered with the odd bit of dog slobber as it was blown back in the wind. However, I had a sneaking suspicion that if Shilo had thought he could get away with it, he would have nudged Bernice out of the doorless Cruiser and into the nearest thorn bush. Ever the gentleman, he restrained himself and maintained a modicum of decorum, but – though I didn't understand it then – I believe he may have felt his personal space was being encroached upon. Bernice may have appeared to be a threat to pack stability: he didn't know where this new member was going to fit in, and perhaps I hadn't gone through the new pack member introduction procedure as I should have.

* * *

Bernice appeared to be enjoying the rugged wilderness of Tuli. Having worked at the Sabi Sands Game Reserve a few years previously, she was no stranger to the bush, unlike Uncle Ed, who – apart from a brief visit to the Kruger National Park – had spent most of his time in the Orange Free State and the Eastern Cape. An outdoorsman most of his life, he knew more than most about gun dogs, wildfowling in the wetlands, or fishing for giant carp in the Vaal River, but big game country was new to him. It was a wonderful new experience to walk in elephant country along the Limpopo River floodplain, with hippo grunting at the intrusion and the air filled with the smells of the bush. To see his excitement when we drove in the open vehicle on night drives with a spotlight, spotting nocturnal animals he had never seen in his life before, made me happy. I was pleased – it was the very least I could do to repay him for the wonderful experiences and warm friendship he had shown me in my youth. He made a point of saying how impressed he was with Shilo's behaviour and discipline, particularly when we were out in the bush together – which, except for when paying guests were taken on a drive or walk, was most of the time. Uncle Ed had a wealth of experience with gun dogs, so I knew how significant that compliment was. It meant a lot to me, coming from him, and it made me really proud of Shilo.

One evening I saw Uncle Ed's jaw drop in amazement when we came across a pride of lions on a wildebeest kill. Bernice had seen the awesome power of these huge felines at work many times during her stint in the Sabi Sands Game Reserve, so she turned anxiously to see what Shilo would do. True to form whenever we came across these big cats, he quietly slid under the back seat and remained there without making a sound. To cover for his trepidation and possible embarrassment in these situations I'd always say he was checking the spare wheel under the seat to see if was correctly inflated. As big as his heart was, so was his brain – Shilo knew his limitations and Uncle Ed admired that too.

* * *

It was a memorable week: Uncle Ed didn't want to go home, and not surprisingly, Bernice and I found we still had a lot in common; there was still a great deal to talk about and not much time left. Naturally I found myself dreading them having to leave the next day, and we lingered over our last lunch longer than I usually do. I broke the slightly melancholy mood by suggesting that we have a siesta and meet at four o'clock for tea, after which we'd pack a cooler and head off to the Matloutsi Ruins for sundowners.

With that Uncle Ed stood up and started down the pathway. 'Okay,' he said. 'See you guys at four.'

Looking across the table at Bernice, I suggested she join me for an afternoon nap. She raised her eyebrows: 'Just a nap?'

'Really, just a nap; you can trust me, I'm only half-Italian,' I said.

The smirk she gave me said it all … 'So, Mario, what you're saying is that it's a 50/50 gamble …'

I grinned sheepishly. (I've never been able to think quickly on my feet.) By this time Uncle Ed was already halfway down the path to his chalet; if he'd heard any of that, he wasn't letting on.

I led the way down to my cottage, Shilo scampering on ahead of us. By the time we arrived, his nose was already nudging at the screen door, which I quickly opened, letting him in. Bernice followed him into the cool, dimly lit interior and looked around for somewhere to sit. Casting her eyes around, she could not have failed to notice that besides some bookshelves, a small coffee table, my desk and a couple of chairs, my huge double bed dominated the décor of the sparsely furnished cottage.

Bernice didn't say a word, but the look I received and her wry smile spoke volumes. I tried to explain it to her: unlike most bachelor pads, this bed wasn't a statement maker; rather it was a practical sleeping arrangement for Shilo and me. There was nowhere else as comfortable or inviting – and as if confirming this, Shilo claimed his spot immediately, in the middle of the bed. This was the same spot he'd slept on since he was a little puppy, the same spot where he lay trembling in fear as a leopard sawed in the darkness close to the cottage, and where he felt my hand as I reached out to give him a reassuring pat. It was where he grew confident and no longer quivered in fear at the sounds of things going bump in the night. Here, on this very bed, he had learned through my reassurance to grow confident and feel safe … with me.

Bernice went over to one of the chairs and sat down, a disconcerted look on her face, then her voice took on a tone I'd last heard years before from a schoolmistress.

'I'm not sharing a bed with a dog!'

I was more than a little taken aback by that, but when I saw she meant it, I tried to bridge the awkwardness with a short lecture on animal behaviour. Bernice needed to know how this had come to be Shilo's territory, his comfort zone, and that it would be wrong to throw him off without an alternative – for example a doggy basket next to me on 'my side' of the bed, where I could reach out and touch him … that sort of thing. I didn't venture into the pack concept pertaining to domestic dogs; I knew only a little of it then, and somehow suspected the explanation would not be too convincing. I was sure it would have been lost on Bernice, as there were only two of us.

Reluctantly, I shifted Shilo to my side of the bed and sat down in the middle with my back up against the headboard. He was OK with that; at least it was close to me.

I patted the large space I'd created for Bernice next to me on the bed.

'C'mon – after all, it's only a nap,' I said – and this time I meant it.

She came over and lay down on the bed next to me, but though I closed my eyes I couldn't fall asleep. My mind was racing. I realised then that Shilo was never going to take second place in my life … not ever, not even to a beautiful woman. Given the circumstances and the fact that I am half-Italian … that was saying a lot.

11

LOVE AT FIRST SIGHT

By the early eighties the timeshare concept, which was well established throughout the world's leisure resorts, had begun to rear its ugly head in wildlife safari destinations. Tuli Lodge was approached and soon affiliated itself with a timeshare consortium. This was a dramatic change, shifting the emphasis from an exclusive wilderness and ecotourism destination to a high-occupancy, high-volume leisure destination. As I had no inclination to become a glorified hotelier, it was time to make a career move and accept a long-standing offer from our neighbour, Brian Gilfillan.

Descended from a family of conservationists, Brian was passionate about the bush and had purchased land in Botswana at every opportunity until he owned a huge tract of the Tuli bushveld, a portion of nearly 16 000 hectares. In fact it comprised the majority of the Tuli Game Reserve, including approximately 20 kilometres of the Limpopo River, and boasted the largest number of elephants on privately owned land in Africa at the time. Other features of particular interest within this reserve included the historically important Pitsani Valley, Nel's Vlei and Rhodes Drift. Ecological management of such a large area promised to keep me enthused and busy, and as if that wasn't enough, Brian now wanted to share what had been an exclusively private bush destination and establish an ecotourism destination – he'd decided to go commercial. At the same time he was a pragmatic man, and realised there was a lot that needed to be done to make that

THE MAN WITH THE BLACK DOG

possible. Knowing I had gained years of experience at arguably the best such establishment in the world, he'd approached me with the proposition of working for him. He needed me to help develop the infrastructure that would support an exclusive game viewing safari business, and then run the operation, an exciting challenge indeed.

I was based at Majali, which when I arrived was a small camp with rather Spartan amenities, belying the fact that it was to become the flagship of the operation, which would soon consist of three camps spread over the reserve, known as Bushfillan Safaris. Perched on a steep-sided plateau overlooking a small dry watercourse, Majali was a compact camp, comfortable and easy to manage. The basic layout comprised seven traditional thatched rondavels, shortly to be upgraded to luxury bush units. They effectively surrounded the larger communal area in a cosy semicircle; the popular design was simple and intimate, a combination the guests empathised with and loved.

Working in this remote area was fraught with obvious difficulties, exacerbated by the fact that virtually everything required had to come through customs from South Africa. Every item of hardware required formal documentation for importation, which was time-consuming and frustrating, to say the least.

Needless to say, it took a combination of creativity, hard work and enthusiasm to get the camp renovated and upgraded to the standard where it was ready to accept paying guests – now all we needed was a caterer. While the Johannesburg office interviewed prospective candidates for the post, I began to tidy things up at Majali and to make preparations for starting the renovation of Limpopo camp, situated on the other side of the reserve, right on the banks of the Limpopo River.

* * *

As with most building projects, there were piles of rubble and left-over building material to be cleared. Not only unsightly, these create ideal shelter for rodents and snakes, particularly the latter, which was confirmed by the shouts of a number of labourers one morning. Removing bricks from a pile, they had come across a nest of small adder-like snakes – in fact, egg-eaters. Although this species is totally harmless, they can put on an extremely aggressive show when threatened. These feisty little snakes don't have a tooth in their mouths, so they need to be quite convincing to ward off any would-be threats, and this they do by striking repeatedly with their mouths agape, so vigorously that their whole body leaves the ground and moves forward with each strike.

I thought this would be the perfect opportunity to teach Shilo about snakes, so I called him closer. Curiosity soon overcame his natural fear, and he approached to give them a sniff. As he got too close, a couple of them struck out, hitting him on his nose, and at the same time I uttered: 'Uh-uh!' Surprised at the speed and ferocity of the snakes, he leaped back to a safe distance, his backside in the air and his forequarters on the ground, and barked ... and this time I encouraged him to bark again.

'Poeffie! Shit snakes!' I said sternly.

After that he wouldn't go near them without barking. I didn't really know what the hell I was doing at the time, but hoped that this would make him exercise caution instead of trying to sniff at a cobra or puff adder when he came across them – which, while he lived in the bush, was as certain as death and taxes. Despite the rubble pile being removed completely, it was only when the rains came and natural growth restored the bare patch that Shilo stopped giving it a wide berth. Importantly, he had also learned that it was acceptable to bark in certain situations – and coming across a snake, any snake, was one of them.

*   *   *

Head office hadn't kept me fully in the loop regarding the employment of a caterer – though to be fair, we had no telephones or telex machines at the time. So when a Land Rover pulled up at the back of the camp one afternoon, I naturally assumed it was one of the rangers from Limpopo camp, retuning from the border post with staff he'd given a lift to – and sure enough it was. However, besides the staff members I knew and recognised, there was a rather elegant, beautiful young woman I'd never seen before stepping out of the passenger side of the vehicle. My immediate thought was that she was a paying guest, so naturally I panicked – there were no rooms prepared and I had no one to do the catering!

The young ranger quickly saved me from making a fool of myself: 'Mario, this is Meagan,' he said, 'Majali's new caterer.'

The glamorous apparition smiled and shook the hand I reflexively thrust out at her, and for which I apologised, because it was more than a little grubby. I'd been working in the generator room all morning, which was one of the reasons I hadn't heard the radio call to say Meagan was on her way. If I'd known, I would have had half an hour to clean myself up a bit, put on a shirt, kick off the sandals that had been repaired with copper wire stitches and put on my vellies, but it was not to be. No wonder she ignored the dishevelled grease monkey in front of her and lavished her attention on the handsome dog that followed her around like a puppy. Knowing Shilo, I was sure this change of allegiance wasn't out of disloyalty to me, even if he did somehow suspect that she was soon going to be the person in charge of 'snootchies' and other delectables from the kitchen. I wouldn't accept that he'd sell his soul for a sausage … was there something about Meagan that also drew him in?

Shilo and I were in one of the six rondavels that would soon be converted to staff quarters, so Meagan would occupy one of the guest lodges until I moved to Limpopo camp in a few weeks' time. In the meantime I took it upon myself to familiarise her with the surrounds, the safari routine and – given the limitations – what would be expected meal-wise: in essence she would be running the camp and planning the menus. Catering under those conditions was going to be difficult at best, and I could see her standards were high, though not unrealistically so.

Within a week Meagan had grasped the reality of life in the bush, and appeared to be more than happy to adapt and improvise with what was available. This included preparing primarily game meat dishes. At this point I pushed her straight in at the deep end and introduced her to the bush kitchen, explaining that most of the meat would come from the reserve in the form of fresh carcasses, which would be hung in the cool room and allowed to age. I also explained that venison is usually tougher than meat from domestic animals, so this process was necessary. As I later found out, as a professional caterer Meagan already knew that, but ever the lady, had not interrupted my babble. I watched her face closely, expecting some negative reaction, but there was none: if this sophisticated Joburg girl was the least bit shocked at the prospect of staring eyeball to eyeball with tomorrow's roast, she hid it well.

At times whole carcasses were simply gutted and then hung, particularly animals culled at night. These would then be skinned and quartered when time and labour permitted. Interestingly, as Meagan began using game on a daily basis, she became convinced that animals shot at night were better table fare; she maintained the venison was easier to prepare and more tender. I suspect there may be something to Meagan's observation, perhaps to do with the animal's lower metabolism at night. Animals taken cleanly while in a relaxed state would be subjected to minimal or no prior stress, therefore adrenaline and lactic acid build-up in the bloodstream would be negligible.

When Meagan was done with the catering for the day, she would join me and the guests for pre-dinner drinks. The transformation from slaving chef to sophisticated hostess came easily and naturally to her. Meagan looked beautiful in khaki ... she would look beautiful in anything, I thought – or indeed, as sometimes flashed across my mind, nothing. Hey, I'd been in the bush for a while ... but you have to believe me when I say it had nothing to do with the fact that I telephoned Brian a couple of days later and told him he'd found a gem.

Meagan still makes a point of reminding me that it was Shilo she fell for, and that I just happened to come with the package. However, I like to think she knew only too well that getting close to Shilo inevitably meant getting closer to me ... hello!

* * *

Majali's main feature was the waterhole I established below the camp. Its specific location, which proved to be both practical and popular, was chosen by the elephants of Tuli. One moonlit evening Meagan and I found ourselves sitting on the rock ledge on the edge of the camp. Shilo lay between us, his belly flat on the still warm rock surface; he'd heard the elephants long before they arrived. Together we watched as a small breeding herd quietly trundled in, as if out of nowhere. Grey and ghostlike, they were suddenly below us, the dust slowly settling to reveal some really young calves among them, small enough to walk under their mothers' bellies. Perched up above the herd as we were, the wind carried our scent high over their heads; they were unaware we were there a few metres away. We watched in silence as they spent nearly an hour milling around below us. At first I didn't understand what they were doing, but after a while, I realised the elephants were eating soil – not just any soil; they appeared to be focused on a particular spot. The soil was relatively pale, which made me suspect it was the base of an ancient termite mound that had been flattened over time. Naturally we were fascinated; neither Meagan or I had ever seen this before, I could clearly hear the mushy crunching as they ground the soil between their huge molars. Patiently they took it in turns according to hierarchy; there wasn't the jostling one expects, it was as if they knew there was enough for all and that there was no need to fight over it. At first I thought it was a one-off; however, closer inspection the following morning revealed years of regular use by wild animals, particularly elephant. It was obviously a mineral lick of sorts, which sadly I don't think anyone has ever analysed. However this motivated my decision to incorporate a waterhole off to one side, slightly downslope of the lick itself.

Establishing a waterhole in the middle of a desert was easy to conceptualise and talk about, but getting it done proved to be no mean feat. However, I knew it would be worth the sweat, so despite water supply limitations I persisted. Soon, under floodlight controlled by a dimmer switch, it would be possible to view game right through the night. Perched 15 metres above the waterhole on a sheer-sided cliff, guests would comfortably use the open-sided thatch-roofed hide, unescorted and at any time. This feature gave life to Majali ... and I believe still does, to this day.

* * *

Inevitably, as with even the most reputable airlines, at some point commercial lodges get overbooked. True to tendency, this happened when a booking for twelve people for Majali was confirmed. This camp was built to take eight people comfortably, and ten at a push. Understandably the enthusiastic marketing team could not turn the group booking away, but this meant Meagan and I would have to sleep elsewhere, without it being obvious. It would have looked rather unprofessional if the staff had pitched a tent on the lawn, or slept in the pantry. Instead we used a rustic old hunting camp about four kilometres away, which consisted of an old caravan and a lean-to with outside ablutions. Although it appeared comfortable enough for Shilo and me, it was a little rough on Meagan, but seeing as it was only for the long weekend and we would only need it to sleep in for a few days, we thought we'd be fine ... that was until we came to trying to settle down for the first night.

Keeping cool is a constant challenge in the bush, particularly when trying to get a good night's sleep in summer. Besides a corrugated iron shack I once had to live in for a few days, I'd never experienced any structure as impossibly hot as this caravan. Both Meagan and I found it unbearably cramped and uncomfortable; sleeping inside this contraption was out of the question. However, it is never too hot in the bushveld if you sleep in the open air, and that is what we opted for. We pulled our mattresses outside and rigged up our mosquito nets, fastening them to the struts which support the thatch under the roof's overhang. Then we tucked them underneath our respective mattresses and slept under the stars. Shilo simply dug himself a hollow in the cool sand at the foot of my bed, curled up nose-to-tail and settled down for the night.

I knew Shilo would sleep with one eye and one ear open. He

never slept soundly when we were outdoors and this was confirmed when he awakened me later that night, standing between our two mattresses and growling deeply. I reached out and put my hand on his back: the hair on his ridge was stiff with apprehension. Sitting up, I shone the flashlight into the darkness: in the beam two pairs of yellow eyes reflected back at us. As my sight slowly adjusted, I could make out the round-eared silhouettes of two spotted hyenas as they casually slunk away, swallowed by the darkness. My mind raced back to when a young colleague of mine, a well-known raptor expert from our Mala Mala days, Roger Ellis, had his ear torn off by a hyena while camping in the Kruger National Park. He was fast asleep in a tent when the hyena clamped the side of his head in its powerful jaws and tried to drag him out. As vivid as the memories of the trauma it caused him were, I consoled myself with the fact that I had taken my rifle to bed with me.

I was woken the following morning after a comfortable night's sleep by Shilo insistently nudging me through the net. His cold wet nose on my bare skin was better than any alarm clock. I sat up, lifted the net, and let him in for a hug. As he turned to face me, I saw his face looked a little strange. The skin on his head was rumpled in loose folds; he resembled that strange dog breed native to China, the sharpei, pictures of which I'd once seen on someone's birthday card, I think. Besides that, he appeared to be his normal, happy self, but I wasn't happy, I wanted to know what had caused this reaction – and more importantly, what it would develop into.

Before slipping my boots on, I gave them a good shake. This was something I hadn't done for ages, but the sudden thought of my toes meeting with a scorpion's sting had me well focused on caution, so I banged the heels on the ground and shook them out once more, just to be sure. Peeling the net back slowly, I got up and checked the foot of the mattress and the hollow Shilo had dug for himself. I didn't know what I was looking for, but I certainly didn't expect to see what I saw.

Scattered about the periphery of our mattresses were at least a half a dozen solifugids. These huge and ferocious-looking sun spiders are harmless, so although Shilo had bitten and killed a number of them, and had possibly been bitten in the process himself, I knew it had to be something else ... something toxic. There was no suitable stick to hand, so I took my rifle barrel and carefully lifted the end of my mattress ... and there it was. A huge, shiny, dark green centipede, easily the size of those realistic rubber ones the kids buy in novelty shops. Although it appeared to have been bitten and chewed to the point that it could hardly move, it had found the strength in its dying throes to wriggle under my mattress.

I quietly disposed of the mangled centipede and most of the solifugids before waking Meagan. If there is one creature on earth that terrifies her, it is a centipede; also, I figured it was going to be easier telling her about the drama without the visual props, which were still giving the odd twitch as they were being scraped out from under our mattresses.

Meagan focused on Shilo and immediately began rummaging through her well-stocked first aid kit. Soon we'd managed to get him to swallow a couple of antihistamines. Whether they did the job, or his natural immune system did, by mid-morning the swelling had gone down completely. Needless to say, from then on, Shilo slept under the net with Meagan. What can I say; he was her hero, her protector, and as much as I envied him I simply couldn't compete. There would be other ways, I thought; ways that didn't include having to chew centipedes.

* * *

Everything was going really well and the guests appeared to be enjoying themselves. We'd split the group into two vehicles for comfort on the game drives; this also enabled us to cover more ground, resulting in much more game being seen. As is true everywhere in Africa's big five country – show people lions and they're happy. To this end the Motabola pride had played their part, and as if rehearsed, had killed a zebra in full view of everyone there on the morning of the second day. Back at camp, everyone was most impressed with the standard of catering, and no one suspected a thing about the overbooked accommodation situation ... well, almost no one.

The guests had just finished lunch and were heading to the pool or to their rooms, when one of them approached me and quietly called me aside. Checking to see that none of the others could hear her, she smiled. 'Mario, I think my husband and I are in your rondavel,' she said.

I tried hard to look surprised: 'What makes you say that?'

'Well, I found this packet of Camels on the bathroom window ledge, and I know you smoke Camels. However, we simply assumed you could have left them there at any time while checking the room, and initially we were comfortable with that assumption. That was until we lay down for a siesta, and Shilo leapt in through the open window in one smooth practised movement, wagged his tail then curled up on the bed between my husband and me and nuzzled down ... that clinched it, we knew,' she laughed loudly.

Thoroughly embarrassed, I began to explain the overbooked situation, but before I'd finished, she stopped me, insisting they had merely been curious; there was absolutely no problem at all – Meagan and I were welcome to take turns using 'their' shower.

'What's more, we're more than happy to have Shilo join us for siesta; after all, it was his bed too,' she said.

* * *

No question about it, if you want to live comfortably in Botswana's remote bushveld, you need to take Lord Baden-Powell's Boy Scout motto, 'Be prepared', quite literally. In addition to being self-reliant and innovative, a basic knowledge of first aid, together with knowing how to look after your own and others' health, is essential. Preventative vehicle maintenance, the ability to find simple faults, to improvise and make minor repairs when necessary, could mean the difference between life and death – no dramatics here, it's true! If you happen to live in

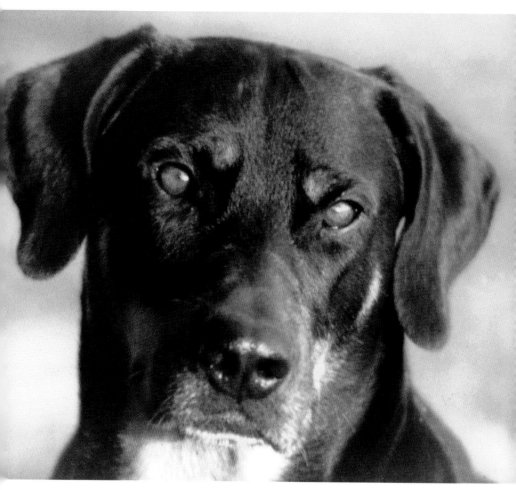
A dog in a million – Shilo, in a portrait by Alan van Rooyen.

Above: An epic feat – Shilo with the wounded kudu bull he tracked down in Tuli Game Reserve.

Left: Three leopard cubs I raised at Thornybush: (left to right) Purdey, Bulu and Delilah.

Above: Tuli, Botswana – Mario with the horns of a huge kudu killed by lions. These stately animals have a special place in my heart – there is no more majestic antelope in Africa.

Left: The bare patch Shilo is lying on was to become a lawn fit to delight all the animals of Tuli – donkeys included!

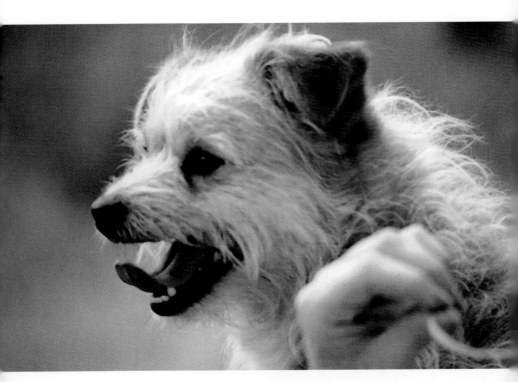

Top left: The look Shilo gave the donkeys when they came into camp ...

Top right: Love at first sight ... Meagan with Shilo in Botswana.

Above: Squealer owed his life to Meagan – and repaid her with total devotion.

Top: Caught in the act of burying a bone … Shilo at Mbali Game Lodge in the Timbavati.

Above: In the stockade where Shilo cornered the honey badger.

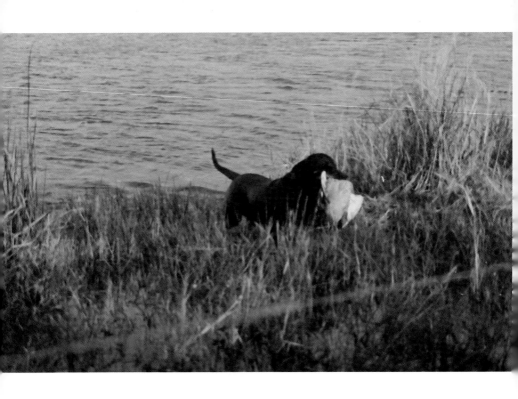

Duck-hunting at Underberg. Shilo thought nothing of swimming in icy cold lakes and ponds, in water so cold that it hurt to touch it. He was a natural, a powerful swimmer, and he loved to retrieve objects from the water.

Shilo's finest hours – waterfowling in the KwaZulu-Natal midlands.

Underberg – waiting for the next flight of duck.

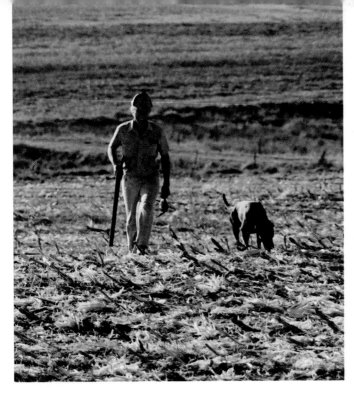

Shooting in
the uplands of
Himeville.

Shilo tolerantly
shares the photo
of his impala
with my young
nephew.

Taking a splash in the pool at Mbali … Shilo loved the water.

Fishing for tilapia in Mbali dam.

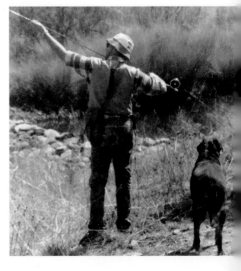

Above: Terminally besotted with the gentle art ... setting up a trout rod.

Left: Trout fishermen may be conservationists first, but this beauty is for the pan ...

Above: The team: Motswari and Mbali game lodges were looking for a general management couple. The location was great, but what decided it was when, on enquiring further, we learned that a well-behaved dog would be welcome!

Left: My parents in their restaurant, called 'Roma', Johannesburg, 1965. My father never took heed of the sign behind him.

Left: Meagan, Shilo and myself standing in front of our Land Rover at Timbavati Game Reserve, 1990. Eleana was born a couple of months later. Photo by Alan van Rooyen.

Below: During the first winter in our new home, the small birdbath I'd built in front of the house was visited regularly by a leopard in the dark of night.

Left: Many tourists have been so spoiled by the visual media and have such high expectations that they often treat an otherwise rare phenomenon, such as a leopard sighting in broad daylight, as an everyday occurrence. Photo by Eric Borcherds

big five country, besides needing the confidence that comes from a knowledge of the local wildlife and their habits, it is also a huge advantage to possess and know how to use a weapon. Naturally then, I thought Meagan needed to become acquainted with using a firearm.

We were expecting a busy festive season, and a stock-take of Majali's meat supply showed that it was running low, down to half an impala carcass in the cool room and twelve guineafowl in the freezer. Replenishment was urgently required.

I believed at the time there was a need for Meagan to understand there was more to procuring meat for the lodge than simply going out into the bush killing animals at random in a gung-ho fashion. More importantly, I felt that she needed to know there was nothing macho about shooting an antelope for the pot. Though Meagan had made it clear she disliked shooting for sport, I thought it was sound practice for her to learn how to shoot. In fact, I believe anyone living in a remote wilderness area, or farming with livestock, needs to know how to shoot a weapon safely, so that if and when the need arises, they will feel confident enough to use it correctly. This is particularly helpful when the humane destruction of an injured or suffering animal is called for and you're miles away from veterinary help. In these situations there is often no time to wait around for someone who knows how to shoot, while an animal writhes in agony or has time to crawl away into thick bush, where it cannot be found, only to die a lingering death.

We drove about two kilometres from camp to the spot I always used to sight in the rifles. It was a secluded section of the Majali's dry riverbed with steep sides; a safe backstop for any stray bullets. Shilo went and lay in the shade under the vehicle. He was waiting for the real thing.

I allowed Meagan to 'dry fire' the rifle, something I don't normally like doing, but she needed to know the trigger tension and how much 'creep' there was before the sear released the firing pin. Once she was familiar with that, and after we'd managed to determine which her dominant eye was, I then showed her how to squint through the scope until she was comfortable enough to fire a live round, which didn't take long. From a dead rest on the Cruiser, Meagan's first shot with a high-power rifle was impressive. At 50 metres she hit the target squarely, about a hand's width off-centre of the bull's-eye I had drawn on the cardboard box we were using as a target. Remarkable – not everyone is able to compose themselves enough to do this with their first shot.

After she'd pulled off a few shots, I could see Meagan was more than capable of taking things to the next level.

Even some expert target marksmen are unable to shoot and kill a living animal, so not surprisingly, this was something she really didn't want to do. However, I managed to convince her that it was important to know that she could do it if necessary.

'One shot, that's all it will take,' I said, trying to trivialise the issue.

Taking out my notebook I sketched a side view of an antelope, and drew the area covering the vital organs on the shoulder. This was where I wanted her to position the cross hairs of the telescopic sight, before squeezing the trigger. Collecting the cardboard box, I pointed out the respectable grouping of bullet holes – a confidence-boosting reassurance of her marksmanship. Leaving it in full view behind the firewall of the Land Cruiser, the three of us drove out to find some impala.

Thinking back now, it must have been an anxious time for Meagan as we drove past a number of impala, all of which I turned down. I couldn't leave anything to chance; I needed to select the right animal, one that would offer the clearest target. Shooting an animal is always taken seriously, even when training: 99% is not good enough, only 100% will do. We didn't drive too long before finding a huge ram standing broadside to the vehicle. I chambered around, then handed the rifle to Meagan, instructing her not to dilly dally, to shoot the moment the crosshairs settled on its shoulder.

Blam! On the impact of the bullet the impala leaped high into the air then took off as if nothing was wrong, but I'd seen this many times in my career and knew differently.

'Teksit!' I hissed, and in a smooth practised jump, Shilo leaped off the vehicle after the fleeing impala.

Meagan's face was the picture of anguish. 'Did I hit it properly?' she stammered.

'Yes, I'm sure you have, don't worry,' I reassured her. 'Shilo will find it.'

I ejected the spent case and re-loaded the rifle, then lit a cigarette, and began to track the faint blood spoor. Looking back I could see Meagan was in tears. I hadn't realised how much pressure I'd put her under, and really hated myself for pushing the issue.

It was starting to get hot, and except for the incessant zizzing of cicadas, it was unpromisingly quiet. It was nearly midday, not the best time to track; however, I continued trying to follow the indistinct spoor. Suddenly the sound of heavy panting broke the tiresome concentration, and seconds later Shilo came into view running back up the game path towards me.

Although he appeared exhausted, I turned him around once more. 'Teksit!' I hissed. This time Shilo didn't dash off; instead he loped easily in front of me as if urging me on, stopping every now and again to look over his shoulder, waiting for me to catch up. Then it dawned on me that he had returned to fetch me; he was making me follow him, which I did for nearly 100 metres. Suddenly he dropped out of sight into a steep-sided donga, and a moment later I heard him yelp with excitement. Looking down I could see a beaming Shilo standing over the dead impala.

Returning to the vehicle, I consoled Meagan, telling her Shilo had found the impala and was waiting for us, and sure enough he was still on guard when we drove in to load it. Meagan rushed up and hugged him, thanking him, but she needn't have – after all, it was her shot that had killed it; Shilo had merely done his job of locating it for us. I turned the impala over and showed Meagan how well-placed her shot had been, and that, although missing the heart, the bullet had hit the lungs, a fatal shot. Despite this, the impala had managed an adrenaline-charged burst of nearly 100 metres before tumbling into the donga, where it fell stone dead.

Although it was the last time Meagan ever shot a rifle, or, fortunately, ever needed to, it wasn't the last time she found reason to hug Shilo.

12

THE GREEN-EYED MONSTER

As Shilo grew, it became increasingly apparent that I'd only begun to scratch the surface of this wonderful animal's character. With the progression of time, and with each new experience we shared, it seemed as though there was always more about his nature being revealed, and the promise of something I had yet to discover.

The fact that Shilo was a good hunting dog was just a small fragment of the whole. I would have been just as happy with him if we'd lived in a big city, where the closest he'd get to doing what he did best would have been to chase the occasional squirrel up a tree, do a few tricks and play fetch. However, there could be no denying it, the fact that he was an excellent bush dog made me very proud of him, and others envious of his abilities.

Shilo's skill in the bush grew to the point where trackers began passing stories about him from one campfire to the next. People were fascinated at his level of discipline and the close relationship we had. Besides his talent as a hunting dog, they admired his quiet confidence and friendly nature. Above all I suspect that many of the locals had never before seen such a level of obedience attained through simple understanding and devotion between a man and his dog. The fact that I could talk to Shilo and communicate using normal tone and selected words must have been a novelty to many. It was no wonder I would often hear his name called in greeting as we drove along the road to the border post or through the neighbouring camp compounds. Eventually this would trickle into the villages, where his extraordinary exploits were much talked about amongst members of the local community.

To those populations of people who subsist off the land, a bushwise hunting dog is of prime importance. Herders and shepherds depend on them to warn of predators threatening their domestic stock or to help with hunting for the pot – in my experience the latter more so. So much so, in fact, that it came as no surprise when I was inundated with requests from local dog owners to have Shilo sire their bitches. One of the Botswana customs officials at Pont Drift actually offered a substantial amount to purchase him outright, or to pay for his stud services. While this was extremely flattering, I declined to pimp my dog out, and as for selling him – there wasn't enough money in the world. So, besides the odd bitch Shilo took a fancy to on occasion, all pro bono liaisons, of course, there were no 'arranged marriages'.

Unfortunately there was another side to this story, and as they say, 'There's always one, isn't there?' It was inevitable. As with most legends, I suspect that Shilo's prowess may have been embellished with the colourful imagination that is the licence of all folklore. Despite innocent intentions, the local renditions of his abilities fell on the resentful ears of the manager of the neighbouring farm. He was a rather envious, small-minded man who hid behind a huge beard, a man with whom I'd never been able to see eye to eye. As a consequence, we had spent no time in each other's company, and it follows that he had never been in the bush with Shilo. However, the green-eyed monster that goes by the name of jealousy, lurking just under the slime, had reared its ugly head. Word soon reached my ears of a malicious rumour that Shilo was a ruthless killer.

Exaggerated accounts of how he would chase animals down at every opportunity, grab the exhausted victims by their throats and kill them, soon found their way back to me. The locals who made up the working community among the various reserves within the Tuli Block all grew up in the same area or village; they knew each other either through being related or as friends, so communication via the 'bush telegraph' and social gatherings between the various farms was excellent. Given the loyalty of my staff, particularly among my field rangers towards me and Shilo, it was not surprising that the source of the unsubstantiated bullshit was soon revealed.

The mumbling of discontent and twisting of facts that filtered through my neighbour's facial hair were of no consequence. Shilo was his own defence. However, I couldn't help but feel a strong paternal urge to protect him. Spurious though the allegations were, it was very frustrating. However, as it turned out my frustration was for naught and Shilo would unknowingly defend his reputation sooner than anyone expected. One evening he spontaneously demonstrated, beyond any doubt, and in front of an independent witness, that he was no killer – in fact, nothing was further from the truth.

* * *

Having dropped off the last of the clients at the border post one afternoon, Meagan and I decided we'd pack a 'TGTG' (thank God they're gone) cooler, and go out for a short evening drive. We would enjoy some sundowners and give Shilo a run. We asked Marc Fraser, our long-suffering mechanic, to join us. Not only was Marc good company, he loved the bush and looked for any excuse to get out of the dingy workshop, so he jumped at the opportunity.

Sunset found us on top of Pitsani Koppie, one of the Boer War battle sites in the area, where poignant reminders of the century-old skirmish were still evident. Old bullet cases and the odd rusted artefact from the time could still be found lying in the dry stony soil. But we weren't there to dwell on the past; rather we watched a herd of elephant silhouetted against the setting sun, kicking up a faint dust cloud as they filed past us over the rise heading to Nel's Vlei to feed in the cool of the evening. We observed how the last cow seemed to hang back, making certain no calf lagged behind, and when the last of their ghostly grey forms had quietly melted into the mopane woodland, we reluctantly began to pack up and head on home.

I decided to drive back via the airstrip and give Shilo a run on its open sandy surface. By this time of the day the warthogs would be safely tucked away in their burrows for the night, and the baboons were already high up in the trees squabbling over roosting spots, so it was relatively safe to give him his head and let him run in the headlights of the cruiser. Although a herd of wildebeest had already moved on to the strip and a couple of them were having a sand bath off to one side, he ran past them with hardly a turn of his head. I backed off a little and watched as his long shadow slowly began to reach the periphery of the headlight beam, fascinated at his fitness and love for running.

Suddenly, from nowhere, a scrub hare shot out of the darkness and into the beam of the vehicle's headlights, practically in front of Shilo. The little hare ran in jerky bursts, picking up the pace when it needed, pulling effortlessly ahead. There is only one dog breed on earth that can match the African scrub hare for straight-line speed, and that is the greyhound. Even so, in a field situation, I strongly suspect that a hare will out-jink the best of them nearly every time.

The hare's excellent hearing could register that Shilo was still running behind it. In an effort to evade its pursuer it began to twist and turn. However, as we got closer, the lights of the vehicle and shadows cast by Shilo, as well as its own bobbing shadow image, must have affected its judgement. The hare mistimed its footfalls and ploughed headlong into some tumbleweed off to the side of the runway. The relatively soft shrubs cushioned the impact, but at a cost – it had lost its advantage and could only freeze and hope to be overlooked. Crouched low to the ground, the hare laid its long ears flat on its dun-brown back, now resembling nothing more than a large stone.

Shilo had been too far ahead and running too quickly to hear me shout 'Uh-uh!' So we all feared the worst for the vulnerable hare. I had a sickening feeling in the pit of my stomach; the snacks I'd munched with sundowners began to well up and sit in my throat. The old Land Cruiser was relatively cumbersome and slow, a handbrake turn would have been the quickest, but I didn't think of it then; instead I brought the vehicle around in a wide turn and drove back to where Shilo and the hare were.

Approaching from behind, we couldn't see a thing except the silhouette of my dog's outline; everything in front of him was blanked out in shadow. Suddenly he jumped to one side and the light then fell on what had been in front of him. It was the scrub hare, but contrary to our worst fears, it was still very much alive. Off to one side now, Shilo had his bum in the air and his fore-quarters on the ground, yelping like he would when he played 'silly buggers' with us. Then it dawned on me, he wanted to play with the hare, not kill it! He could have killed it with a single bite at any time as it lay there at the base of that small bush virtually under his nose.

Shilo knew that the hare was faster than him, and that if it broke cover he'd never catch it, yet he made no attempt to kill or maim it. Not wanting to tempt fate, I called him back to the vehicle, and as usual he responded immediately and jumped up onto the seat between Meagan and me, panting and slobbering all over us. The perceived danger now gone, the hare sat up and straightened its ears. A couple of minutes later, it had composed itself, ears up and alert, and was still sitting there when we turned around and drove home.

Most dogs would be acting unnaturally if they didn't at least attempt to chase a fleeing hare, and I'm sure there are only a handful that would not try to bite or kill one given the slight-est opportunity. This is a natural, instinctive response of most canines, which are, after all, basically predatory carnivores. I will wager that even a poodle straight out of the parlour in down-town Paris, given a similar scenario, would have torn the leash out of its high-heeled, wafer-thin owner's hand and pounced on that hare in an instant, or at least attempted to. The only dogs that immediately come to mind as soft-mouthed and reluctant to kill are Labrador retrievers, and Shilo's behaviour that evening could be attributed to the fact that half the blood in his veins was from his Labrador ancestry.

* * *

Had Shilo been a wild animal, I suppose it would be fair to say that his attributes would have qualified him as potentially dangerous. He certainly had all the physical characteristics that a 'killer' would require, which, if used defensively or aggressively would be capable of inflicting serious wounds ... or indeed worse. Shilo was fast, fit and powerful; he was also equipped with long, sharp canines set in a highly intelligent head. He was also a devoted pet whose attitude had outgrown and dispelled the necessity of these attributes for survival. The wolf in him had been bred out of his temperament thousands of years ago, he was no longer a wild creature, but merely a well-trained domestic animal that had been born and had grown up in the wild. Although Shilo was primarily a bush dog, he was clearly content, and enjoyed the company of people. Basically those I'd meet, he'd meet too, and those who were close to me, were to him, it was as simple as that.

Most people admired Shilo, which made me really proud of him; many grew to love him, and for others, particularly children, it was love at first sight. Not surprisingly, it was usually these 'little people' that showed the most genuine interest in petting him, hugging him, and sometimes overzealously pulling his ears. Naturally Shilo relished the attention, as most dogs do, and he also responded surprisingly well to strangers, but there were moments, as with most dog owners, when I was concerned he may lose his patience and snap at someone. Though nothing ever happened to prompt my reaction, being involved in a commercial operation as we were at the time, this was too much of a risk to contemplate. So without further ado I set about training Shilo to ensure that nothing like that would ever happen.

I realised that the need for Shilo to tolerate the attention of children was more for my own peace of mind than anything else, and although I began teaching him in earnest, I remember approaching the procedure with confidence knowing I could rely on his inherently gentle nature. I had total faith in Shilo. Had there been even the slightest inkling that I might have a potentially vicious dog on my hands, I would never have taken the risk of leaving him around small children, even after his training.

127

Toddlers are particularly fascinated with dogs, even tots that are only able to crawl are curiously drawn to them; unfortunately they also seem to have a penchant for homing in on dog food bowls, why, I don't know, but they do. Needless to say, his response to the training in this regard was what I'd suspected it would be.

Soon Shilo had become so tolerant of having his food messed around with by all and sundry, that it became a bit of a party trick. He would allow children to take his food from him while he fed. Not only that, he'd also let them pull a juicy bone away from between his front paws, while he stared at them, drooling in bemused anticipation of having it returned. I was totally convinced, and any hint of trepidation that I may have had dissolved completely. I knew there were only a handful of dogs that would tolerate this level of interference, even from their own masters ... and my Shilo was one of them.

However, there was something that Shilo could never put up with, and that was having his ears tugged. Fortunately he'd always respond to this unintentional abuse by giving a short yelp and then moving away. Nevertheless, his lack of tolerance at having his ears pulled or rubbed, even gently, concerned me, and it wasn't until I'd consulted my long-time friend and wildlife veterinarian, that I found out and understood why. Gerrit Scheepers, who you will meet later, told me that this was a physiological issue rather than a psychological one, and was due in part to Shilo's love of swimming. Whenever he got out of the water and shook his head to get rid of the water, blood would rush to the tips of his ears under considerable pressure. The constant effect of this would then break some of the smaller capillaries in the tips of his ears, hence the sensitivity.

* * *

Summer's heat was upon us. Most days were hot; some impossibly so. What didn't get done before ten in the morning had to wait until after three. That particular day we were contemplating spending the heat of the day in and around the pool when the base camp radio crackled into life. A report came in from one of the early morning game drives to say that they'd seen an injured kudu bull, which appeared to have broken its front leg. The kudu was on the Tuli circle road close to the Zimbabwe border, a fair distance away, and as it was already nearly 8am, I knew we'd need to move quickly before it got too hot. I decided that if I found the kudu, I would put it out of its misery. To my mind it was preferable to shoot an otherwise healthy animal for rations, one that was doomed to a slow painful death anyway, rather than select a sound individual.

I cursed the fact that it was a kudu. These stately animals have a special place in my heart – there is no more majestic antelope in Africa. To watch a magnificent kudu bull, normally capable of clearing a three-metre fence, hobble around crippled is soul-destroying, to say the least.

When Shilo and I arrived at the spot where the kudu had last been seen, it was no longer there. Knowing how enigmatic these antelope are, I hadn't really expected it to be. They are not known as the 'grey ghosts' of Africa for nothing. At that point I had no idea how far it had gone, so we were obliged to track it down by following the spoor, which I picked up easily.

I was reluctant to send Shilo on the kudu's trail until I'd caught sight of it. I needed to confirm that the observation made by the ranger that morning was indeed accurate – and if so, I was hoping to get a clear enough shot to take it cleanly. However, the kudu, true to this antelope's elusive nature, got wind of our approach. Considering he was only able to use three legs, he was surprisingly agile and managed to keep moving ahead of us. At one point I feared he had outdistanced us, but looking up on the crest of a small rise, I saw the big bull as he stopped to look back at us before taking off again. He'd stood just long enough for Shilo to see him, but not long enough for me to take a shot, so I gave Shilo a gentle shove on his backside. 'Teksit!' I hissed, and with that he disappeared over the rocky knoll after the kudu.

There was no need to keep looking ahead; that aspect was being covered by Shilo, so I was able to stay focused on the kudu's tracks. However, when nearly forty-five minutes had gone by and there was neither sign nor sound of dog or kudu, I began to get a little anxious. Stopping to light a cigarette, I noticed how slowly the smoke drifted away; there wasn't a breath of wind, and I could feel how hot it was beginning to get. As I watched the blue smoke drift lazily away, something other than the incessant buzz of cicadas came drifting through the stifled air, a rapid repetitive sound I'd never heard before. Importantly, it got louder as I followed the spoor of the kudu bull.

Though I didn't know what the sound was, I had a feeling it would lead me to my dog. Homing in on it was really easy: there I found Shilo sitting on his haunches, his lips pulled right back, exposing his rearmost carnassial teeth. It was as if some invisible index fingers had hooked his jowls from behind and pulled them back as far as they would go. His tongue was distended and hanging out to the side. I'd never seen him like this before. He was panting so heavily that each breath was a rapid, throaty effort, and it was so loud that I'd heard it from over 100 metres away! About five metres away from him, in the shade of a shepherd's tree, stood the enormous kudu bull. At my approach he attempted to run, but, tired as Shilo was, he expertly blocked the kudu's escape and it staggered back to the shade of the tree. This time I was ready, and now with his attention on Shilo, the old bull never knew a thing as I put a swift end to his ordeal.

Besides the badly broken leg there wasn't a mark on the kudu – the closest Shilo got to him was after he had been shot, and even then, there was no more than a thorough sniffing out of curiosity. Though the kudu bull must have been in state of exhaustion, it was apparent that Shilo had not attempted to attack it at any point; instead he had tired the kudu out by preventing it from getting any further away. Evidence on the ground showed that Shilo had herded the kudu as a sheepdog would a flock of sheep, keeping an eye on it until I arrived. It was as if he knew the great beast was doomed, and there was no need to make it any worse; come to think of it, I had not heard him bark or even yelp at the kudu.

It was only mid-morning and already the ambient temperature was high enough to make the cicadas stutter and the distant hills shimmer. I knew it was only going to become unbearably hot towards midday, so I covered the dead kudu with a few leafy branches from an evergreen magic guarri bush that grew close by. Their branches are easily broken by hand, hence the Afrikaans name *lekkerbreek* (nice break). This was done in order to keep as much sun off the kudu as possible, and to prevent vultures from scavenging the carcass until we could return to load it. Once done, we began to head back to the vehicle.

I poured what little water I had left in the canvas bag over Shilo's head and neck to help cool him down a little. It pained me to see him suffering in the heat, but he didn't wimp out on me as I have seen other dogs do in similar conditions. I suspect Shilo knew there was no option, so he adapted as best he could by making full use of any available shade. He'd wait until I'd covered some ground, then dash to the next patch, and so we progressed with Shilo leapfrogging across the sun-scorched earth, from shady bit to shady bit, until we reached the vehicle and that priceless second water bag.

Once again Shilo's versatility had shone through. While an inherently compassionate streak in his nature had been revealed beyond any doubt, it had not stopped him proving that he was an exceptional hunting dog. He was simply doing the job which I had trained him for and expected of him. Although it was undoubtedly a job he loved doing, Shilo had proved beyond any doubt that he was a hunter, not a killer.

13

SHILO IN THE CITY

I have no affinity with the city of my youth, none at all, and with each visit I become more impatient to leave its claustrophobic atmosphere, pacing like a caged tiger until it is time to be heading back to the bush again. Meagan, also Johannesburg-born and bred, soon began to feel the same way. Nevertheless, many of our family and friends live in and around the city, and it is always good to see them again. For a while we took turns sneaking away for a couple of days at a time, while one of us stayed behind with Shilo. However, this changed when we were required to take our annual leave of two weeks, which was long overdue. No longer was there a question of doing relays, there was no discussion, Shilo would simply have to come with us on holiday, a prospect that filled me with excitement.

Besides being let out for a pee at a filling station's grassy patch in Pietersburg on the way down, Shilo had never been in a city environment. Despite my initial apprehension, he appeared to be treating the trip as an adventure, taking an obvious interest in everything new he saw and smelled. Like a canine tourist, Shilo spent much of the journey with his head out of the back window, his ears flapping in the wind and a look of eager anticipation on his face.

We arrived to a warm welcome and of course my father's cooking, which you could smell above the carefully tended rose garden. Although she never admitted to it, I'm convinced my mother planted and nurtured those roses so that passers-by would have something to smell instead of garlic, oregano and sweet basil ... But today was special; Meagan and Mario were coming to visit, so my mom didn't mind at all. I suspect she was beginning to realise there's not much that can compete with the aroma of Italian cuisine.

This trip I was making a point of going to visit my good friend Tyrone Stevenson, who happened to be South Africa's 250cc motocross champion at the time. He had invited me to watch him race the national event while I was in town. I told him I would love to, but had a dog I couldn't leave on his own. I explained that Shilo was totally street unwise, not to mention the effect of the high levels of noise that these high-performance machines made at the race track, which I was sure would terrify him.

'That's no problem; he can stay at my house with Tasha,' Tyrone said. 'I'm sure he'd love her.'

'Who's Tasha?' I asked suspiciously.

'She's my dog, a cross Doberman Rottweiler,' he said. Then as if reading my mind, he added. 'But don't worry – she's not aggressive.'

Despite my trepidation at the prospect of Shilo and a strange dog being left together, when they met the next morning it was love at first sight. Tasha was a beautiful dog, although slightly bigger than Shilo, and appeared to have similar energy levels. This would be the first time I would be leaving Shilo on his own with such an attractive lady in unfamiliar surroundings, but the high walls and secure gate gave me a measure of reassurance.

* * *

We returned a little later than anticipated that same afternoon, all of us in high spirits; it had been a successful day at the track for Tyrone. I must admit to being quite keen to see if Shilo had missed me as much as I had missed him. I expected him to be waiting at the gate for me, but when we arrived at the house, I looked through the bars of the top half of the gate ... only Tasha was there to greet us. The blood drained from my head as a cold flood of panic swept over me.

'Hang on here,' Tyrone said. 'I'll quickly check inside the house.'

Returning a few minutes later I could see he hadn't found Shilo. 'I'm sorry, guys, he's not there,' he said, shrugging his shoulders.

Meagan and I went through the gate and walked into Tyrone's yard. We called Shilo's name while searching in amongst the many huge cycads, tree ferns and aloes that made up his father's extensive collection ... nothing!

We were just about to climb into my truck to begin searching the neighbourhood at random, when Tyrone's house maid came out to inform us that when she came back from lunch and opened the gate to let herself in, Shilo took the gap, slipped past her and out into the road. There was nothing she could do to stop him, she apologised.

She pointed to the road that led down to the main road through that part of the suburb, which led to a very busy intersection where the local shopping centre was. My mouth went dry with fear and my heart, which was already in my shoes at that point, sank through the floorboards and onto the road! We had only just come through that very same busy intersection. I also knew that punters who had spent the day at the racecourse and many regulars from the local pub were among those behind the wheels of the cars heading home through that point.

Shilo knew nothing of the dangers posed by vehicle traffic, and now he was exposed to speeding vehicles on busy roads, roads he'd never been on before, and a surface to which he was totally unaccustomed. With no familiar smells or landmarks to guide him, he could have headed anywhere, and without any tracks to follow, who knows where he would end up? Despite searching the suburban roads in the immediate vicinity and calling his name at each corner, we saw nothing; Shilo was nowhere to be found.

Understandably, I began to paint a really negative picture in my mind. Meagan and I decided to drive around the area again, which we did for the best part of an hour, questioning everybody we could. We called his name repeatedly, particularly up dark lanes and alleyways. Of course this aroused every dog in the neighbourhood, which was now filled with the cacophony of barking dogs. When it got too dark to see any more, and hampered by the limited search area allowed by the straight line beam of the headlights, we decided to call it quits. I vowed then never to be caught without a hand-held spotlight ever again, and to this day there is one permanently behind the seat of my pick-up.

Utterly dejected, Meagan and I slowly began driving in the direction of my father's house, which was about six kilometres away from Tyrone's. Resigned to the possibilities, but expecting the worst, we drove in silence through the first busy intersection, where I half expected to find Shilo's lifeless body. Thankfully there was nothing. Approaching the second one, located about midway, again I went through the anguish, and tried hard to swallow the lump in my throat ... nothing.

I was going through the mental process of preparing for never seeing my dog again. I was behaving like a zombie, going through the motions quietly, but with deliberate urgency; there was no wheel squealing cornering and racing around in desperation. Perhaps the way I felt, could be best described as a sickeningly quiet acceptance of the worst, an utterly numbing helplessness. I consciously quelled the upsurge of panic that threatened to explode at any moment, and whenever I looked across at Meagan, her tears told me she felt the same.

Meagan and I were no longer actively searching; instead we found ourselves staring straight ahead. Neither of us said a word to the other; by now there was nothing to say, we'd exhausted every possible permutation. Slowing down as we approached the last turn to my father's house, I suddenly caught sight of a familiar shape in the headlights as they swung in an arc round the corner, the shadow of yet another dog. We'd seen many similar dogs during the search, so it took a while to register that this outline was strikingly familiar. I couldn't believe my eyes initially, but it was no mere illusion – this time it was Shilo, nose to the ground and tail up, and less than 200 metres away from my father's house!

'Shilo!' I called. When he heard his name he stopped instantly, but carried on staring straight ahead, in the direction of the house. I called his name once more; this time it came out softer than I would have liked. Either I was choked emotionally, or possibly some dust from the motocross track had lodged in my throat, but it was loud enough for him to hear from which direction it came. He whipped his head around, turned towards us, and in a flash he'd crossed the quiet street and jumped onto the front seat between Meagan and me. He immediately started licking my face, something he was not normally encouraged to do ... but this time it didn't matter. Shilo also smiled a lot when he was happy or embarrassed, which made him sneeze, so it was lick-smile-sneeze, lick-smile-sneeze, the short distance home to my father's house.

So what is so extraordinary about this? Countless domestic dogs throughout history have been known to run home from hundreds of miles away, but Shilo had been in the city less than two days, hardly enough time to familiarise himself with this strange environment. He had never set a paw on the ground between Tyrone's house and my father's, nor had he ever walked more than a few metres on a tar road in his life, let alone amongst so many people and cars. He had come straight out of the Botswana bushveld through to Johannesburg's concrete jungle in the back of a truck. His only experience of this crowded environment was what he'd seen out of the rear window of my vehicle. What scent he was following or trying to pick up when we found him was a mystery, yet therein lay the only possible physiological explanation. But how a bush dog without any car sense had negotiated two busy intersections without mishap on a Saturday afternoon, only Shilo himself will ever know.

* * *

The following day found us winding through the western suburbs of Johannesburg on our way to the Magaliesberg. It was peak hour on Main Reef Road, and the traffic was bumper to bumper. Shilo was fascinated, if not a little overwhelmed with the hubbub around him, particularly as we spent a lot of time at a standstill, or crawling at walking pace in the heavy traffic. This gave him the opportunity to stick his head out of the back windows of the canopy, which I'd opened as wide as they'd go, to allow as much air in for cooling as possible. When he did, I couldn't help wondering what a wealth of information his nose must have been picking up from what was around him.

The traffic light changed to amber and I slowed down and pulled up to the line as it went red. A newspaper vendor with an armful of papers tucked under his left arm and a folded one in his right hand approached my open window, but I politely declined. Meagan had already bought a paper at the filling station a few kilometres back. Moving down the narrow gap between the stationary vehicles, the vendor began making his way to other potential customers. He appeared to be in a jovial mood, his head and shoulders bobbed from side to side as if in time to some private beat. As he went by the rear window of my truck's canopy, he slapped it a couple of times with the folded newspaper.

Shilo could have had no idea what this meant; there was just too much happening around him. Possibly he was looking out of the opposite window when this sudden slapping noise in an unfamiliar environment frightened him. It was loud enough that my attention was drawn to the noise as it reverberated around the largely empty fibreglass canopy. He had to have felt threatened, or felt I was being threatened, and for Shilo the best form of defence was to attack.

Glancing in my rear-view mirror, I was just in time to see Shilo leaping out of the window. He sailed through as effortlessly as a trained seal through a hoop, and hit the road running as he set off after the vendor, who instantly discarded all the newspapers in his wake as he fled screaming. Realising he wasn't going to outpace Shilo, the poor chap leaped up onto the high running board of a huge eighteen-wheeler truck just as the traffic began to move, and hung on for dear life.

Abandoning the Cruiser with Meagan sitting in the passenger seat, I ran out into the road after Shilo, and as I did, the traffic on both sides of the line I'd blocked began to move. The impatient drivers in the lanes on either side were totally unconcerned with the drama. They continued rolling forward with no apparent concern for any peripheral activity, and drove zombie-like with their minds elsewhere, as if wearing blinkers. Despite my attempt at signalling my dilemma with gesticulations, the drivers of the stationary vehicles that were now backed up behind my truck were hooting intolerantly. Fortunately, amidst the din, Shilo responded to my call, and leaped through the now opened door and into the back of my truck. With his tail wagging and a huge grin on his face, he popped the occasional sneeze; the look on his face said it all, but I'm sure if he could have spoken he would probably have said. 'Hey, dad, the city looks like it can be just as much fun as the bush.'

I have no idea when that vendor eventually alighted from the running board of that truck, but when we caught up at the traffic lights, he was still clinging to the rear-view mirror struts. As we drove past, all I can remember seeing were his eyes, now as wide as saucers, staring past us at Shilo's head sticking out of the rear canopy window.

When we got home, I screwed two horizontal black plastic conduit tubes onto the inside of each of the canopy windows, and although the back of my truck may have resembled the prison on Alcatraz, it gave us peace of mind. Shilo could still comfortably get his head out, but not his shoulders, so we could now leave the windows fully open when it was warm … And the newspaper vendors of Main Reef Road would be safe.

14

GOODBYE BOTSWANA

Bushfillan Safaris' reputation as a big game wildlife safari destination was soon well known and we were proud of what we had helped achieve – but we couldn't help feeling that our prospects in Botswana were as ephemeral as the Tuli Block's summer rains. A persistent, underlying uneasiness had never really allowed me to feel welcome. We tolerated the politics, the endless restrictions and bureaucratic red tape imposed on us in order to live in Botswana, but it seemed that begging, bowing and scraping at every turn was part and parcel of a South African's life in that country. I guess we always hoped things would improve with time and trust; we'd grown to love the Tuli area, its people and its wildlife. The difficulties we encountered had been overshadowed by our enthusiasm to make a meaningful contribution to the Tuli wilderness and its conservation. Limited though it was, we knew that the time we were spending providing training and creating meaningful employment opportunities in ecotourism and the associated hospitality industry was well worth it. It was rewarding, it kept us motivated, and lifted our spirits when things got us down.

The red tape was enough to crush the most dauntless spirit. In order to legally work and reside in Botswana we needed endless documentation, and with each renewal there was the humiliation of continually having to justify our presence. The administrative offices in Gaborone were at least six hours' drive away from the reserve and often we would be turned back for some small omission on the renewal application form. Invariably it was for some petty reason that could have been rectified there and then with a modicum of effort. These delays would result in days wasted, which was both counterproductive and demoralising; the petty officials knew this and capitalised on it. If subtle 'grease my palm' hints were ignored, their blinkered view would fail to take in the bigger picture, and instead of exercising their discretion at times, they dwelt fixedly on onerous, petty procedure.

Slowly but surely our enthusiasm began to erode, eventually reaching the point where the short-sighted abuse and wanton, petty corruption blighted our days. Soon the sacrifices being made began to outweigh the benefits. Extensions to residence permits could be obtained at the local border post, but this 'convenience' often involved having to part with whatever those in authority could wheedle from us disguised as a 'loan' – and all this in exchange for the inescapable rubber stamp. For example, the border post authorities at Botswana's Pont Drift requested I leave Meagan's portable TV with them 'on loan' while they extended her temporary residence permit. I obliged, of course, without hesitation, naturally assuming, or rather hoping, that they would return it once her paperwork had been processed at Gaborone. But, when they requested an aerial and booster to be installed a few days later, I knew the TV was history. Then there was the fibreglass supply canoe we kept at the border post, which a customs official 'borrowed' and then forgot to secure at its mooring. It was never replaced; nor was there any apology or acknowledgement of wrongdoing from the individual concerned.

'It was the river that took the boat,' he said.

Technically speaking, I guess he may have had a point.

* * *

Open aggression, particularly towards young South African men, was worrying. We were always particularly circumspect with the military, and not without good reason. Only a couple of years before, in a widely publicised and controversial case, two young South Africans running Safari Camp in the Northern Tuli Block had been shot by members of the Botswana Defence Force, just a few miles north of Majali camp on the Shashe River. The killing was rigged to look as if they were shot trying to resist arrest on suspicion of spying. But in the soldiers' haste to cover their crime, they didn't pay enough attention to the smaller details – for example, bullet holes in the ill-fitting Rhodesian army camouflage clothing found on the dead men, which didn't correspond with the bullet wounds on the bodies. Subsequently a detailed investigation revealed the truth. Both men had been shot in the back.

Evidently the soldiers had been drinking when they found the two men hunting only a few metres inside Zimbabwe. The physical boundary line between the two countries was only 300 metres from the camp and was virtually impossible to discern, so with no fence or stone cairns, and only a faint vehicle track as a marker, it was an easy mistake to make, especially when concentrating on spoor. Popular conjecture had it that because one of them was wearing his old South African army bush hat, they were suspected of being 'Boer' spies. In those days, the BDF were unofficially at war with the 'apartheid' army of South Africa, so understandably there was a lot of mistrust … but this was murder!

The negative publicity was relatively short-lived, and as the months went by, tourism resumed with renewed impetus. Tuli Lodge in particular began picking up to the point where we were turning people away due to a shortage of accommodation. We needed to find a venue to cope with overflow bookings, and Safari Camp provided the infrastructure we needed.

Although the situation had now returned to 'normal', the owners of Safari had never returned to their property in the Tuli Block; it had simply been left to the elements. I can clearly remember the day I arrived at the deserted camp two years after this tragic incident. The once-beautiful lawn that stretched down to the small but clear Motabola River was now knee-high in grass and weeds, and some of the thatched roofs of the chalets had been damaged by baboons; otherwise I found the camp pretty much as it had been left two years previously. Nothing had been vandalised and not a soul lived there now; it was eerie and quiet. Apparently the rest of the staff at Safari Camp, fearing they might be implicated as cohorts and treated in the same manner, had run for their lives. The families of the two men had left with little more than the clothes on their backs and their passports – they simply got up from the table, climbed into their vehicles and drove back to South Africa.

Poignant evidence of their hasty evacuation and terrified state of mind was clearly evident. Pots and dishes lay heaped in the kitchen sink waiting to be washed, the kitchen table chairs were left as they'd been pulled out when those who'd sat on them got up and fled, none had been pushed back in under the table, and one of them lay where it had fallen, its legs sticking in the air like those of a sun-bloated carcass. I stood there trying to imagine what it must have felt like to be so terrified that you simply got up and ran from your home, your refuge, a bastion of safety … where now only the smell of fear clung to the air, like the mould that was now growing on the dirty dishes in the kitchen sink.

The owners of Safari Camp have never returned to Botswana.

*   *   *

'Temporary residents' – the first word of that classification had summed things up all along. We knew that we were merely tolerated and our stay in that country was going to be a measured one. However, the sustained disdain of the BDF made the surliness of the customs and immigration officials seem a mere routine hassle.

One incident that comes to mind took place when I had driven across the reserve to supervise some work at our Limpopo Camp one day. It was one of only a very few times I left Shilo behind, but Meagan was alone in camp that day and I thought his being there would give her some measure of comfort and company. The breeze of political unease blowing at the time was threatening to reach gale force. Zimbabwe's opposition leader, Joshua Nkomo, was on the run from Robert Mugabe's followers, and was rumoured to have been planning to enter Botswana through the Tuli Block from the Bulawayo region. This gave the BDF an excuse to patrol the area and visit the camp more regularly, where they would creep around in their camouflage gear making an elaborate show of searching all of eight small buildings and surrounds. To me it appeared to be just a good excuse for them to intimidate us and to cadge free cool drinks and snacks from the lodge. Midday was a favourite time, usually when we were about to sit down for lunch. It was absolutely terrifying for the guests, some of whom needed quite a bit of PR from us to reassure them that these weren't their last moments on the planet.

Meagan heard the familiar sound of a Land Rover approaching. Looking out of the window, she was expecting to see me arriving back with my team of workers. Instead she saw a vehicle load of men in camouflage, and recognised them as BDF. They were approaching Majali fast, then as always, ground to a halt in a huge cloud of dust. This time the body language of the occupants flashed a warning. Meagan didn't step out to welcome them into camp, instead, acting on an impulse of dread, she climbed under the bed with Shilo and lay there clutching the 30/06 ... the only rifle she had ever used in her life. She admitted it gave her only a modicum of comfort while she hid under the bed, one arm around Shilo and the other on the rifle. They lay together like that until eventually she heard their vehicle drive away.

Later, on my return, Meagan was visibly shaken.

'What were you thinking, Annie Oakley?' I asked flippantly. 'Were you going to take them on with your rifle, and all of four rounds in the magazine?'

Meagan's solemn expression remained resolute; my weak attempt at humour was completely wasted.

'I don't know, but when I saw that bunch driving like they did, I just had a feeling they might have been drinking,' she said. 'I suddenly felt vulnerable.'

I was going to give her a reassuring hug, but before I could, Meagan bent down with tears in her eyes and hugged Shilo. Then she stood up; now it was my turn. I hugged her.

'Shilo was an absolute star today, you know,' she sobbed. 'I felt

143

so safe with him as he lay there with me – I simply whispered, 'Uh-uh!' He didn't utter a sound, even when one of them opened the door, walked in and looked around briefly. The arrogant bastard didn't have the decency to knock first!'

Meagan didn't need to elaborate – it was written all over her face. She didn't want to stay in Botswana any longer. I believe if it hadn't been for me, she would have left that same day.

A couple of months later the police added their own display of audacity when they arrived on a 'routine visit' and requested some meat for Christmas. Congenially hospitable, Meagan explained that there was a kudu and two impala hanging in the cool room, but because our bullet permit was nearly due for renewal, we had only four cartridges left and therefore could only offer them one impala. Assuming that, being policemen, they could be trusted, she excused herself and went back to the kitchen to prepare lunch for the guests due back from the bush.

When I returned later that day I found only one impala hanging in the cool room, and naturally asked Meagan where all the meat had gone. She looked shocked, initially, but giving the officers the benefit of the doubt, began doubting herself, thinking that she may have been too vague, and they, not understanding her, had taken the kudu and one impala, leaving only one impala. The Botswana Police speak and understand English, so they had understood Meagan, but chose to ignore her request. Naturally I was simmering at the way they had taken advantage of her, and to add insult to injury, when I went back into the coolroom and checked, it was the smaller of the two impala they had left for us. We had four bullets and one small impala to see us through the entire festive season!

* * *

When weighed against the rewards of working in such a beautiful environment, the occasional hassles appeared to be worth it, for a while anyway. For me, the added prospect of building a camp from nothing, with nothing, in the middle of nowhere, was a creative challenge; it got me up long before dawn each day. Best of all I had Meagan's support and a well-trained team of staff – and most importantly for Shilo, he was able to be with me all the time, wherever I went and whatever I was doing.

What turned out to be the last straw started out as a relatively boring project for Shilo to sit through, which happened to be landscaping. Besides Nel's Vlei and the Pitsani Valley, green grass is a rare sight on Tuli's open plains and although visitors to this arid environment love the rugged beauty, nothing is as soothing to the eye as returning from a sun-drenched game drive to see a green lawn surrounding a cool, sparkling swimming pool. To this end I painstakingly transplanted some hardy *Cynodon dactylon* lawn grass from the Pitsani Valley and established it around the pool at Majali Camp. A little organic fertiliser mixed into the soil and subsequent regular watering was all that was needed: the small patch of lawn responded really well, soon reaching the point where it needed regular mowing. In a couple of months we had a tiny piece of turf to be proud of, and which the guests enjoyed lying on around the pool. Unfortunately there were some unwelcome guests that not only enjoyed lying on the lawn but also took nourishment from it. One morning I woke to find the culprits in the form of two donkeys on the lawn and chased them off immediately, but not before their hooves had done extensive damage.

The donkeys' owner was known to me, so I asked him to keep them on his property, which was just outside the reserve, some ten kilometres away. Needless to say the request fell on deaf ears, and the following day the donkeys were back. However, this time when I chased them off the lawn, I sent Shilo after them, hoping he'd be more persistent. Starting the donkeys at full gallop, he maintained the momentum and succeeded in chasing them for a quite a few kilometres, something that would make them understand they weren't welcome, at the very least they wouldn't be back in a hurry, I thought … wrong. The next morning we woke to find them back on the lawn, and although Shilo knew the routine, he glanced back at me, waiting impatiently for the word. He didn't have to wait long.

'Teksit!' I hissed through clenched teeth.

With that Shilo took off from the front door and ran straight up to them, but this time the donkeys stood their ground. Shilo was flummoxed; this had never happened to him before, normally when he gave chase the quarry ran, so instinctively he did the next best thing and went in to nip the hock of the donkey that was cheeky enough to carry on grazing. As Shilo tried to bite the donkey's lower leg he was swiftly kicked in the face. Reeling, he howled in pain, which of course got my undivided attention – you hurt my dog, you hurt me! I immediately saw red, even through my bleary morning eyes. I grabbed the nearest stick I could find and ran up to the donkeys still clad in only my underpants. Never mind their reputation for stupidity, these two donkeys could see this screaming, stick-wielding, semi-naked man was ready to kill, so they made an intelligent decision and took off at a gallop, though not without gouging more craters in my precious lawn. I have to admit being somewhat relieved they'd moved off as quickly as they did, for fear that Shilo would go in for a revenge nip and get kicked again.

After checking to see that he was okay, I put on some clothes, climbed into the Land Cruiser and drove out of camp after the donkeys. Shilo and I soon caught up with them strolling along the road at a leisurely pace which we gently encouraged until they were running. The pain all but forgotten, Shilo yelped with delight as we continued chasing them along the road at a steady canter all the way back to their owner's house, where they came to a stop blowing and quite exhausted.

Two uneventful weeks went by, the swelling above Shilo's eye gradually went down, the lawn began to recover and the donkeys weren't seen again. I suspected that their owner realised I was serious about not having them in my camp, and had honoured his promise to keep them out of the reserve ... Wrong again. He arrived one day accompanied by the police, and demanded that I buy him two new donkeys, accusing me of chasing all the power out of the old ones, which were now so lazy they wouldn't pull his cart any more. I politely replied that all they needed was some decent food and rest, and they'd be fitter than before. He remained adamant, supported by the police, who issued the ultimatum that charges would be laid against me if I didn't pay up.

There was no reasoning with this! I paid him the required 40 pula (about R50) which would enable him to replace his tired donkeys in cash while the two policemen stood looking on. The man accepted the money with a smile; this was case closed as far as I was concerned.

Then a couple of weeks later I returned from the border post one morning to find a cart parked near the lodge under the shade of a large shepherd's tree, with two harnessed donkeys that were somehow familiar to me. Only when I saw their owner standing at reception did I put two and two together. They were the same donkeys that we'd chased out of camp, looking none the worse for wear, I might add. Their owner didn't mince his words; he came straight to the point, saying he wanted money for another two donkeys.

'But I've paid you!' I exclaimed. 'We had a deal, don't you remember?'

The man simply looked right past me, arrogantly repeating his demand. I refused again; this time our eyes met, and his were clearly filled with anger as he vowed to bring the police.

Sure enough, at lunchtime the following day the police arrived accompanied by the 'complainant'. They too apparently had no recollection of the transaction they'd witnessed only two weeks previously, so I simply repeated to them what I'd told the donkeys' owner.

'Well, then he is going to lay a charge against you and your dog for taking the power from his donkeys,' they said.

I could see where this was going, so I simply shrugged and gave them a wry smile. With that they left.

I had reached the point where I could no longer push against this relentless tide of unpleasant anxiety. It had begun to erode the edges of what I'd come to love, and the line between love and hate was beginning to blur. The veiled threat against Shilo cut me to the quick; it was the catalyst I needed to make the decision. That afternoon, I told Meagan I thought it was time to leave Botswana, and her smile spoke volumes. That evening we packed our belongings and loaded the car. The following morning the three of us were the first to drive through the border post into South Africa ... never to return.

* * *

Whether Shilo and I had become fugitives we never found out, but apparently the donkeys returned and continued to eat what little was left of the bedraggled patch of lawn. But that wasn't the end of the story; not long after we'd left, I received a call from Ockie to tell me that he had heard that both donkeys were killed by lions just outside Majali camp one night. This time their owner had called the Botswana Game Department and laid a complaint against the marauding predators. The fact that these lions were on private property in a game reserve at the time meant nothing. In the eyes of the law, lions that killed somebody's livestock were classified stock killers. Apparently, where the stock happened to be at the time they were killed was immaterial.

I knew the two Game Department Officials in charge of that area quite well. 'Peter game scout', as he was known, was a stocky chap, fond of his food, quick-minded and always ready with a joke, I also remember the poor man perspired a lot and was forever wiping his neck and forehead with a handkerchief. The other man was his opposite, not the brightest button in the tin. A tall and slim man with the longest neck I have ever seen on a human being, he was nicknamed 'Giraffe'. He didn't smile or say much, I suspect he may have fancied himself as the silent deadly type. He was armed with a rusty old .303 Lee Metford rifle, which spent most of the time strapped to the crossbar of his bicycle by means of strips of inner tube. Having already seen a couple of world wars, this old weapon was indeed a veteran of death. However, given its age and state of neglect, I'd always had grave doubts about its ability to function properly. Of particular concern was the fact it had a bent front sight, almost certainly the result of a head-over-handlebar accident, where the front of the barrel had taken the brunt of the fall.

According to a witness who helped them track the three lions, it wasn't long before they found them in the riverbed close by, whereupon 'Giraffe' took the old .303 and proceeded to loose off a number of shots, wounding one of them in the jaw. Eventually, nearly a week later, one of the resident professional hunters was called in to finish the game department's botched attempt, mercifully bringing a swift end to the lion's misery.

15

A CHANGE IS AS GOOD AS A HOLIDAY

Shilo had never seen the sea, and neither Meagan nor I had been to the coast in years. Before looking for a job in South Africa, we decided to take a short break and head for the seaside. We had an invitation to visit Mkambati Nature Reserve, which was managed by old friends – and as a bonus, boasted excellent fishing. More importantly, Shilo would be more than welcome. I couldn't wait to introduce him to the surf and beautiful secluded beaches of the Transkei Wild Coast.

On the way down to Mkambati, we put aside an extra couple of days to take ourselves off the beaten track. Truth be told, most of the time we didn't know where the hell we were going, but this simply added spice to our forays. Long before decent roads and GPS navigation threw cold water on the spirit of adventure, there were some exciting times to be had travelling this way, as we found when we ended up on a sand dune footpath that dead-ended at the edge of a secluded beach.

Though crafted solely by the hand of nature, the tiny bay was a veritable scene from the chronicles of fantasy, a set tailor-made for rum adverts, pirates and buried treasure, or the backdrop for a romantic scene played out in a crystal-clear lagoon. Never in our wildest dreams could we have envisaged the 'Survivor'-type location that we found on that remote Wild Coast beach. Naturally, as with any survival strategy, I couldn't wait to rig my fishing rod and catch some fresh fish for supper, lest we starve to death. Sigmund Freud believed men can only concentrate on one thing at a time, and right now I was in provider mode.

Pulling up under a huge milkwood tree on the edge of the dune, I went straight around to the back of the truck and let Shilo out. He needed no encouragement whatsoever and ran across the small beach straight into the sea, biting at the foam and jumping out of the way as the waves broke close to him. I actually saw the look of shock on his face when he tasted the saltiness of the water – he didn't try that again.

Watching dogs on any beach anywhere makes me suspect that the taxonomists have it wrong; dogs are just frustrated, landlubbing, wannabe seals. I don't know of a single one that doesn't enjoy the beach, nor have I seen dogs more playful or happier with life than when they are at the beach. Even though Shilo was born and bred in the arid bushveld, he was no different, he loved the seaside ... and I found out later that, like seals, he also loved raw sardines!

Shilo chased the sand crabs that buried themselves faster than he could dig, and despite his highest leaps into the air snapping at the seagulls, they still managed to steal some of our bait, but he was having a great time. I waded into the surf and cast my line into the sea. I didn't have to wait long for a bite: setting the hook, I could feel I was into a fair-sized fish. After a brief struggle, it surfaced, showing itself as I slid it up onto the beach. The late afternoon sunlight reflected off its flank, a silvery pink hue with a hint of mother of pearl – a beautiful fish, perfection in every sense. Bending down to get a closer look, I recognised it as a kob, and estimated that it weighed about five kilograms, a relatively small specimen. Nonetheless, overjoyed, I grabbed my prize and ran back up the beach to where I'd left Meagan, calling out to her as I approached what was now a really comfortable-looking camp.

Holding the fish high, I proudly displayed it for her to see that I'd provided supper for us – we would survive the wilderness. Instead of the expected accolades for my piscatorial prowess, there was only silence; nor was there a smile or simple kiss offered; instead, my accomplishment was greeted with a scowl of disdain. Then it dawned on me: I suddenly realised why there was no sharing of my joy. I'd completely neglected to get the priorities right, and she had been left to single-handedly rig our tent, unpack the truck and make things really comfortable while I had been intent on getting a line in the water and playing on the beach with Shilo. Later that evening, after I had prepared the fish and spoilt Meagan with a delicious meal on the beach, washed down with white wine, she mellowed and forgave me ... but even though I washed all the dishes, and unpacked everything single-handedly the next day, we don't camp together any more.

Sunrise found us all up and about, in anticipation of a beautiful day. It would have been sacrilege to squander this gift and lie in. It was also the time we saw the first people on 'our' beach. We were busy tidying things up and preparing for breakfast when a low growl from Shilo alerted us. With the sun rising behind the figures it was difficult to make them out at first, but as they got nearer I could see two young white men and a Xhosa youth carrying long fishing rods and wearing backpacks. Then, as they carefully laid their rods down, I could now see by the wear and tear and the type of fishing equipment they had that these guys were serious fishermen. They walked over to our tent, but seeing Shilo standing next to me, hung back a little and politely greeted us in Afrikaans, then, with a note of genuine concern, asked if everything was okay.

Shilo saw there was nothing to worry about – perhaps he recognised that these guys were the adventurous type – and made friends with them immediately. Touched by their concern and impeccable manners, we invited them for coffee, which they eagerly accepted. As it turned out, the two young men were the sons of a Kokstad farmer. A little fishing cottage close by had been their family's holiday home for over fifty years, and was cared for in their absence by the youth, who was from the local village.

The conversation turned to fishing, and I learned that they were angling mainly for sharks off the rocks. Although they had only a day left before heading home again, they invited me to go along with them – although not suitable for sharks, my rod and reel would be fine for gulley fishing. Before I could answer they looked at Meagan again, clearly concerned about our rough abode, saying they didn't think it was right for a lady to camp on the beach. I prayed Meagan wouldn't tell them who it was that set up that camp, and thankfully she didn't. In the same breath, they invited us to stay with them in their cottage, adding that once they'd left the following day, we could stay there for as long as we wished.

The Transkei Wild Coast is aptly named: the coastline is rugged, untamed and very dangerous. Every time we crossed a steep-sided gulley, I feared Shilo would lose his footing and tumble into the sea, where the next incoming wave could easily smash him against the rocks. The thought terrified me and I was beginning to think it was a bad idea to have brought him along, but Shilo negotiated the gullies as if he'd been born on those rocks. Then, just when all fears of losing my beloved dog were dispelled, we came to the mother of all gulleys; I could see this was going to test my resolve to the limit. It was well over 15 metres deep, sheer-sided, slippery and narrow; the only way across was a thick wooden plank that was narrower than a railway sleeper but three times as long. It was simple; if you fell off into the sea in this gully ... you were dead!

The three young men had already crossed; they'd obviously done this on countless previous occasions. All the same, there was no way I was going to let Shilo attempt it. But before I could call him back, wave farewell to the fishermen and head back to the relative safety of 'my' blue lagoon setting, he followed them, trotting across the plank as if the gulley wasn't there. Now compelled to follow, I shuffled across on all fours, my rod clamped firmly between my teeth ... for balance, you understand. Relieved that nobody made a fuss of my rather unorthodox way of 'walking the plank', least of all Shilo, I still found it difficult not to think of the return leg. Needless to say, everyone except me crossed back again just as casually as they did that morning. This time I had a few fish to carry across as well.

The beach cottage was one of a few situated on a larger bay about three kilometres away from where we had pitched our tent. It was equipped with all the basic necessities, so Meagan and I spent a couple of days in relative luxury, conducting the definitive test on the various species of fresh fish we caught, to determine which was the most delectable. Meagan prepared each fillet in exactly the same way and the results, in order of most delicious to the least, were as follows: rock cod, grunter, shad, bronze bream, musselcracker, kob, blacktail and karanteen. That's our verdict and we're sticking to it.

*   *   *

Mkambati Nature Reserve is named after a species of palm tree native to Madagascar, from where their huge seed pods, oddly shaped like a giant pig's scrotum, floated across the Indian Ocean on powerful currents to end up in this bay. Here they encountered all the necessary environmental conditions to germinate and flourish. The reserve also comprises beautiful mangrove swamps, a wonderful diverse coastal-marine reserve where limited fishing is allowed, and an inland reserve with an impressive variety of birdlife and numerous species of antelope. Mkambati had also been a leper colony for decades; the solid sandstone buildings that were built by the lepers to service their colony are still standing and in use today.

Fishing off the rocks on the edge of the lagoon one morning, we were totally engrossed in the task at hand. The incoming tide would be bringing in the shad, a particularly good sporting fish. As usual, Shilo was on guard duty, keeping our bait from becoming seagull food, and though there were no seagulls about, I thought he'd hang around anyway, just in case. However, when I turned to bait up, I noticed that he had abandoned his post and was a couple of hundred metres away, wading across the shallow lagoon mouth. Across on the opposite side I saw the reason for his sudden dereliction of duty – a pretty tan-coloured bitch belonging to one of the local villagers was coursing up and down the water's edge. It appeared as if she was frightened of the water – or, as I suspected, she knew the local conditions better than Shilo did. I was sure she could sense what I now feared, that the incoming tide would quickly flood the lagoon mouth. If Shilo was caught in the backwash, no matter his excellent swimming ability, he would be swept out to sea.

When Shilo did something he was not entirely sure of, he would look back at me, either for approval or reassurance. I don't know why I called to him, the sea was so noisy he could not possibly have heard me, but at the same time I beckoned for him to return with repeated exaggerated full arm movements much like bowling a cricket ball. To my utter relief, Shilo turned around and came back half-bounding, half-swimming through the rising water. Although I'd seen him react immediately, and that there was no need to carry on with the gesticulating, I continued beckoning reflexively. It was as if an invisible cord was attached between us and with each bowling motion I was pulling him closer in towards me and safety. In a couple of rather anxious minutes he bounded up the rocky ledge and was at my side. After a vigorous shake he looked up at me wagging his tail and smiling, sneezed once or twice, clearly a little embarrassed that he'd snuck off, but oblivious to the danger he'd been in. Shilo had no way of knowing that had another fifteen minutes lapsed with him on the other side of that lagoon, there would have been another ending to this story.

The lifestyle of a beach bum really suited Shilo; he'd clearly loved every minute of this adventure. He came away looking lean and muscular from all the exercise and his coat glistened from a combination of regular swimming and raw sardine titbits the seagulls didn't steal. But Meagan and I needed to get back to reality and earn a crust, so we bade a sad farewell and headed back north.

* * *

Having returned from holiday to Johannesburg, we knew we'd be unable to adjust to the claustrophobic environs of suburbia, even temporarily, so we began hunting for 'country' accommodation, somewhere quiet where we could regroup and give ourselves

155

enough time to send out our CVs to prospective employers in preparation for returning to the bush as soon as possible, somewhere Shilo could stretch his legs in relative safety. Fortunately, we made contact with a 'weekend farmer' who needed someone to keep an eye on a Brahman stud farm in the Magaliesberg for a few months.

In exchange for free accommodation and a small retainer, Meagan and I were expected to run the farm in a mainly supervisory capacity, as the farm workers knew the basic routine but simply lacked mechanical and bookkeeping skills. Less than an hour's drive from Johannesburg, it was ideal, and the pace of country life allowed us to focus on job-hunting.

It was here, at the back of the stud bull's feedlot, that Meagan found a little 'furball' rummaging through old cowpats for the bits of crushed maize. This tiny dog's plight tore into Meagan's soul; she just had to rescue it from a life of certain neglect and imminent starvation. We later found out that the ginger-haired waif had been born to a pedigree white Maltese poodle that in a moment of illicit freedom from its kugel owner had a one-night stand with a pavement special somewhere along the leafy avenues of Greenside. Owning a mongrel in this posh suburb was just not kosher, doll, so it was summarily dumped on the farm in the hope that one of the labourers would take it in. Little did they know that unless the dog was of whippet or greyhound extraction, mixed with a bit of jackal and a smidgen of hyena, the locals would have no interest in it; they wouldn't want it, nor would they care for it. If a dog couldn't hunt and run down small game for its owners, and be able to survive on watery porridge, they'd have no use for it.

Meagan called him Squealer, because he yelped rather than barked, and the name – unflattering as it was – sounded a lot better than 'Yelper'.

I have no doubt that somehow Squealer knew that Meagan had saved his life. He lived for her and to his dying day never left her side unless it was beyond his control. It was as if he tried to show her just how grateful he was, the only way he knew … through his utter devotion to her and no one else. Although Squealer became an inseparable part of the family, he never joined Shilo's 'pack' in the field.

Shilo adjusted to farm life quickly; there was always something on the go, rats to sniff out in the feed shed, or the cat-and-mouse game he played with the cheeky geese that kept nipping his tail when he lay asleep on the lawn. The Magaliesberg and environs had a relatively mild climate, and the four of us would be able to walk for miles in the field. On occasion I'd grab my shotgun and Shilo and I would go out and collect a couple of guineafowl or francolin for the pot. Shilo really enjoyed these excursions, which he treated as missions of purpose; he took any outing that required a weapon seriously – he couldn't help himself, the desire to hunt was inescapably tattooed on his genes.

The worst things about conventional farms are the barbed wire fences and the endless gates to open and close. I never got used to that. One day while negotiating a fence at a run Shilo nearly cut his penis in half as he dived between the strands. Thanks to a late-night emergency operation he was saved, but my hatred of barbed wire probably goes back to that day. Later, when I became Warden of Olifants River Game Reserve, I would be instrumental in removing hundreds of kilometres of this scourge in wildlife areas, particularly between the big private nature reserves and the Kruger National Park, and between the individual reserves themselves. Of course this had less to do with my long-standing hatred of barbed wire as a threat to dogs and their nether regions than the fact that the removal of these old veterinary fences would partially restore old migratory routes in free-ranging ecological systems, allowing huge areas to slowly return to the natural order of things.

* * *

Our sojourn in the quiet countryside lasted no longer than we meant it to: our search for a bush job was successful, and less than three months later we were excitedly packing for the Timbavati Game Reserve. During our time in the Magaliesberg we had become close to the owners and their farm, and had built up a great working relationship with the farm hands. Not least of all, I had become attached to the livestock, particularly the massive stud bulls, some of which would come running up to me at the sound of my voice. But the call of the bushveld was simply impossible to ignore ...

16

TIMBAVATI

Having included a couple of dogs in our lives, Meagan and I were carrying a little excess baggage, which narrowed our chances for potential bush jobs. Motswari and Mbali game lodges were looking for a general management couple. The location was great, but what decided it was when, enquiring further, we learned that a well-behaved dog would be welcome! Our interview with owners Paul and Mechtild Geiger went very well – we got on from the word go. Motswari and Mbali had become their lives – and for the next nine years, they became ours too.

Initially we would be based at Mbali, the smaller of the two camps. This was a particularly attractive option: firstly we would both be employed in senior management positions answering directly to the managing director, but most importantly for me, Mbali was located smack bang in the famous Timbavati Game Reserve's white lion territory...

I'd read so much about the area and recalled a brief but memorable visit to the southern Timbavati when I was sixteen. Although the north was quite different in terms of vegetation, I had some idea of what to expect. Meagan and I could hardly wait to get packed. Not surprisingly, the fervent pace and excited babble must have rubbed off on Shilo, and he could tell something exciting was happening. I am convinced that had I been able to communicate the detail of where we were going, he would have been impossible to live with for the two days it took to pack up. Even so he wouldn't let us out of his sight, he'd lie there watching as we packed, like he used to when he was a puppy in Botswana. Busy focusing on packing, we largely ignored him this once, which in itself was unusual behaviour from us, but it wasn't enough to cause the involuntary, almost imperceptible whimpers that sneaked out every now and then ... I am convinced Shilo had more than an inkling of what was happening.

* * *

We left Magaliesberg long before dawn, reaching the edge of the Drakensberg escarpment at midday. Having driven through the Strijdom Tunnel I looked down into the lowveld far below the seemingly endless bush that stretched all the way until it faded into the hazy horizon. That is when the reality hit me, and for the first time in ages it felt as if I was really coming home. Winding our way down into the warm lowveld, nearing the bottom of the pass, my ears popped open with the sudden drop in altitude, and rang to the incessant, monotonously brittle buzz of cicadas; it was beautiful music. Once through the twisting turns, I put my foot down. The big baobab we shot past, the most southerly of the species, was exactly as I remembered it. The huge tree didn't appear to have grown an inch since I'd first laid eyes on it.

Arriving at Motswari main camp just after lunch time with our worldly possessions in the back of my Toyota pick-up, we declined the offer of lunch, saying we'd really like to get to Mbali and unload as soon as possible. I wanted to settle in and take it all in quietly, and I could see by the wagging tails and Meagan's smile that I wasn't the only one.

I could immediately feel that I was in one of the last remaining unspoilt areas of the lowveld. The bushveld of Northern Timbavati and Umbabat Nature Reserve comprises predominantly mopane woodland. Born of shallow nutrient-poor soils, these hardy trees are apt to form dense thickets of scrubland in places which can make for difficult game viewing, particularly in the summer months. Occasionally breaking the monotony, especially in areas with deeper soils, we find taller specimens of mopane trees interspersed with red bush willow, knobthorns and marula trees, which have combined to form a rich mosaic of varied woodland habitat. Although many people find mopane veld monotonous, I don't, I happen to know different. From the moment I arrived in the area I was tingling with excitement; I knew from my time at Letaba Ranch that mopane woodland meant big game country; in particular it was home to big bull elephants.

Between Motswari and Mbali the road wound its way through some relatively thick stands of typical mopane woodland. As we slowed to negotiate the sandy crossing of the Sohebele River midway between the two camps, we came across an enormous herd of buffalo resting up in the shade, while two huge elephant bulls took it in turn to demolish a stand of wild date palms in the middle of the sandy wash. I looked across at Meagan and smiled in silent confirmation. Shilo's nose couldn't stop twitching – as the wet dung splashed up against the wheel arches of my truck he may have remembered this bovine smell from the stud farm we had left and wondered for a moment what we were doing on another farm. But I was wrong; his nose had picked up smells that unequivocally told him he was back in the bush. Shilo stuck his head through the interleading sliding window, whining softly and pressing his icy cold nose against my ear every now and again, while his tail constantly thumped against the fibreglass canopy. This was his way of letting me know he was excited too. It wasn't long before we were crunching our way up the sloping gravel road and driving into Mbali.

We decided to park at the staff quarters around the back of the camp, then walk down to the main area so as not to make an overly conspicuous entrance. Meagan held Squealer under her arm as we walked past the kitchen and the quaint admin office, but Shilo scampered on ahead of us and in effect saw the camp and fell in love with it moments before we did.

Not quite knowing what to expect as we rounded the reed screen that shielded the guest area, my jaw dropped at the sight. Mbali was everything we'd been led to believe it was, and then some. Perched on a hill overlooking the Nhlaralumi River below, it commanded a spectacular 180 degree panoramic view of the bush. While we stood there taking it all in, Shilo ran straight to the pool and jumped in, as if he'd done it countless times before. After briefly swimming around and biting at the odd floating leaf, he clambered out, shook the excess water from his coat and dried himself off by rolling around on the lawn. Despite shaking himself vigorously, dried bits of grass still clung to his coat when he went to lie down on the cool cement floor of the open verandah.

Shilo's demeanour gave every indication of belonging; he'd made himself completely at home in less than five minutes. Lying there on his chest, his back legs straight out behind him, he surveyed the scene in utter contentment. Shilo's body language spoke volumes: every wag of his tail, each territorial marking and investigative sniff was done with enthusiasm. As if to reassure me about things, he would come back to me briefly, give me a nudge and then resume what he was doing. There was no doubt that Shilo was letting me know that he too was happy to be back in the bushveld.

* * *

Squealer didn't mind where he was so long as Meagan was there. He did have to make one very unwelcome adaptation to life in the wild, however. Although the ugly little mutt wasn't much bigger than a lion's furball, and was covered with the same, mousy, gingery coloured fur, Squealer was still classified as a dog, and veterinary law required that any domestic dogs brought into the reserve be vaccinated against rabies. This horrible disease rears its ugly head from time to time in this area, and any dog living among wild animals is at risk. Although Squealer spent most of the time in camp with Meagan, he could not escape the needle; he also had to be jabbed.

These were the days before the dog whisperer Cesar Millan's techniques could be employed to calm Squealer down, so the very sympathetic vet we discovered in Phalaborwa bore all the fury of his quite unexpected and repeated attempts to bite him.

We had no option but to muzzle Squealer, and it proved to be far from easy. The back end was remarkably similar to the front, unless the tail was wagging, which it most certainly wasn't at the time. The only other longitudinal identification was teeth, which we waited to emerge from somewhere deep within the tangle of fur, and which we used to locate the head and the target for the muzzle.

It's strange; while Shilo and I related to Dr Gerrit Scheepers from our very first meeting, Squealer never did. A year later, when Meagan took him for follow-up jabs at the mobile clinic behind the Fort Coepieba Hotel in Hoedspruit, he began growling as she turned the corner to the hotel. Gerrit was quick to point out to Meagan that this little dog was incredibly perceptive, gifted with an unusually acute memory, one that might have enabled him to do some complicated tricks had she got him young enough.

Gerrit became one of Shilo's greatest friends, and mine too. While he administered the necessary vaccinations we discovered a common interest, namely fishing, and he regaled me with an account of his last trip to Vilanculos in Mozambique (demonstrating a remarkable fisherman's arm span). This was the beginning of a professional relationship and personal friendship that has spanned nearly twenty-eight years and is still going strong. If anyone had any idea how much Shilo meant to me, it was Gerrit.

* * *

Shilo always enjoyed running, not necessarily after anything in particular; he simply loved to run, and would yelp with delight when he was let out of the Land Rover to run behind it for a while. He would often hit the ground running; in his eagerness to get off, sometimes he'd miscalculate the depth and yield of the sand and land on his nose; even so, I would always have to make a point of pulling well ahead of him when he took off. I didn't want him running next to the vehicle – the roads were narrow and I had an abiding fear that if he ran close to the vehicle and lost his footing, he'd fall under the back wheels. Also, if the road surface was good and I wasn't far enough ahead of him, he'd turn on the pace and catch up to me when I was compelled to slow down for a bend or a sandy drift.

That particular summer's day was warmer than usual, and the cooling effect of the wind driving in an open Land Rover was deceptive. Relenting to Shilo's cold-wet-nose-against-my-ear pressure to run, I let him out and drove on ahead as I usually did. At this point we were about three kilometres from camp by road. A few minutes later I began climbing the gentle slope that led up to Mbali. Glancing over my shoulder I expected to see the familiar sight of Shilo, ears pinned back in the wind, running up behind me ... but save for a faint trail of dust that hung in the hot air, there was nothing.

Fear gripped my throat like I'd imagine it would that of a mother who turns to look at her baby's cot and finds it empty. I turned the vehicle around and drove back along the road to where I'd last seen him ... still nothing. Checking for his tracks, I found the unmistakable prints of where he had run down the road, then on a bend a few hundred metres later, where they veered off and disappeared into the bush. I began calling him, trying at least a couple of dozen times until fear dried up all the saliva my mouth, and soon I could no longer utter a sound. There was no response, so I went back to the last track I could find, hoping for a clue as to the direction he took. It had become considerably hotter, the midday sun beat down bright and brassy, quite possibly the worst time to try and follow spoor. This only added to my anxiety.

Thinking he might have headed back to camp by taking a short cut through the bush, I drove home and started the generator and water pump, hoping he would be guided home by the familiar sound of the thumping diesel motors. However, not satisfied with the noise level being created, I began hooting in desperation (something one doesn't normally do in the bush). This alerted my concerned staff, who came in from their lunch break to find out what the problem was. Before I'd finished explaining what had happened there were groans of sympathy; everyone there knew what Shilo meant to me.

Timbavati bristles with large predators – a domestic dog had no chance of survival in that environment. Despite Shilo's bush sense, I knew that I had to find him before nightfall at the latest. Choked up with dread and almost in tears at the thought of what could happen if I didn't, I climbed back into the Land Rover and headed out to look for him again.

At the time Motswari didn't employ trackers or game scouts at the lodges, and there wasn't time to hire one from elsewhere. Time was running out, and in my impatience to get going I spun the wheels of the vehicle on the loose quartz gravel of the road surface. This brief delay allowed the camp gardener, Phinias Sibuyi, to step into the road and motion me to stop.

'I can help you find Shilo, if you show me where you left his tracks,' he said.

In situations like this, one clutches at straws. I wasn't expecting much more than a sympathetic pair of eyes to help me scan the bush – well, that was until Phinias took the spoor ... and he literally did 'take the spoor'. Cupping his hands on either side of one of Shilo's prints, he scooped the soil that had contained the track and put it in a small plastic bag, which he closed and promptly pocketed.

'We will not lose him now,' he said.

I remember thinking at the time how weird that was, but as I had a much more pressing issue to worry about, I decided on adopting an 'any-port-in-a-storm' attitude, which thankfully didn't last for long. As Phinias proceeded I detected a definite change in his attitude and the way he moved. Despite his baggy, soil-stained overalls and oversized gumboots, there were subtle behaviours that were hauntingly familiar ... then it suddenly dawned on me. Years before in the Sabi Sands Game Reserve I'd seen game scouts with the same mannerisms conjure the same magic – I was witnessing a master tracker at work! This man was no longer the humble labourer tending a garden, which at best was what the warthogs and crickets didn't want to eat, or the man who depended on me for a meagre wage each month. I was clearly in the hands of an expert and totally dependent on him now for something no amount of money could buy.

Clasping his hands together behind his back and bending over slightly, Phinias studied the spoor. He proceeded frustratingly slowly, but with such confidence that it completely renewed mine. Nearly an hour later he turned to me with a broad grin on his face: '*Nangu!*' (there) he said, pointing to Shilo, who lay softly panting in the cool shade of a magic guarri bush. Besides a sheepish grin that broke into a toothy smile which made him sneeze when he saw us, he looked rather comfortable. This is probably where he would have lain until it cooled down later in the afternoon, and who could blame him. I was the one to blame, having horribly underestimated the heat that day, and the sheepish grin was mine too.

* * *

Our first year at Mbali flew by. We had to apply ourselves in order to run both camps from the relatively remote Mbali, but we settled into a comfortable routine and immersed ourselves in the work we loved. From the outset both Meagan and I loved the Timbavati, particularly Mbali, where we settled in quickly. A year later, in 1985, we decided to get married. As a team we began to earn the respect of owners Paul and Mechtild; I believe they could see their business was in competent hands. I'm sure it must have also been a relief for them to know that, true to our word, Shilo was well behaved around guests (though I somehow suspect that it was his Doberman heritage and disciplined behaviour that appealed to Paul).

Not surprisingly, our social life took strain, so given the time that had lapsed since we'd last seen each other, my good friends Tyrone and André decided they'd drive up from Johannesburg and visit me one weekend. Even though it had been over a year since I'd seen them, I have to admit to greeting this prospect with more than a little trepidation. I knew these guys well, I'd grown up with them, and I also knew that when they got together, they redefined the boundaries of what we, in the sane world, generally understand to be practical jokes.

We were invariably fully booked at the weekend, so Tyrone and André had to share the pilot's quarters. There was also no space on the game-viewing drives, but I'd always try to make up for this when I returned from the routine drives by taking them on a short drive straight to some of the big game we'd found. The location of Mbali meant one could see for miles around, and there was always something coming down to drink at the dam below the camp, or wandering across the clearing; anyway, there was never a dull moment. So I didn't feel guilty leaving Tyrone and André alone back in camp – maybe just a little apprehensive.

* * *

It had been a long day and it wasn't over yet. A faulty gas oven in the kitchen 'blew back' and singed Meagan's eyebrows, the camp was full of guests, and the Geiger family was coming for dinner that night. Tyrone and the owner's son Roland raced motocross bikes together, so they knew each other well; nevertheless I begged my friends to behave themselves.

Shilo was waiting for me on the stairs of the reception area on my return from the afternoon game drive, his tail swinging from side to side so hard that his whole bum swayed with the momentum. He knew the sound of my Land Rover over all the others, and knew I was coming home long before I saw him. Shilo's greeting was just as enthusiastic, whether I'd been away for a day or a couple of hours. He was always smiling, sometimes when he was embarrassed, but most of the time because he was happy. I knelt down and hugged him in response; I always let him know how happy I was to see him. Shouldering my rifle, I told the guests I'd see them later, then Shilo and I made our way to the kitchen and called Meagan.

With a heavy sigh Meagan threw her apron on the counter, and smiled, she looked rather relieved to have a reason to take a break. Together, the three of us walked up to our cottage to freshen up and change for dinner. When Meagan was really busy in the kitchen, Squealer would be left at home away from the bustle, an arrangement that suited him. He was happy as long as he could curl up on her shoes or her handbag; I guess somehow he knew she'd go nowhere without those two items.

Sitting reflectively in the bathroom, I heard a call from the bedroom, an urgent: 'Mario, come quickly!'

I sprang up and bounded out into the dimly lit bedroom, my trousers still around my ankles.

'I think it's a snake,' Meagan said. 'But I'm not sure.'

Grabbing the nearest weapon I could lay my hands on, which happened to be a small fold-up military-type camping shovel. I hobbled closer, approaching the foot of the bed, where Meagan stood pointing at a pile of neatly folded, freshly ironed laundry.

Meagan began to explain: 'Shilo jumped on the bed as he always does, but then leaped off again, as if he'd trod on hot coals, and he hasn't stopped staring at the stack of washing since, so whatever it is, I'm sure it's in there!'

As I shuffled closer, Shilo began to growl, a low warning growl, so I knew this was serious. Using the point of the shovel I began to flick each item of clothing off the pile, one after the other, until half the pile lay in an untidy heap on the floor. In anticipation of the next lift, Shilo, who hadn't taken his eyes off the spot once, growled louder, and sure enough, when I lifted the next item, there it was!

The huge snake lay tightly coiled on the freshly washed and ironed clothing, so I knew that in order to neutralise it I would have to hit very hard indeed, as the cushioning effect of the clothes would act as a shock absorber and allow it to escape unscathed, or only injured. 'Mad as a snake' came to mind. I couldn't afford to have an angry wounded snake thrashing about in the confines of the small room. Lifting the shovel high above my head, I brought it down with enough force to knock a musk ox unconscious.

The snake didn't move after that ... But in fact it couldn't have gone anywhere. It was the dead rufous beaked snake killed in ignorance by one of the guests earlier, which Tyrone had carefully placed in between our laundry hours before. In the poorly lit bedroom, even to the trained eye, it bore a striking resemblance to a large Mozambique spitting cobra.

At the time Meagan didn't see the funny side; instead she raised what was left of her singed eyebrows: 'I happen to know that Tyrone is petrified of spiders,' she spat. 'I'm going to get him for this.'

Tyrone now thoroughly checks his bedclothes whenever he comes to visit. I guess he knows that hell hath no wrath like Meagan scared witless, and that one day, that spider *will* be there!

I have since designed a snake stick that will save me having to resort to the 'shovel method' again – I now make a point of removing live snakes from similar situations quite safely and releasing them back into their environment completely unharmed.

17

TOUGH, TOUGHER, 'TUFFY'

Has your dog ever gone without food or water for longer than a day, or horror of horrors, a whole weekend, through some unforeseen and unavoidable circumstances beyond your control? Are you are still racked with guilt, unable to forgive yourself, believing you have damaged your faithful pet for life and broken his or her trust of the very hand that is supposed to feed?

This book would be incomplete without a remarkable story of survival. The following is a factual account of working dogs that will hopefully put your concerns regarding the inherent endurance capabilities of dogs in perspective. It concerns two Jack Russell terriers I knew, named Tuffy and Badger, which were born and bred right in the heart of 'Jock of the Bushveld' country, a slice of picturesque mountainous bushveld situated between Pilgrim's Rest and Bourke's Luck Potholes, as pristine today as it was back in the days when Sir Percy Fitzpatrick gazed upon it.

The huge valley was carved out by the beautiful Blyde River, which flows clear and cool in a series of riffles and runs, the sound of moving water quietened only occasionally by the interruption of deep languid pools as the river wends its way down towards the escarpment where it becomes one with the Olifants River. The area was once racked by gold-rush fever, filled with the daily din of prospectors driven by hope and a pioneering spirit of adventure – a spirit that still lives on, as apparently some of the claims are worked to this day. Though more than a hundred years' worth of water has tumbled over the river stones and swirled through Bourke's Luck potholes, the bush here remains relatively pristine. Steeped in history, it is littered with poignant reminders of the endeavours of those hardy pioneers seeking a new life and good fortune. Although the sound of their tools breaking rock and splitting shale no longer echoes through the valley, a few silent reminders of their dashed hopes and deserted efforts are occasionally and unintentionally revealed.

* * *

Tuffy had already been around the block once or twice. His aptly chosen name was self-explanatory and he had the scars from a number of encounters with bush pigs and baboons to prove it. At six years of age he had three years' experience on his three-year-old son, Badger, so named after the legendary honey badger, whose reputation for toughness needs no further elucidation. Father and son were an inseparable pair, as thick as thieves, and always up to something. The little reprobates would frequently sneak out into the bush chasing after something, and a more formidable and persistent pair of 'ratters' you'd be hard pressed to find: they would spend hours digging at some burrow or hollow log in which some unfortunate rodent sat shivering in terror.

Although chiefly ratters and rabbit dogs, Jack Russells have more guts than are good for them. Whereas rodents ranging from striped field mice to cane rats are quarry that are considered to be in their league, they will think nothing of upping the ante to include anything from bushbuck to baboons, all of which abound in this slice of doggy heaven.

Badger was being taught everything that Tuffy knew: a lot of it was fun, not all of it good, and most of it decidedly dangerous. The two of them would frequently disappear for most of the day, returning near supper time bedraggled and completely exhausted. Sometimes they were just dirty, yet other times they would limp home scratched up by thorns or bleeding from wounds inflicted by an irate bushbuck's horns. More often than not, they'd also be reeking to high heaven from having rolled in some rotting carcass or the scent gland markings of a civet. But the open-mouth panting smile that pulled their lips almost back to their ears, said it all, Tuffy and Badger were clearly having a great time, burning the candle of life at both ends, in an environment where it most certainly wouldn't see the night through, but, fuelled by their adventurous spirit, was making one helluva flame.

The dogs' owners, Mark and Sharon, ran the huge conservancy which included Buffelsfontein, a game reserve that lay in the heart of the region owned then by Barloworld. Mark knew the area like the back of his hand, he knew of its pleasures as well as the dangers that lurked out there, and although he kept a tight rein on the dog's forays into the bush, there was only so much he could do. It was usually when he wasn't around that they'd take the gap; otherwise they would spend a lot of time with him in his Land Rover out on the reserve somewhere, or back at home with Sharon and their three-year-old twins, Dale and Julie. Here the dogs would keep themselves occupied by investigating all the nooks and crannies in the confines of the huge garden, persistently digging and nosing around until they were satisfied that any resident rodents that hadn't been chewed to pulp had at least been evicted. But sometimes this wasn't enough for them, there was always the lure of bigger game in the bushveld beyond the fence.

It was time for the annual fishing expedition, a week set aside for when Mark and some of his old agricultural college buddies would head way up north to try their luck for tiger fish and nembwe bream on the Zambezi River. Sharon would stay behind to manage things and keep an eye on the dogs while he was away, as she always did, which wasn't easy, the twins were mobile now and quite a handful to watch and care for, and they quite rightly took priority. Left to their own devices, Tuffy and Badger took full advantage of the situation; no sooner had the dust settled to indicate the coast was clear, than they began to plan a little expedition of their own.

The next morning Sharon left to check the lodges, and knowing what happy wanderers the dogs were, carefully closed the gate behind her. This measure proved to be no deterrent to the experienced Tuffy. As soon as she was out of sight he led Badger across the lawn to where porcupines had dug a hole under the fence the previous evening – there to prove it, half buried in the sand, lay a few loose quills that had been brushed off when they squeezed through under the wire. Slightly smaller than the prickly burrowers, the dogs crawled through this convenient escape route easily, and quickly disappeared into the undergrowth as the bush swallowed them up.

Night fell and although Sharon was concerned that Tuffy and Badger hadn't come home, she was sure that they'd turn up any minute; after all, this wouldn't be the first time they'd come home after dark. Having fed and bathed the kids, Sharon then put them to bed and went outside to take one last look around for the dogs. Except for the crickets and the wail of a black-backed jackal down the valley, there was no sign of life out there, nor was there any response when she called their names. The next morning there was still no sign of Tuffy and Badger, and despite an organised search by the farm labourers, neither hide nor hair was found of either of them. To add to Sharon's dilemma, Mark was in the middle of nowhere, out of cell phone range and only due back in six days' time.

* * *

In a shrouded glade deep in the thick forest of a narrow gorge, a tiny bushbuck fawn lay on a bed of leaves. It blinked slowly, unable to keep its lids open as they slid down over its big brown eyes, eyes that were now droopy with sleepiness. Having suckled greedily it was now sated and ready to doze off, while its mother, ever alert, stood vigil over her precious baby. Ears like radar for any blip on the airwaves, her nostrils flared inhaling the air, testing for the scent of danger, a routine check before she bent down to nuzzle the fawn as it curled up on the soft leaves tucked away in the undergrowth. No sooner had it settled than the doe lifted her head again, sharply. Her acute hearing had picked up the yelps of the dogs way off in the distance. Although fully alert to the danger, she took no immediate evasive action, knowing from previous experience that there was always the possibility they'd be distracted and end up heading in another direction, which they sometimes did. However, as it happened, this time they were getting nearer; soon the dogs were too close for comfort, and she now needed to make sure they would focus on her rather than the fawn.

Wasting no time, the bushbuck doe uttered an alarm call, a hoarse bark, a sound not unlike that of a large dog's. Noisily she bolted out of the thicket, lifting her bushy tail to reveal its white underside enticingly as the dogs got close enough to see her. To keep the dogs distracted; she slowed down a little, with just enough inducement to allow them to catch up and think they might have a chance. For Tuffy and Badger, that fluffy tail was too much to resist, they focused on the fleeing doe, the chase was on. Though the terriers could not outpace the bushbuck in the thick tangle of undergrowth, it was nevertheless always great fun and excitement to try.

As their name indicates, bushbuck are completely at home in thick bush, right down to their dark coats with contrasting lighter spots which emulate the shadows and the slivers of blinking rays of sunlight that penetrate the glades they love. In this habitat it is almost impossible to follow them at their pace; even in seemingly impenetrable bush, they seem to glide through its matrix in an effortless undulating gait, hardly ever having to double back on themselves.

The longer strides of the bushbuck took her easily through familiar terrain and over obstacles which the relatively short-legged terriers had to negotiate through or around. Eventually frustrated at this handicap, the dogs tried to follow the doe as she leapt over a hole that was too wide for them. Unfortunately it happened to be an opening to an old exploratory mine shaft, one of many that had been hand-dug over a hundred years before by some hopeful gold prospectors. Shafts such as these yielding little or no promise of gold were simply abandoned and another one dug. Over time, a veil of plant life had grown over the entrance, effectively obscuring it from view. This natural covering emulated the technique used by primitive hunters, who would conceal purposefully dug pit traps into which unsuspecting animals fell and were then impaled by sharpened spikes.

This was the doe's back yard; she knew every path and every obstacle ... she also knew the hole was there. Tuffy and Badger were already committed to the jump, and were in mid-air when they realised they wouldn't make it. Falling through the 'trap door' of undergrowth, they tumbled more than two metres to the bottom of the pit. Dazed but unhurt, they stared up through the gloom, wondering what had happened. Dust stirred up by the disturbance created columns as the particles swirled in the few streaks of sunlight that penetrated the leafy shroud overhead. Due to the vegetation covering the entrance and the depth of the hole, the warmth and light from the sun they could see now would only last for a few hours a day.

Repeated attempts by the dogs to clamber out failed; all they succeeded in doing was to loosen more shale which fell in, making the floor area more uncomfortable than it already was. The desperate yelps and barks that punctuated these futile efforts were also to no avail; there was no one to hear them, and there would be no response. Later, as the sun began to set and the hole quickly grew dark, the temperature dropped quite dramatically. Real fear now gripped their stout little hearts; this was going to be their first night in the hole. Despite their desperate situation, they grew accustomed to the darkness, which seemed to have a calming effect on them, and soon they resigned themselves to settling down. I guess they must have known there would be no one out there looking for them in the dark anyway. Scratching away some of the shale, the dogs dug a crude bed where they lay down. Confined by the size of the pit, they were obliged to curl up tight against each other, and soon the shivering stopped as they began to share the warmth of each other's bodies. Exhausted from all their effort, it wasn't long before Tuffy and Badger fell asleep, as dogs do, with one ear open.

Awakened by the raucous Natal spur-fowl which heralded the dawn as they scratched around in the leaf litter near the lip of the pit, the dogs began to feel the full cruelty of the early morning cold. They would have to wait until midday for the direct rays of the sun to provide a tiny bit of warmth. The shocking reality of their predicament was exacerbated by gnawing hunger and a desperate thirst.

All dogs are essentially pack animals, and though Tuffy and Badger often sneaked out on their own for hours on end, these forays were of such a nature that they could usually depend on each other for support. Needless to say, they also drew comfort from belonging to the bigger human pack where they enjoyed the other creature comforts that this relationship brought – a warm fireplace, regular meals and a warm soft bed. Understandably then, they were terrified, utterly miserable and uncomfortable with their present lot. Little did they know it at the time, but it would be how they were able to cope with these difficulties that would determine whether they would survive their ordeal or not.

Suddenly Tuffy leapt up onto his hind legs, his front legs against the side of the pit, his head cocked slightly to his good ear side, his little stump of a tail wagging. Badger was at his side in an instant. The vehicle they could now both hear faintly in the distance was Sharon's diesel-powered double cab, which she drove through to the lodge virtually every morning. There was no mistaking the familiar sound; Badger had virtually grown up in it. Both dogs began barking frantically, which soon escalated to a crescendo of high-pitched yelps. Dancing on their hind legs now, their front paws against the side of the pit, they desperately tried to throw their calls for help up and out, as it were. They continued barking even though the vehicle had long disappeared; they barked and yelped until their dry throats began to hurt and their tongues stuck to the roof of their mouths. Eventually the best they could do was to cock their ears in the direction of the sound and whimper pitifully.

As each day went by, the dogs got weaker, their tongues began to swell with dehydration, and soon they were unable to stand up on their hind legs any longer. Most of the time was spent curled up next to each other shivering with cold and drifting in and out of sleep. Every time a vehicle droned in the distance, they forgot the terrible thirst that seemed to shrivel any resolve to move, and each time their spirits were momentarily lifted with renewed hope; it helped to carry them through.

*   *   *

A week later Mark returned from a successful fishing trip on the Zambezi, and although happy to be home, he was devastated by the news that Tuffy and Badger had been missing since his departure. Despite the time lapse Mark began the search anew; he wouldn't give up, employing every resource at his disposal to try and find them. However, being a pragmatic man, he eventually resigned himself to the likelihood that the dogs had been killed by baboons, or tangled with a poisonous snake – the list of perils in that neck of the woods is endless. The contemplated mind pictures were dreadful. Both dogs were small and easily approached, so there was also the vague possibility that they had been stolen. Mark and I spent quite some time on the phone discussing the various scenarios, looking at all the permutations of possibilities and trying to get a more positive perspective, but mostly trying to instil a modicum of hope. As much as I wished I could help my friend, there was not much more than sympathy that I could offer Mark.

Sunday was a beautiful day, and if the weather forecast was to be believed, it was going to be quite warm later on. Mark tried hard not to dwell on the fact that Tuffy and Badger had been missing for almost nine days; he knew it was time for acceptance now; it was time to move on. In an attempt to lighten the prevailing mood, he decided to take everyone for a picnic at a small lake on Buffelsfontein, located a couple of kilometres from the house. The lake was popular with the family; there were always plenty of fish to catch, frogs to chase and crabs to feed, and best of all no one else went there – it was their 'private' little spot. Placing the twins into their respective three-wheeler prams, Mark and Sharon began pushing Dale and Julie along the road to the lake, the same road that Sharon took when she drove to the lodge each day.

Both Mark and Sharon make a point of keeping fit – to this end they'd look for any excuse to walk or to climb in the surrounding mountains, and often did. Having pushed the prams for most of the way to the lake, the tedium began to get to Mark, so he challenged Sharon to a pram race over the remaining few hundred metres. The twins squealed with pleasure as the prams bumped over the gravel road; running next to each other just added to the excitement. Slowly coming to a stop not too far from the lake, they both stood catching their breath.

Suddenly Mark stopped breathing, and even with his heart thumping in his ears, there it was once more, weaker, but nevertheless an unmistakable short high-pitched squeal. He later described it as sounding like the noise he'd heard dogs make when caught by their throats in a wire snare ... a strangled scream. Initially he thought his mind was playing tricks on him, he had dreamed of his lost dogs and had heard them in his mind often enough during the last few days, so his first response was to dismiss the sound, thinking it may have been a bird. However, that was until he heard it once again: this time, although much fainter, he knew it wasn't the sound made by any bird he knew.

Leaving Sharon with the twins, Mark made his way through the thick bush to where he thought the sound came from. With his heart in his throat, he followed the faint game trail as it wound through the thicket, in places so overgrown that he had to go down on his hands and knees to get through. Mark was expecting to find one of the dogs slowly dying in a poacher's snare, but all he could see was an old shale heap off to one side just ahead of him, and next to it an overgrown miner's pit, much like many of the other pits he'd come across in the area. Parting the growth that partially concealed the entrance Mark peered into the gloom, and immediately recognised the two familiar small faces peering up at him. The wide-eyed fearful stares dissolved instantly at the moment of recognition, he could see how their jowls moved rapidly in excitement, but hardly a sound came out ... it was a pathetic sight. Overcome with joy, Mark slid into the pit and carefully lifted the dogs out one by one, then using an old ledge as a foothold he climbed out moments later, gathered a dog under each arm and made his way back to Sharon.

Apparently what Mark had initially heard was the guttural barking cry from their throats, as the sound squeezed past their swollen tongues. Actually it was an absolute miracle they'd managed to make any noise at all, and it is quite possible that the strangled scream Mark heard was the last sound those little dogs would have been able to make. Tuffy and Badger were alive and didn't appear emaciated, but dehydration had caused their tongues to swell up so tightly against the roof of their mouths that they couldn't lap water or pant.

Despite the severity of their ordeal, careful nursing and nutrition brought both dogs from the brink of death within a week. Tuffy recovered completely; however, Mark, who knew these dogs better than anyone, was able to detect that Badger appeared to have undergone an imperceptible character change. Perhaps he had suffered some form of psychological damage, due to the effects of severe dehydration. Incredibly, Tuffy and Badger had spent eight nights and nine days in a five-sided grave without any food or water and survived!

* * *

Given the fact that a large percentage of dogs are well nourished, many to the point of being dangerously overweight, a day or two on a diet or without any food at all might in fact be good for them ... But it wouldn't be fair to ask them to chew their celery sticks in a dark, dank hole in the ground, in freezing cold conditions, far away from home.

18

TO CATCH A POACHER

For the most part, modern day poachers no longer fall into the category of hungry peasants providing a tickled trout or snared rabbit for the family table – today it is mostly about money, big money. Needless to say, the craftier they are, the more successful and lucrative their business is. Most of them possess an enviable knowledge of the local wildlife, and bushcraft second to none, and they use this to maximum effect when plying their despicable trade. Depending on the circumstances, they can also be extremely dangerous, particularly when well-armed, organised gangs target rhino and elephant, where the stakes are high and the consequences of getting caught are justifiably dire. Although there is nowhere safe from this scourge, it appears that until recently, the majority of illegal trapping activities on private reserves in the lowveld comprised mainly subsistence and bush meat poaching.

The steel wire or cable snares that are set to capture wild animals are quite possibly the most deplorable and indiscriminate of all illegal hunting methods. Death usually occurs by slow strangulation, which is relatively merciful if compared to what happens when larger animals caught by their limbs manage to break the wire or steel cable after a desperate struggle that pulls the snare tighter and tighter before it parts – often at the cost of a hoof, a leg or a section of trunk, at which point the prognosis for a wild animal is not good.

Maimed by the snare, the animal can linger in this state for weeks and without intervention a slow, agonising death from infection and gangrene is inevitable. To this end, all our anti-poaching efforts go into removing whatever snares are found, and then sitting up over carcasses, waiting in ambush for the poachers. Remember, these reprobates are extremely wary, so meticulous concealment is vital ... but if all goes according to plan, arrests are made when the poachers return to inspect their snares. In fact, our anti-poaching units are some of the best at outwitting poachers, and have a solid reputation for getting their man most of the time.

Sometimes a little outside help is invaluable, particularly when deviously inventive poaching methods defy all but the most skilful detection methods. This chapter in particular might never have been written had it not been for Shilo's inquisitive nature and keen sense of smell ...

* * *

Much of the Timbavati Nature Reserve comprises individually owned tracts of land where landowners employ caretakers to manage their properties in their absence. The vast majority of these people are trustworthy individuals whose family has been in the owners' employ for generations. Many, having been born and bred on the property, know the lie of the land better than anyone else. Unfortunately this knowledge was put to mischief by one of them ... There's always one, isn't there?

The farm Brazilie, in the extreme northeast of the Timbavati, enjoyed a common boundary with the Kruger National Park for some four kilometres (though separated by a fence at the time), and it was here that Lamson plied his trade of treachery in a most unconventional way. Unlike many of the other caretakers who used bicycles to get from A to B, Lamson had been entrusted with an old Land Rover pick-up for running around in. Recognising the value of this perk, he kept it in good running order. A regular visitor to our workshop, we'd see him about once a week when

181

he brought the old Landy in to refuel or for minor repairs, and I couldn't help noticing how fastidious he was about keeping it clean.

One morning I noticed Lamson's Land Rover parked under the baobab tree that grew close to Motswari's garage. According to the pump attendant, Lamson had just refuelled and then gone down to the staff store to buy some supplies. Shilo had trotted ahead of me, reaching the vehicle before I could stop him from doing his usual embarrassing peeing on tyres routine. However, this time he ignored the tyres and went straight to the front of the vehicle, where he seemed to be totally engrossed with something underneath. He'd lowered his forequarters and crouched with his chest on the ground under the vehicle, his bum in the air, nosing the steering arms under the engine area. Naturally I was curious, and bent down to see what it was that he had found so interesting.

Steering arms on Land Rovers are situated in front of the differential, and so are exposed to damage from time to time. They are vital components, particularly from a safety aspect, and so all joints and linkages making up the system use what are known as castle nuts and split pins. This reliable feature ensures the nuts don't rattle loose or fall off, and Shilo was showing an unusual interest in one of these joints. In fact, his nose was pressed so hard against one of these nuts, I thought he would cut it on the split pin that jutted out slightly.

Looking closer at what he was sniffing so intently, I noticed a minute amount of fine grass-like material that had been caught in between the turrets of the castle nut and the split pin, not unlike dried buffalo dung. Taking some between my thumb and forefinger I brought it up to my nose. The unmistakable acidic smell of fermented vegetation left me in no doubt as to what it was. There are only a few smells that linger as long as the rumen contents of ungulates, and there is only one explanation for how rumen contents could have ended up on that nut. No ungulate can survive with a ruptured rumen, so clearly the animal had to have been killed or mortally wounded by the vehicle.

But Lamson hadn't reported anything to me, which he was

obliged to do – it was routine protocol. Accidents can and do happen; he really had nothing to fear, so I could only assume that his non-disclosure meant he was trying to hide something. With my suspicions suitably pricked, I decided to do a surreptitious investigation when he went off on his monthly four-day break, which he was due to take in a few days' time.

The owner of Brazilie, besides being a busy corporate banker, was also a private pilot. His 900 metre landing strip ran right up to his camp – a very convenient situation. Jan loved the bush, and he managed to fly in and visit at least once a month, although sometimes only for a day or two, which left Lamson with heaps of time on his hands between visits ... and we all know what the devil does with idle hands.

Landing strips in the Timbavati bushveld are magnets for plains game such as impala, wildebeest and zebra. This is due mainly to the fact that these open patches are usually situated on the higher lying warmer zones, which provide relatively safe and comfortable night-time rest areas. However, their concentrated activity inevitably leads to the deterioration of the landing surface, and it becomes necessary to check the condition of the strip from time to time. More often than not we needed to level the wildebeest sand bath depressions and fill in the odd porcupine excavation. It was on such a routine check one morning that we noticed vehicle skid marks and other indications of unusual and suspicious vehicle activity.

Closer examination by Shilo, using his wonderful nose, enabled us to find a patch of dried blood, a couple of partial boot prints and the unmistakable tyre tread patterns of Lamson's Land Rover. All the signs appeared to be related. I felt a prickle as the hair on the back of my neck started to rise.

'On the back,' I said quietly, patting the seat, and with that Shilo leapt onto the passenger seat in one smooth movement. We drove down the airstrip to Jan's camp. Pulling up at the rear of the camp, I called Shilo down and motioned him to start sniffing around the staff quarters, which he gave a cursory once-over. He then went over to where the implements shed stood and homed in on a spotlessly clean wheelbarrow propped up against the side. I could see nothing suspicious or out of place there; in fact everything was suspiciously clean, neat and tidy, so calling to Shilo to jump on again, I drove out to the boundary road that runs parallel to Kruger Park's fence line, which was only about 300 metres from Jan's camp.

The fence was an unsightly eight-strand barbed wire veterinary cordon fence; it had no electrification, and was actually more of a cruel hindrance than an effective barrier. The fact that it was frequently damaged by game and required repairs on a daily basis proved this.

Out of curiosity, I always checked the small drainage lines and dry stream beds that the fence traversed; it was at these points that the fence was found to be least effective, and where one would usually find signs of large predator movement into and out of the respective reserves. Clues were often clearly imprinted on the soft sand, or in the form of hairs left by the animal on the barbs of the lower strand of wire as it squeezed through. In fact this was how we knew where the white lions had entered the Kruger Park when they disappeared for nearly two years, and where and when they came back in again. A few innocuous white mane hairs caught on a barb were all that was needed to identify the individual, and the paw prints told us where they were headed and when.

Finding evidence of the most dangerous predator on earth crossing this boundary fence was the last thing on my mind that morning ... But there they were, the unmistakable bare footprints of a man in the same small drainage line. As I stopped the vehicle Shilo jumped down and started nosing around what appeared to be small tyre marks, about twice as thick as a bicycle's. These went up to the fence line and no further, then they doubled back along the game path they had come along. When I realised that the barefoot spoor was superimposed on the wheel imprint, it dawned on me they were the tracks of a man pushing a wheelbarrow. Somebody had pushed a wheelbarrow through the bush from the direction of Jan's camp, right up to the fence and then back again ... why?

In the meantime, Shilo had wriggled through the huge gap

in the fence, entering the Kruger National Park, and now stood there waiting for me, his tail wagging. Expectation gave way to impatience as he turned, sniffed the ground and gave a short yelp as if to ask: 'Come on, what are you waiting for?'

It is Kruger's policy that any domestic dog found wandering in the Park will be deemed to be hunting or abandoned by poachers, and as such could be shot on sight. But of course Shilo was blissfully unaware of this; as far as he was concerned he was helping me, and that was all that mattered to him. I suspect he may have detected a total lack of angst in my tone of voice and body language, knowing that anyone intending to harm him would have to come through me.

It was late in the morning, and I could see from the bicycle tracks that the Park's fence patrol rangers had been past that point earlier, which meant they'd only be back after lunch. This gave me about two hours to investigate what Shilo's nose was itching to sniff out. I drove the Land Rover off the cutline road and out of sight into the thick mopane bush. Shilo, thinking I was leaving him behind, came back through the fence and followed me, somewhat bemused – it must have been confusing for him when we walked back to the fence again.

Double-checking up the cutline road and down again, checking that there was no one watching … I was about to trespass onto conservation's equivalent of holy ground. To obtain the required permission and escort rangers would have taken days and endless red tape, by which time the trail we were on would have gone completely cold, and the faint tracks we were following obliterated completely. So with much trepidation about the legal technicalities of any evidence so procured, I crawled through the fence and joined Shilo in the Kruger Park.

On the eastern side of Kruger's fence patrol road, Shilo put his head down and stuck to a moderately used game path. Here, in the relatively soft sand, I found the partial prints of a barefoot person, a toe here, a heel there, much of which had already been obscured by wildlife … they had to have been made by the same person that had crossed through on the drainage line. I estimated the tracks to be approximately two days old, yet it was apparent that there was still enough scent left for Shilo to follow. Shilo's scent memory was kicking in, and he was possibly making associations with the scent from Jan's camp, or was there something else he smelled, something he had no way of communicating to me? Only now did I realise that these could be Lamson's prints ... but why was he barefoot, and what was he doing going so deep into the Kruger?

A barefoot human moving with stealth would leave only very faint tracks, and walking carefully on the compact surface of the graded road would make them all the more difficult to see – possibly the reason why they had gone undetected by the routine fence patrol unit. Unless they were specifically looking for spoor, the ranger's eyes would normally be on the fence itself, checking for breaks. I was just about to turn back to fetch expert tracker and ranger Phinias Sibuyi, when Shilo began to pick up the pace and I had to break into a slow jog in order to keep up with him.

The soft sandy trail and surrounding mopane scrub soon gave way to thicker mixed bushveld woodland, as we moved down into a depression of lower-lying ground. Fresh dung and tracks revealed that a small herd of buffalo and a single elephant bull had moved through the area earlier that morning. For the first time since we started out, I was acutely aware of how naked I felt without a firearm. However, Shilo continued unperturbed, which was comforting; his nose was the best early-warning system. I knew that with him along there would be no surprises and we'd have time to take evasive action if necessary ... then, as if to confirm this, Shilo suddenly stopped, lifted his head and looked intently ahead. An impala ram, barely visible some 30 metres ahead of us, gave a harsh rasping alarm snort as he noisily broke cover and fled, taking his harem with him. Shilo had picked the impala up long before the attendant red-billed oxpeckers warned the herd of our approach

We had been following what appeared to be a well-used game trail for approximately half a kilometre, when rather unexpectedly it ended abruptly on the edge of a secluded clearing roughly the size of a tennis court. It was shaded for the most part by a number of huge rain trees which grew in a semicircle on the lower periphery. The typical broad-leafed canopy of these trees formed a protective shroud, which afforded welcome respite from the sun, yet was high enough to allow cooling air to flow unimpeded through the glade. On the other side of the clearing was a gently sloping mound, which I recognised immediately as an old, time-worn disused termite mound. Evidently it had provided an ideal nursery den for a variety of creatures over the years. However, the plethora of fresh hyena and jackal tracks we found in the immediate vicinity had nothing to do with carnivores on a house-hunting spree; these predators had been attracted to this particular spot by something else.

Nothing appeared out of the ordinary until I happened to look up and saw numerous strands of wire which had been strung taut between the trees like washing lines. Jolted by a shock of recognition, I knew immediately what I was looking at; I'd seen similar set-ups a few years before in Botswana. Shilo and I found ourselves standing on the edge of a poacher's meat-drying camp! However, unlike the typical camps I'd seen, this was no random makeshift spot in the bush, the location had obviously been carefully chosen. It was remarkable, in that – except for the wire – nothing appeared out of place; it was the neatest poacher's camp I'd ever seen. Most significantly, I noticed there was no smell of putrefaction from the discarded skins and entrails, which is often associated with these bush kitchens, despite the well-worn path and the bare earth trampled under the lines, which showed that it had been used frequently. The complacent permanence of it riled me, and I felt my Italian blood starting to simmer as I began to realise the extent of what had been going on undetected for quite some time, right under our noses – well, except for Shilo's nose, that is.

Obviously Lamson had drawn confidence from the fact that much of the evidence was in the Kruger Park, so he wouldn't be investigated from within the Timbavati, as he'd left no evidence to link him with the meat-drying camp. Most importantly, he knew it was taboo for anyone to enter Kruger without the prerequisite reams of red tape. The only risk as far as he was concerned was getting past the fence patrol rangers, who had a regular scheduled beat, and whose primary concern was fence repair, not anti-poaching. However, as well thought out as his devious operation was, his calculations hadn't factored Shilo into the equation, and Shilo wasn't finished with his investigating nose yet.

Digging furiously at a concealed entrance at the back of the old termite mound, it wasn't long before Shilo located more evidence. Two machetes, a knife and a small hand axe wrapped in an old fertiliser bag were hidden behind a boulder that had been wedged into the entrance hole. I rewrapped them and shoved them into my backpack, then, calling Shilo over to me, I knelt down, took his head between my hands and kissed it lovingly.

'Good boy, Shilo, well done!' I said, and then I stood up and turned to head out on the path, motioning for him to follow close behind me. We still needed to get back into the Timbavati unnoticed, and I could ill afford to have my cover blown at this stage ... not to mention the dire consequences it would have for my dog. Reaching the edge of the bush, I told him to sit. Now with Shilo well hidden, I slowly edged forward and checked the road; I looked up the fence line, just in case the patrol was making its way back and returning sooner than anticipated. It became apparent how well Lamson had chosen his point of entry and exit, you could see for miles in either direction. There was no sign of the fence patrol unit, so crossing quickly I called to Shilo. Pulling the lower strands apart I created a gap which allowed both of us creep through the barbed wire fence and back into the Timbavati without a snag.

All in all, we had spent a little more than an hour in the Kruger. But it was all the time necessary to assess the situation and obtain the evidence we needed to challenge the suspect when he returned from leave in a few days' time. It had proved to be well worth the risk. Even though technically I'd procured evidence without a warrant, and on property I had no jurisdiction over or permission to enter, I regarded this as a 'hot pursuit' operation. Given the circumstances and time constraints, there was no alternative.

Later that afternoon, I asked Phinias Sibuyi to carefully examine the tyre tracks and other physical evidence on the runway itself. I needed confirmation of my initial findings from an expert. He concluded from the small amounts of hair, blood and rumen found on the hard-baked surface that it could only have come from impala. All indications – including the stop–start tyre marks – pointed to them being run down by a vehicle wearing a particular set of tyres, tyres with the same tread patterns as those on Lamson's Land Rover. It was too much of a coincidence … there was no doubt; Phinias had confirmed that the callous sod had used the Land Rover entrusted to him as a weapon! Lamson probably knew that if he was ever caught in the act of driving over an impala, he could cover the impact as an 'accident'. Blinded by the headlights, the unfortunate antelope were easy targets; those that did not die on impact could be summarily slaughtered and taken back to camp. There the carcasses would be quartered, loaded onto the wheelbarrow, and pushed through the bush to the Kruger fence … The rest, according to the evidence we had accumulated, was history.

* * *

Lamson duly returned from his monthly leave, alighting along with a number of Motswari staff members from the minibus taxi. He was wearing sunglasses and grinned broadly when he saw me, his white teeth in stark contrast to his dark complexion. Lamson greeted me in his usual friendly way, then loaded his luggage aboard his Land Rover and drove out of camp with a wave. I was sure from his relaxed demeanour that he didn't suspect a thing, so I decided to give him a few minutes' head start to let him get back to camp, unpack and settle down before confronting him. In the meantime I collected the evidence Shilo and I had found in the Kruger, and carefully placed it behind the seat. As the dust from Lamson's vehicle settled, Phinias, Shilo and I slowly drove out to Jan's camp. Although we were in no real hurry, I had waited a long time for this moment, and was more than a little anxious to put the issue to bed.

189

It was nearly twilight as we approached Jan's camp, those precious minutes before sunset when shadows are accentuated and everything is bathed in that beautiful late afternoon glow, a time when some creatures begin to settle down for the night and others begin to stir. Crossing the peaceful expanse of the runway, I couldn't help thinking how its serenity belied the killing field it had become.

Having heard our vehicle approach, Lamson walked out to meet us as we drove into the small courtyard. As usual he wore a huge grin, and appeared pleased to see us. Coming straight to the point, to ensure there was no possible misunderstanding, I had Phinias translate what I had to say into Lamson's mother tongue. There wasn't too much to say; moreover the translation wasn't really necessary, and even as I spoke, I saw the smile fade from his face – otherwise nothing else gave him away. I was careful not to make any direct accusations – there was merely a tone of enquiry as to his possible awareness of this activity going on so close to camp. Though we already knew, and suspected that he knew we knew, he was well aware that without evidence we couldn't pin anything on him. Most importantly, I wanted to see his reaction to our inquiry, which came in the form of a rather sombre, head-shaking denial, much as I had expected.

At that point I stepped back and reached in behind the seat of our vehicle and produced the evidence we'd found in the Kruger. Shilo jumped down immediately, and kept his nose stuck up against the package.

There was no need to reveal the contents to elicit a telling response from Lamson: when he saw the dirty white bloodstained fertiliser bag containing the tools of his trade – with his fingerprints all over them – his confident arrogance faded and he turned ashen grey. The game was up and he knew it. In an effort to get his hands on the evidence he casually bent down and reached for the bag, saying he'd like to see what we had found.

Up to this point Shilo had sat next to me, tightly guarding the package; after all it was his, he'd found it ... so when Lamson reached out, he uttered a low throaty growl and bared his teeth menacingly.

Turning away slowly, Lamson began to walk towards his room, I called after him to stop, but he ignored me, breaking into a sprint and disappearing into the bush behind his house so quickly that within seconds all we saw were a few mopane branches moving in his wake to show where he'd rushed past. It was getting dark, and I had no desire to track a cunning poacher through thick bush at night; also I knew Lamson carried a sheath knife and doubtless wouldn't hesitate to use it.

'Teksit!' was all I needed to say to Shilo; it was what he'd been waiting to hear, and even though this was not his usual quarry, he knew exactly what was required of him.

Although Phinias and I were relatively fit, Lamson was younger and leaner than both of us. Added to his list of advantages, he was supercharged with adrenaline, driven of course by the fear of being apprehended. I knew no man could outrun Shilo – Lamson didn't know my dog was bearing down on him until it was too late. We would never have caught him but for Shilo, who amidst much screaming and growling, had already ripped the back end of the man's overalls by the time we found them, and was now tugging at his trouser leg while Lamson tried in vain to kick himself free from Shilo's canines. Thankfully he had not attempted to use his knife on Shilo, although I somehow suspect he knew that if he had, he could expect no mercy from me. I called Shilo off the moment Phinias had handcuffed Lamson.

* * *

Six years later, while standing in line at the cashier's counter at our local hardware store in Hoedspruit, I noticed something familiar about the man standing in front of me. Despite the new cashier at the till doing the best she could, the queue was moving slowly, slow enough for me to study the man closely as he placed his wares on the counter to be tallied up. Then he turned, looked straight at me and broke into a wry smile ... it was Lamson. He nodded in greeting and I returned the gesture, but without a smile. In the brief, uncomfortable conversation that followed, I learned that his two-year sentence had been reduced to eighteen months for good behaviour, and that he had since found another job working as a temporary labourer mixing mortar on a construction site in Phalaborwa.

'I hope you have learned your lesson,' I said grimly. 'What you did was cruel and greedy, you also broke the trust of a good man … you could have had a secure job with Jan for the rest of your life.'

Lamson couldn't look me in the eye, instead he appeared to focus on the counter as if checking his change.

'I know I made a big mistake,' he mumbled. Then a few moments later he turned to look at me again and asked, 'Do you still have your dog?

I nodded.

'Eish, that is a good dog!' he exclaimed.

'Yes, he is – as a matter of fact, I think he's the best dog in the world,' I said.

With that he hurriedly picked up his stuff, gave me another wry smile and walked out without a backward glance.

It was the last time I ever saw Lamson.

19

THE WOUNDED LEOPARD

I suspect the South African lowveld is not unlike any number of other places in Africa where people converge due to a mutual passion for the bush and its wildlife. Whatever the motivation or interest, the bush has acted like a magnet, attracting a liberal sprinkling of interesting and diverse personalities. The lowveld has had its fair share of legendary characters and personalities, though not all of them drank copious amounts of whisky, rode a horse and could shoot a rifle ... or smuggled ivory. Some had other claims to fame.

According to Dr Marie Luttig, she was South Africa's first female gynaecologist. She and her husband, Ambassador Luttig, also happened to own a huge portion of land situated in the far northeastern corner of the Umbabat Nature Reserve. Adjoining the Kruger Park to the east, and the Timbavati to the south, it was ideally located, wedged between these two great bastions of wildlife. The abundance of a wide variety of big game animals that frequented her property, particularly large-tusked elephant bulls, reflected this. Wise old elephants are quite picky about where they choose to roam, and being undisturbed ranks high on their list of preferences.

When her husband died, Dr Luttig hardly ever came to visit the farm, nor would she allow anyone to traverse the property. No one, not even state conservation officials, policed the area. To say she was an eccentric old lady was putting it mildly, and it was clear that everyone was petrified of her legendary ferocity, so who was I to act the hero? Like the 'haunted house' of our child-hood, we would only observe her forbidden wilderness from a distance. Of course I suspected, or rather hoped, that some of the rumours of her reputation were exaggerated. However, imagina-tions ran wild and speculation was rife, and I'm loath to admit I didn't have the courage to take a chance and see for myself if the perilous phantom I'd conjured in my mind was real.

Notwithstanding all the conjecture, it was regarded as a strictly no-go area; not even the intrepid rangers of Motswari dared ven-ture there. The result of this was that much of her property's infrastructure fell into disrepair. Roads deteriorated into tracks which then gradually grew closed; at best, some became well-used game paths, yet others that had been badly placed became little more than erosion gulleys. Some of the rusting windmills that stood silhouetted against the skyline had rusted solid, others that were still able to move creaked and screeched with a metal-lic agony you could feel. Most of them were beyond repair, their joints and mechanisms no longer able to do the job they were designed for. Sun-baked clay depressions that were once filled with life-giving fresh water pumped up from deep below the earth's surface now lay cracked and dry.

Her enormous house was a quintessential example of the co-lonial-style homesteads of the time, complete with white walls, red corrugated iron roof and the typical surround stoep. To me it always looked so out of place, perched on a stony piece of high ground; instead of assimilating with the surrounding bush, it was arrogantly grand and dominating, reflecting the era and its attitudes. Over the years the lack of maintenance, exacerbated by the ravages of the elements, had taken its toll, and despite its solid architecture, the old house was deteriorating rapidly. In the surrounding garden, the vestiges of its former splendour still clung desperately to life despite the attention of elephants and baboons.

You may well wonder, at this point, how I could possibly have known all this if I never went there ... Read on.

*　*　*

Only one man was allowed on Dr Luttig's property. To this day, nobody knows how this arrangement came about, nor has anyone ever asked. Pieter was a middle-aged man, a staunch Afrikaner with a passion for hunting; he was also a prize-winning cattle breeder from the Thabazimbi area. Although not related to Dr Luttig, he was given *carte blanche* over her property for the brief periods he came to do some big game hunting. These visits were seldom longer than a week or so, and usually occurred twice a year when he'd arrive, more often than not, on his own.

Pieter kept himself to himself, and didn't socialise when he came to stay, primarily because the majority of the surrounding landowners were anti-hunting. Even then, among the up and coming crowd of ecotourists, there was just about zero tolerance of people who hunted for sport, and many took this sentiment to the point of absurdity, particularly members of the developing share-block type reserves in the area. The macho image epitomised by the big white hunter of yesteryear had become an instant turn-off in most social situations. But Pieter didn't care what people thought of him; he loved to shoot big game, so much so that he became known as 'Skiet Piet', ('Shoot Piet'), or 'Fok Piet', the latter for his liberal use of the 'F' word as an adjective in general conversation, and his oft verbally expressed attitude towards anti-hunters, which was, 'F..k them!' Not surprisingly most of the private reserves in the area refused to sell Pieter supplies or fuel, or help him in any way; as far as they were concerned he was a foul-mouthed pariah.

*   *   *

One morning I heard a vehicle coming down the road into camp, and looking up from my desk saw the unmistakable shape of an old short-wheel-based Land Rover pull into the parking area of Motswari's reception. Climbing out of the vehicle the man removed his hat, and I recognised him immediately. It was Pieter. We'd met a couple of times on the boundary road between our two properties, and exchanged greetings, the odd snippet of small talk, nothing much more. After a cordial greeting he came straight to the point. It soon became apparent that he had come to me out of sheer desperation; no one else would help him, particularly when they heard what he needed. Holding out an old sweat-soaked felt hat in his hand, he gestured eastward to Dr Luttig's property and told me that he had wounded a leopard and needed help finding it.

Apparently Ingwelala had refused to let him in their gate, and the Umbabat Nature Reserve didn't have a warden in those days; there was simply no one else he could turn to. Pieter explained that he didn't want to leave the wounded leopard to die a miserable slow death; nor did he want to go in after it with only an inexperienced tracker as backup. I winced, not at the thought of the consequences of an attack by a wounded leopard, but at the fact that such a beautiful animal had been shot in the first place. I had a glimmer of what made the neighbouring landowners angry; it is difficult for most people to understand what motivates a man to kill a leopard for sport. However my decision that morning was motivated in no small measure by the need to help bring a swift end to a magnificent animal's suffering. Phinias Sibuyi was on leave at the time, and though I really could have used his masterful tracking skills in this situation, there was no time to send for him.

Pieter explained that he was more afraid of being shot by his tracker if things went pear-shaped than of being mauled to bits by the leopard itself. He had heard that I had some experience hunting dangerous game – would I help him, would I act as a back-up for him?

The relief on his face when I agreed was unmistakable; clearly he had not anticipated an immediate positive response. My thoughts were now preoccupied with bringing the leopard's misery to an end. Then Pieter's eyes settled on Shilo, who had just come into the reception area. His toenails clicked softly on the cement screed floor as he trotted up to sniff the strange man. It was the first time Pieter's face broke into a broad smile.

'Man, this is a nice dog, what is his name?'

Before I could answer, he bent down and began to stroke Shilo affectionately, gently rubbing his chest with his strong calloused hands. I couldn't help thinking that these were the same hands that were reputedly stained with the blood of countless big game animals.

'Shilo,' I said. 'His name is Shilo.'

Despite the attention he was getting from Pieter, when I said his name Shilo turned, tail wagging, and came to me, possibly thinking I'd called him. Pieter stood up, but the smile had faded from his face; instead he now wore a rather sombre expression, though his attention was still focused on Shilo.

'Can Shilo follow spoor?' Then he qualified his question: 'Is he a hunting dog?'

'As a matter of fact he is an excellent hunting dog, but he has never tracked a wounded leopard before,' I said.

At this point I didn't want to elaborate on Shilo's exceptional skill at retrieving birds; anyway I suspected it would have been lost on Pieter, because in those days most Afrikaners were not keen wing shooters. They were more familiar around rifles than shotguns; well known for their marksmanship, as the British learned to their cost during the Boer War. Nevertheless, I told him I was confident that Shilo would help us track down the leopard.

* * *

Knowing these tracking forays could take an indeterminate amount of time, I packed what I thought we'd need, then Shilo and I jumped into a Land Rover and followed Pieter along a faint bush track that took us deep into some thick mopane bushveld. Half an hour later we came across Dr Luttig's camp attendant Willias, whom Pieter had employed as a tracker, standing on the side of the track waiting for us. Pieter pulled up and stepped out of his vehicle, then reaching into the back he grabbed his rifle and beckoned to Willias, who took the lead. The bush was so thick we were compelled to walk in single file, and so Shilo and I followed close behind. Within a few minutes we reached the spot where Pieter had wounded the leopard. Now all heads turned to my dog – it was Shilo's turn to take the lead.

I bent down and pointed to the blood spoor. 'Teksit, Shilo,' I whispered.

With his nose to the ground, Shilo began to sniff the dark red-brown blood spots. The spoor was getting old now. The few droplets we found on the odd dry leaf cracked like shellac, but the faint scent still spoke volumes to him. As it began registering, an instinctive alarm must have caused Shilo to turn around and look back at me: the quizzical frown on his face seemed to say, 'Are you out of your mind?' However, despite his initial apprehension, he moved slowly but steadily along the blood trail – it was almost as if he was tip-toeing.

'What guts he has,' I thought.

Shilo had smelled leopard many times in his life, but never the scent of their blood, and as daunting as this must have been for him, he knew there was some serious work to do. My apprehension was short-lived. As we began to track the leopard, Shilo's presence and attitude gave me immediate cause for optimism. Instead of fear, his excitement and enthusiasm moderated the imminent danger we faced, which helped to lift our spirits considerably.

Shilo was much more than a working dog to me, he was my best friend, and I would never have been able to live with myself if any harm had come to him. Fortunately, I could tell from his body language that his eagerness was tempered with a measure of caution. His earlier training would stand him in good stead, I was confident he would not rush into a confrontation with any big cat. I was also confident that he would somehow warn us of the leopard's close proximity, giving us time to prepare for an imminent attack; in fact, I was relying on this, otherwise I would never have exposed him to the risk of facing a wounded leopard.

Within a couple of hundred metres the blood droplets had disappeared completely, Shilo and Willias were now relying only on scent and tracks respectively. A cat's pads leave very little impression at the best of times; these were no exception, the leopard's tracks were faint and progress was painstakingly slow. We couldn't risk leapfrogging the spoor, we had to go track for track. However, when the trail was lost, we saved considerable time by moving to where Shilo had nosed on ahead, and where sure enough we'd pick up the leopard's tracks again. This continued until the trail took us down a steep embankment and into a narrow sandy wash that could more accurately be described as an overgrown erosion donga, and where for the most part the soft sand was no more than five metres wide. Pieter and I dared not look down, even though the prints in the soft sand were now obvious, too obvious perhaps.

Leopards are extremely cunning, so understandably we found our minds racing with the suspicion of being led into a trap, and this donga was an ideal venue for a showdown ... ideal for the leopard, that is. We knew he could be anywhere waiting to pounce, so we left the tracking to the experts while we focused on every shadowy nook and cranny that could render its dappled form invisible, every possible thicket that could have concealed a house cat from us was scrutinised. Never mind how carefully we walked, every footfall crunched in the loose sand of the wash, which was getting wider as we moved along.

Suddenly Shilo stiffened his motionless tail straight, the hair on his back bristling. Craning his neck, he leaned forward, nose in the air, and as he did so his front paw lifted off the ground in a tentative point. I'd never seen him in this pose ever before; I knew he could either see the leopard or smell it. Trusting Shilo's instincts, Willias slowly sank down to his knees, getting out of the line of sight in case of a charge. Straining our eyes, we scoured the bush, searching for any clue, the involuntary flick of an irritated ear, or anything out of place. But even though the bush was relatively sparse, none of us could see any sign of the leopard.

The most prominent feature nearby was an old disused termite mound, and except for a huge boerbean tree growing through it, there wasn't much cover in the immediate vicinity that could conceal an adult leopard. However, Shilo remained fixated on that dome of hardened soil. I turned to Pieter and pointed to the termite mound; in response he shrugged, pointing to the tracks that appeared to continue past and up the riverbed and silently gestured that we follow the spoor. I suspected that he too could see nothing at that point, it was also clear from his body language that doubt was beginning to creep into his mind … but Shilo knew different.

I pointed again emphatically, then motioning for Pieter and Willias to step back, I bent down and gently patted the sand in front of Shilo, who lay down immediately. Leaving Shilo and Willias behind, Pieter and I straightened up, and virtually shoulder to shoulder we slowly crept ahead. Holding our rifles at the ready, we moved in a wide circle of the mound, hugging the opposite bank of the donga in order to approach it from the side. As we did so I noticed the huge aardvark burrow in the side, which was not visible from the way the tracks were leading us. It lay at eye level facing the opposite direction to our approach. Crab-walking sideways up the donga, we reached a point where the entrance of the burrow was now square on to us … precisely where our backs would have been had we continued on the spoor and passed the termite mound. Now almost face on, we stared at the ominously quiet dark space only five metres away.

Only the sound of cicadas pierced the still, hot air. My eyes were glued to the entrance, which was abuzz with small black flies, but before I could count their wing beats, a hollow guttural growl resonated from deep inside the hole. It was all the warning we were given.

The leopard exploded from deep within, filling the gaping black hole with a yellow blur in a nanosecond as it launched itself at us. Both rifles went off as one, killing the huge cat instantly; it crumpled in mid-air, almost knocking Pieter over as it fell virtually on top of him. Had we been facing the other way, focusing on its tracks, which it had doubled back on, the leopard would have attacked us from behind, as was the cunning animal's intention. God only knows what the consequences of that might have been.

Now lying dead, inert, like a diffused bomb, the leopard posed no danger, yet Shilo tentatively walked around the huge cat, moving in to give it a sniff now and again, his neck craned, stretched to its limit, like an impala drinking from a crocodile-infested river. He clearly admired this carnivore he'd never seen before. Then, looking back at me and catching me proudly studying him, he gave a modest wag of his tail as if to say, 'Hey, did you know this was what we were tracking?'

This time there was no typical canine jubilation, no biting and worrying of the dead adversary or game ... just quiet, cautious respect – it was as if Shilo knew what incredible potency had just been quelled.

After examining his shot that had wounded the leopard, which as it turned out was high on the shoulder, Pieter looked at me: 'That explains why there was so little blood,' he said, then turning to look at Shilo, who was still fascinated with the leopard, added, 'F..k! That dog knows his stuff.'

Pieter turned to me again, shook my hand and thanked me. Willias stood there, his mouth agape, and although he had done an excellent job of tracking himself, he couldn't help but admire what Shilo had done that morning.

I was relieved that we had all come out of the situation unscathed. I was also consoled by the fact that a magnificent animal which I felt did not deserve getting wounded in the first place, was at least spared a slow agonising death in some dark hole in the ground.

* * *

Six months after the leopard incident, Motswari obtained traversing rights on some prime wilderness in the northern Umbabat. It was well known as superb big bull elephant country, thousands of hectares of remote and wild mopane woodland, and as a bonus there were also a few roan and sable antelope that came through from Kruger occasionally. Exciting as this was, we needed to be realistic, since having to drive around the Luttig farm to reach it meant a prohibitively long 'dog's-leg'. So, although every piece of traversable land was an asset to our safari operation, this particular piece would only be of practical use to us if we were able to access it by cutting across a small section of Dr Luttig's farm.

I'd mentioned this to Meagan a few times, but one morning at the breakfast table, the frustration boiled over.

'She can only say no,' I said. 'What's there to lose?'

Meagan shrugged: 'Who's going to ask her?'

I smiled ... Meagan knew what that meant. 'Uh-uh! Not me,' she protested.

'Pleeeze, pretty pleeeze,' I begged.

Call me chicken, if you like, but the soft touch worked, as I knew it would. Meagan used her charming phone voice and successfully got Dr Luttig to venture beyond her usually short, non-committal greeting. More than that, in the same breath, as it were, she managed to set up a meeting for the Doctor's next visit to the farm, which happened to be only a couple of weeks away.

Tea-time on the day had my tyres crunching the gravel on her driveway a little ahead of time. I was comfortable that we had arrived a couple of minutes early, just in case Dr Luttig was a stickler for punctuality – most of the 'old school' were. Although I suspected that eccentricity can work both ways, I thought it better to be myself, and for me, that meant arriving a little ahead of time or on time. Since being expelled from the fashionably late club, I'm pleased to say that Meagan now feels the same.

Dr Luttig was waiting, and gave us an unexpectedly warm welcome. She was a small sprightly woman with a naughty twinkle in her eye and a dry sense of humour. 'I'm not good with farm matters,' she said, then turning to Meagan with a smile and a wink, she added, 'But from the waist down I'm an expert.'

There was nothing about her demeanour to confirm the rumours; no fire spewed from her mouth when she spoke, and instead of drinking blood, she sipped tea and nibbled biscuits with us on the stoep. She reminded me so much of my grandmother in many ways, except that my Grandma never called me 'Lovey'.

It didn't take long to wade through some small talk and get around to the purpose of the visit. Not wanting to try her patience, we tried to explain as briefly as we could why this was important for Motswari from a traversing point of view. Although this took longer than I intended, she nevertheless let me ramble on, appearing to listen intently. When I'd finished talking, there was no response, instead only a silent nod to indicate she'd understood. I have to admit there were some uncomfortable moments as she paused for a while, staring straight ahead into the bush beyond. When she turned and looked at us, her solemn expression gave nothing away: 'I will let you have my answer before nine o'clock tomorrow morning,' she declared.

At this point Meagan and I knew our visit had come to an end, so we politely said goodbye and drove back to Motswari feeling a little flat, but pleased that at least we had made personal contact with the old lady.

*   *   *

At eight-fifty the following morning Dr Luttig phoned to say that she had consulted with Pieter, who had only good to say of us, and had told her we had helped him when no one else would. She went on further to say that she had decided we were not only helpful, but could be trusted on her property, so she would grant us permission to use the access road to the north, as well as the rest of her farm if we wished.

I was so ecstatic at Dr Luttig's response that I almost didn't hear what she said next, and in light of the importance of what had just been said, I found it difficult to believe the old lady when she declared herself intrigued by the dog that Pieter had told her about, and asked if we'd bring Shilo around when we came for tea on her next visit ... Wow!

This was the beginning of a long, mutually rewarding relationship between Motswari Game Reserve and Dr Marie Luttig, which lasted until her death, nearly ten years later.

20

HONEY BADGERS AIN'T HONEYS

Honey badgers have a power-to-weight ratio that justifiably earns them their standing as one of the toughest mammals in the world: there's nothing out there with fur and fangs to touch them. Although there's not much in weight between them and their European cousins, who are tough creatures in their own right, the African honey badger is in a league all of its own. Primarily omnivorous, they are cunning hunters and scavengers, but their name is derived from a voracious appetite for honey and their well-known relationship with a small bird known as the honeyguide. These little birds will locate bee hives, then find a badger and guide it to the location. As a reward the bird is always left some of the spoils, mainly bee pupae, their favourite, and of course, scraps of beeswax.

Although happier foraging for relatively small prey items, honey badgers are powerful predators with a formidable reputation – they're notorious for going for the groin rather than the throat, and have been known to rip the testicles out of larger animals like buffalo which have subsequently bled to death. This inspired the title of big game hunter Robert Ruark's famous novel, *The Honey Badger*, which tells of American women's tendency to rob men of their masculinity. But these dreadnoughts are not only capable of dishing out ruthless attacks; they are built with muscles of steel wrapped in sheaths of thick loose skin, which allow them to absorb incredible punishment themselves, and as if that wasn't enough, they are also immune to potently toxic snake venom. It is small wonder that the South African Defence Force named its toughest armoured go-anywhere troop carrier the 'Ratel', which is Afrikaans for honey badger.

* * *

Winter evenings in the lowveld can get decidedly nippy on occasion. After supper on one of these rather crisp evenings at Mbali, we moved our chairs from the wider dining circle to huddle closer together around the blazing camp fire. There we sat gazing into the flames, which threw just enough light to give everyone's cheeks a healthy glow. Nobody was saying very much, there was no need to. Private thoughts brought contented smiles to each one there as we reflected on another successful day in the bush. Natural wood fires have a mesmerising effect on man, never mind your status in the modern world; as human beings we cannot help but be drawn to fire, fire awakes a primal sense of basic comfort deep within us, sometimes holding our focus and thoughts in an almost hypnotic limbo state.

There was no moon that night. Beyond the flickering light from the fire, there was little to see, except the silhouettes of the trees around us, which appeared to grow in front of a black wall we couldn't see through. It was only when someone threw a new log onto the fire that we were reminded of some of the potent solar energy trapped by the tree when it was alive. As the wood burned it popped and spat when its latent energy was released, the sparks exploding into the night sky like a mini fireworks display, then calming in intensity, the wood slowly burned down to glowing coals. Some of the denser leadwood would smoulder red hot under the grey ash until morning. Then, with only a minimum of effort the fire could be coaxed into life again, to boil water for the morning's brew.

Shilo loved to lie at my feet or next to my chair, but when the fire got too warm he would move to the outside edge of the circle and lie there looking out, appearing relaxed, but always alert. In the dark people were apt to trip over him, so to help make him more visible I would tie a white bandana or a serviette around his neck in the evenings, which solved the problem for the most part.

In spite of this measure, I didn't notice when his ears pricked up, and I didn't see him test the wind; nor was I aware when he got up and quietly walked past me in the dark to investigate something he'd heard just behind the lapa.

Moments later the mesmeric peace was shattered by a guttural rattle, a harsh staccato sound that seemed more mechanical than animal ... I'd never heard anything like it before. Instinctively I called out to Shilo, but there was no response. Pinpointing the source of the noise at the back of the kitchen area, I grabbed the flashlight next to my chair, got up and went to look; one of the young rangers followed me. I feared Shilo was in some sort of danger, but as I heard nothing from him, no yelping or barking, I didn't know what to expect.

Adjoining the kitchen complex was an open-plan pantry area where the fridges and freezers were kept, walled in by a stockade of treated poles no thicker than your arm. This enclosure was accessed via a flimsy gate through which deliveries were made directly to the kitchen's back door. Approaching the 'delivery' gate I found it standing slightly ajar. Using it as a shield, I slowly pushed it open and shone the light to where the sound was coming from. Shilo was standing there with his back to me, his tail held stiff as a rod. In front of him, against the stockade wall, was the source of the blood-chilling sound I'd heard earlier ... a black and white bundle of snarling fury. Shilo had disturbed a honey badger!

I went cold with fear, astounded that even though it was cornered, the badger didn't launch itself at my dog. I screamed at Shilo to come back, and without turning his head away from the badger he reluctantly stepped back a couple of paces. This was enough to allow the badger to take advantage of the withdrawal, whereupon it spun around and squirmed through under the stockade and into the night.

I was shaken but utterly relieved that the badger and Shilo hadn't tangled physically. At the time I could only assume the stand-off was due to the fact that he hadn't initiated an aggressive attack, and my intervention had been timely. Months later I learned the real reason for the badger's relatively composed reaction.

A glance around the small courtyard revealed the extent of the chaos. The fridge containing the cheeses and cold meats had been opened, and most of its contents lay strewn on the ground. There was evidence of rummaging around, but the badger had apparently been selective. Nothing of any consequence appeared to have been eaten, except for a huge salami sausage, the remnants of which lay in the corner where he and Shilo had the stand-off.

The following evening the badger returned. The lure of salami was too much to resist, and even though the fridge door had been wired closed to prevent him from opening it, he managed to break into it again – on two more occasions.

Unable to tolerate these relentless raids, we took a decision to trap the badger and translocate him to an area as far away as possible from Mbali.

A specially designed trap cage was obtained from the warden and baited with the favourite salami; needless to say, the badger was caught the following evening. When we approached the cage he made the same guttural rattle we'd heard a few nights ago. From close up he really looked and sounded every bit as ferocious as his reputation had led me to believe. I couldn't help thinking of what injuries this potent animal might have inflicted had he and Shilo tangled physically. Frankly I didn't care much about the damage to the fridges or the loss of foodstuffs … it was Shilo that was irreplaceable.

We drove across the Timbavati cutline, northwards up into the mopane veld of the Umbabat Nature Reserve, up through Dr Luttig's area to the furthest extent of this reserve, and then along the fence line until we reached the point where the Kruger National Park's boundary cuts due west, forming our northernmost border. At this point we were about 28 kilometres away from Mbali – far enough, we thought.

'Super badger' as we'd named him, was then unceremoniously

released, but not before we'd sprayed the top of his coat with gentian violet. This was in the scant hope that should the rangers who traversed the northern region come across him in the next few days, they'd be able to see the purple marking easily.

The following evening at Mbali passed without incident. We were sure the badger had found a new home, some place without dogs, traps and people, but unfortunately our respite was short-lived – two nights later he was back! Although nearly 30 kilo-metres of travelling through the bush had worn away some of the violet stain, there was still enough of it on his fur to leave us in no doubt that it was indeed 'Super badger'.

In the interim we had moved things around a little, so he no longer had access to the fridges. It took a couple of hours of sniff-ing and scratching, but once he had accepted that he was finally beaten, he wandered off back into the bush and never returned – though not before digging a huge crater in the corner where he had been apprehended by Shilo with the salami, and where the tantalising smell of that delicious sausage still lingered.

Although we never came across 'Super badger' again, he wasn't the last honey badger Shilo would meet.

* * *

Later that year tourism took a turn for the worse in South Africa, which compelled us to downsize the operation and close Mbali camp, a temporary measure until things improved. Reluctantly, with heavy hearts, we mothballed everything and moved down to the main camp, Motswari, which was the 'administrative capi-tal' and larger of the two camps. Both camps traversed the same area, so essentially the bush experience and game viewing they offered were identical; it was only once back at the respective camps that the differences were obvious. Being more spread out, Motswari was somewhat less intimate and more formal than Mbali. At Motswari, guests would eat in a dining room during the day and at night everyone ate in the large boma seated in a circle around a cosy fire in the centre. While both camps offered

facilities and service excellence in keeping with the bush atmosphere, we had been spoiled rotten with the rustic, easygoing style
of Mbali, where there was no boma or formal dining room.

As with any conventional safari camp in the bush, the eating
areas were laid out in close proximity to the kitchen for practical
reasons. However, as with all commercial kitchens there was the
inevitable smell of food being prepared, as well as the leftovers
and food waste generated, which in turn attracts wild creatures
of all descriptions. Despite care and stringent waste management
procedures, we were kept on our toes and constantly challenged.
During the day it was mainly baboons and vervet monkeys that
would use their thieving cunning to try and outwit us. At night,
myriad creatures would use the cover of darkness to raid the bins.

We were primarily concerned with hyenas and honey badgers,
which were the chief scavengers, and although both were quite
brazen, the latter was more so. Outside the kitchen a number of
forty-four gallon drums were used to contain the garbage until it
could be removed to be processed. Secured together so that they
couldn't be overturned and the contents spilled, this measure
kept all but the most determined scavengers from gaining access.
But, as we were constantly reminded, they don't come more determined than a hungry honey badger.

We'd just finished eating supper one night when Prince,
Motswari's head chef at the time, came into the boma and beckoned me over to the kitchen access. Once outside, he told me
there was an animal trapped inside one of the rubbish drums,
and it was making a terrible noise.

'Wait here for me, Prince; I'll be back in a minute,' I said.

Crossing to the far side of the boma to where Meagan sat, I
bent down and instructed Shilo, who had been following me
closely, to stay with her, then I grabbed my flashlight and followed Prince as he led the way to the refuse depot.

Long before we'd reached the drums, I could hear the unmistakable rattle of a highly pissed-off honey badger, accompanied
by desperate scratching noises as claw and metal met, punctuated with deep short grunts of rage. This time there appeared
to be much more noise than I'd ever heard one of them make. I

209

assumed the badger had climbed onto the lip of the drum, lost its balance and fallen in. The only option was to undo the drum, tilt it, and allow the thief to escape. This I did, but before the drum reached full horizontal, two adult honey badgers and what appeared to be three sub-adults leapt out, tumbling over each other as they hit the ground, and scampered off into the night. Incredibly, five honey badgers had been trying to feed together in an area not much bigger than a baby bath – no wonder there was a little family dispute over dinner.

* * *

Shilo's second and last encounter with a honey badger occurred a few weeks later, and I suspect the culprit was one of the badgers we'd rescued from the drum outside the kitchen. It was getting late, and as I was on duty that particular evening, I was among the last to leave, everyone else had trickled out of the boma and headed off to bed already. I locked the bar, picked up my rifle and windbreaker then called to Shilo as I headed out into the en-closed walkway that led out of the dining area. Shilo rushed past me as he usually did when we retired for the evening; he would always scamper ahead up to the cottage. On his way he'd often stop to pee against the tyres of the Land Rovers which made up the fleet of game viewers parked outside the boma. He had per-fected the timing of this, so that by the time I reached the door, he would already be there, tail wagging, bladder emptied and ready for snooze time in his basket next to my bed.

Motswari camp was open to the surrounding bush and its wild creatures, so covering this stretch from the boma to the house at night with Shilo was always a worrying few minutes for me. The camp lawns and gardens between the buildings were a particularly popular resting area for waterbuck at night; the resident lions knew this and would often hunt them in the camp environs using the chalets as cover. However, any thoughts I may have had of lions evaporated immediately as an all-too-familiar spine-chilling rattle filled the still night air. Again, there was a very angry honey badger close by, and it sounded as though the noise was coming from under one of the game viewers.

Running around to the back of a Land Rover, I saw Shilo standing in the dimly lit carport straddling something between his legs. Then it registered that underneath him was a honey badger, it lay flat on its back, baring its teeth and uttering that now familiar rattle. Thinking it would launch itself at Shilo's groin or belly area and rip him open at any moment; I forcibly nudged Shilo over to one side with my knee then tried to scrape the badger away in the opposite direction using my rifle barrel. However, by doing this, I now had the badger positioned directly between MY legs! Still on its back snarling up at me, I was pretty sure that it could see which of the Highland clans the tartan weave of my Jockey briefs represented. Suddenly I became acutely aware that the family jewels were in a vulnerable position, and the 'Italian stallion', as I have been referred to on occasion, was only a bite away from being gelded. Fortunately, before it could live up to its fearsome reputation, the next swift scrape with my rifle barrel had the badger roll over onto its feet and run off in that characteristically cocky (no pun intended) waddle, tail in the air, grunting and growling. Despite my left hand shaking uncontrollably, I held Shilo by the scruff of his neck, just in case he wasn't convinced by the sluggish retreat of the badger.

*   *   *

Why did these fearsome animals appear to submit when confronted by Shilo – and me, for that matter? The answer to this question plagued me for ages. Although I still have no definitive answer, the fact that these were two similar incidents involving two different badgers in two separate locations, within the confines of Shilo's territory, makes me suspect it has more than a little to do with territorial respect. It may be that even in a savage animal's world, there is respect for the sanctity of another's space.

21

INGWELALA – WHERE THE LEOPARD SLEEPS

'Beware of what you wish for, you may not want it when you get it' or something to that effect – to be honest, I never understood the logic of this adage, even when it happened to me, when I found that my desire and fervent wish was still there, but that the practicality of life had stepped in, and what I'd always wanted, I couldn't have, even though it was up for grabs now ... if I wanted it.

If, as an aspirant young ranger, I'd been told that ten years hence I would be offered a post at Cape Vidal with the Natal Parks Board, and would then turn it down, I would never have believed it. Never! It had been my lifelong dream, I would have given my right arm for a career in the Parks Board, even though a one-armed game ranger would be seriously handicapped ... it didn't matter, I would work around it, I wanted in. Yet it happened, and without having to sacrifice any limbs, my wish came true and so did the dream offer, followed by the reluctant rejection.

Meagan and I had reached the stage in our lives where the realities of life's commitments were entrenched. We'd encumbered ourselves with life's small unavoidables, and reached the point of no return. Starting over was not an option; we could not have contemplated starting a family on the salary offered by the Parks Board at the time. Instead we opted for a counter-offer from our company directors, one we could not refuse. It included a share option in Motswari and Mbali game lodges, and our own place in the bush, somewhere we could put our roots down.

Our own home in the bush: it was what we'd always wanted, a modest, solidly built stone and thatch cottage, in the middle of nowhere. Every last stone used in its construction came from the surrounding area, and all the window and door lintels were hand-made using Rhodesian teak and jarra railway sleepers, which we had stockpiled before they became fashionable and prices went through the ceiling. Gnarled, character-filled leadwood posts seasoned by years of exposure to the dry lowveld climate were used as supports for the stoep and interleading archways. Nearly all our furniture was built by Winnias Segodi, a Sotho carpenter, using old Oregon pine floor boards and shipping crates, which he cut, planed and chiselled into tables, chairs, cabinets and bookcases using hand tools and skilled craftsmanship only.

The new thatched roof had been brushed to perfection, and for the first few weeks it shone a pale golden yellow in the sunlight, starkly contrasting with the surrounding landscape. We knew this would be short-lived, and as expected, the shine faded and the sunburned thatch slowly turned from gold to grey, finally, after two months, blending in with its surrounding landscape and disappearing as intended.

Finding a site when we had so much land to locate it on hadn't been as easy as it sounded. After months of consideration, we had finally settled on a spot close to the boundary between Motswari and neighbouring Ingwelala, with the most stunning view overlooking the Nhlaralumi River and its associated floodplain. Cooling is everything in the lowveld, so we built the house facing southeast, into the prevailing breeze. Practical considerations in deciding its location had also been carefully taken into account – it needed to be close enough to Motswari Game Lodge to be convenient, yet far enough away from work to afford some respite from the 'goldfish bowl syndrome' that we had endured for years living in the lodge grounds. Although only a little over a kilometre away, the house felt remote, cut off and private. Looking out of any of the windows offered a different view of the surrounding bush, which was in essence our garden. Except for a few hastily planted aloes and a small bird bath which had also been built from local stone, everything was kept as natural as possible.

Shilo loved the cosy, cave-like atmosphere of the house, espe-cially the cool comfort of the screed floor on the stoep where he'd often lie flat on his stomach, with his back legs stretched straight out behind him while he surveyed all below him. This was his home too, and he knew it. Here he could play silly buggers with me, yelping and running around without disturbing anybody's siesta. The only thing I think he missed about being at the lodge itself was the pool, but for nine months of the year there were natural pools of water in the crocodile-free Nhlaralumi River close by. Exclusively ours, these pools were much more fun to jump into, nobody was disturbed and unlike the lodge pool, we didn't have to sneak a quick swim when paying guests weren't using it.

The 'Old Farmhouse Plain' on Ingwelala lay about half a kilo-metre away downslope from our house, and as with most open areas in thick bushveld, it was a popular night-time venue for plains game. The larger predators, particularly leopard, knew this and capitalised on the relatively easy pickings. Occasionally we would hear their rasping grunts, not unlike that produced when sawing a wooden plank with a coarse-toothed hand saw. These coughs were uttered from deep within the thick riverine bush close by, where the leopards would spend most of their time, and from where they would move out under the cloak of darkness to hunt.

Only in the winter months, when the river stopped flowing and surface water became scarce, did they venture further in search of prey and water. During the first winter in our new home, the small birdbath I'd built in front of the house was visited regu-larly by a leopard in the dark of night. For ages all I saw were its tracks, then one morning she lingered long enough for me to not only see her, but get a photo of her from my bedroom window. Despite the technical detail of the photo being far from decent, I had it enlarged and framed, with an inscription underneath that read 'From my bedroom window'. Though, out of habit, I cast an eye on the birdbath whenever I went past the window, weeks went by and I never saw her again. When I remembered, I'd shine a torch out of the window just before going to bed,

Meagan and Eleana outside our bush house the day we left for Olifants, February 1993.

The Cesare family at Olifants, November 2002.

Jock of the Bushveld country – view of the Blyde River flowing through the open bushveld valley about 3 km north of Pilgrim's Rest. Photo by Mark Jevon.

Phoning the vet: Mario calling Gerrit Scheepers to do an autopsy on a dead rhino. Diagnosis: heart-lung failure. Photos by Louis Brad.

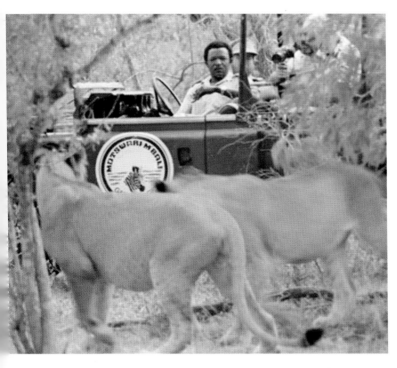

Left: The late Phinias Sibuyi, master tracker and a close friend, looks on as lions he tracked amble past. Tragically he did not live long enough to pass his bushcraft skills on to his sons.

Below: A cheetah family uses a fallen knobthorn tree as a lookout.
Photo by Grant Kassner.

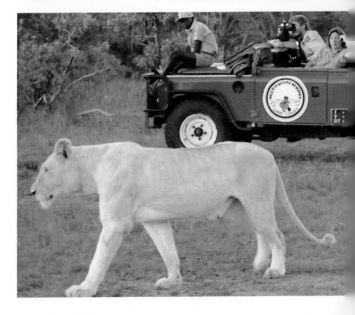

Top: It is ironic that this notoriously sharp bend in the railway line is located in the heart of Olifants' most popular lion nursery area. Nearly every lion born on the reserve takes its first breath within a few hundred metres of this 'death bend'. Photo by Neil Hulett.

Middle: Tragic: lion cubs killed by the train.

Right: One of the famous white lionesses of Timbavati.

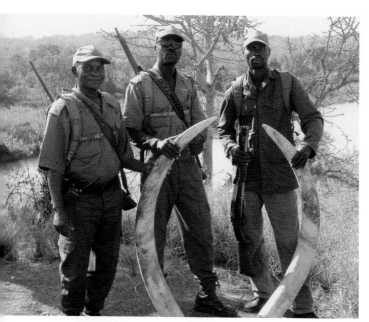

Left: A force to be reckoned with: the Olifants anti-poaching rangers have taken on much of what used to be the provincial authorities' responsibility: (left to right) Jabulaan Makhubedu, Johann Khoza and Januarie Mahlaule display the tusks of a poached elephant.

Centre left: The mopane scrubland of the Umbabat area is a favourite with elephant bulls.
Photo by Neil Hulett.

Below left: 'God's impala'. To this day I have a tremendous empathy for these beautiful 'red buck', and little respect for those in the conservation world who regard them simply as 'goats of the bush'.
Photo by Brendan Feather.

Below: Zebra – our backyard ponies at Olifants.
Photo by Brendan Feather.

Olifants River Game Reserve, 2010: My son Dino and I share
some quality time together in the bush. Being a weekly boarder
and passionate about conservation, Dino always looks forward to
weekends at home on the reserve.

Just in case you thought of sneaking off without me ...
Shilo waits in the driver's seat.

Above: Shilo knew the sound of my Land Rover over all the others, and knew I was coming home long before I saw him. His greeting was just as enthusiastic, whether I'd been away for a day or for a couple of hours.

Left: Giving Shilo a hug. I always let him know how happy I was to see him.

Sunset at Olifants. Photo by Dino Cesare.

In the dark people were apt to trip over Shilo, so to help make him more visible I would tie a white bandana or a serviette around his neck in the evenings.

Shilo's grave. There could never be enough space on a headstone for a fitting epitaph to his memory; instead I found a sliver of granite which I cold-chiselled to clearly mark his grave. It reads, simply, 'Shilo'.

hoping to catch a glimpse of her lapping water in the darkness ... nothing.

* * *

It had been a sweltering hot day in the bush and we were glad to be getting home from the muggy office at the lodge. We arrived at the house just as the sun began to set, which turned the dial of the oven-like temperatures down a few degrees. Hardly had we brought the vehicle to a stop when Shilo leaped off, but instead of rushing up to the back door with his muzzle against the jamb and pushing at it with short impatient nudges, as he usually did, this time he stopped short. With his nose to the ground not more than a couple of metres from the door, I could see the hair on his back go rigid, the same as I'd seen it do on the rare occasion when we were in close proximity to leopard or lion. Head down and tail held stiff, Shilo began to move towards the side of the house, but I called him back immediately. Earlier that week we'd had lions make a kill within a few metres of the house – thankfully it was an impala, which they polished off in less than thirty minutes, anything bigger and the noise they made squabbling over it would have kept us up all night. Knowing there were big cats around, there was no way I would allow him to investigate and risk him walking into certain death. We all went into the house and closed the back door, which meant forfeiting the comfort of a cooling breeze, but as it later turned out, it was a good decision.

Looking out of my bedroom window had become a habit. Much like that particular tree you drive past regularly, the one with the thick shady bough you once saw a leopard lying on, you always expect that one day you're going to see a leopard in it again. Against the hillside our stone-walled abode was so natural looking, it simply melted into the bush, almost becoming part of it. We felt really at one with our surroundings, so it was not surprising that other creatures of nature besides ourselves also found it appealing. Every time I glanced out at the birdbath, I would

215

half-expect, half-hope to see that leopard drinking again. This afternoon, however, I noticed that not only was there no leopard there, but there was not a drop of water in the birdbath, which was surrounded by numerous small birds. Amongst others there were grey loeries, babblers, shrikes, waxbills and fire-finches. This wasn't unusual on such an exceptionally hot day, I thought, assuming, from what I could see that it had been visited by more than the usual number of thirsty birds and smaller mammals that day. With my eyes still on the empty bird bath, I opened the control tap located under the window sill inside the house and watched as it quickly filled again ... just in case 'my' leopard came to drink that night. As expected when the warm water ran in, so the birds swooped onto it. That was when Meagan called me to come through to the tiny 'lobby' area.

'Come quietly,' she urged. 'There's a leopard on the stoep!'

Tiptoeing through, I found her on one knee with her arms protectively around Shilo's neck, both of them staring out of the cottage-paned door that opened onto the stoep. Staring back at us through one of the panes was the unmistakable full-framed face of a leopard! It was clear from its curious expression that it couldn't see inside. Suddenly another movement caught my eye – there was a second leopard lying on the step.

Incredible, I thought, there were two leopards on our tiny stoep! My mind flashed back more than ten years to when as a young man of twenty I had the rare privilege of rearing three leopards. I'd obtained them when they were less than two weeks of age, so I had a fair idea of how to judge the age of a leopard from their appearance. I could see immediately that both of these were young animals; at a rough guess I estimated their age to be no more than twenty-four months. Neither was any of them the leopard that I'd photographed a few weeks earlier at my birdbath, these leopards were both slightly smaller and had distinctively darker coats. The thought did cross my mind that 'my' leopard was in all probability their mother.

Shilo was incensed that these overgrown spotted furballs were on his turf; the stoep was his private 'throne' and they were violating his space. Despite this he only uttered a soft growl, a low

216

rumble that Meagan said she could feel more than hear when holding him.

'Let Shilo go,' I whispered, curious to see what interaction there was going to be ... if any.

Instead of rushing up to the door as expected, Shilo moved with the same stealth as if stalking a covey of francolin, but with less conviction – he clearly wasn't sure what to make of these spotty intruders. Every molecule in his genetic make-up must have screamed warning signals to him, but courage and curiosity got the better of him. Cautiously, and with the longest outstretching of a dog's neck you can imagine, his nose touched the pane that the leopard's face was framed in. The leopard must have seen or sensed something, because it pushed its nose against the same pane. Meagan and I were witnessing a meeting of extreme opposites in the animal world; something that only Walt Disney could have thought to bring together – a domestic dog and a wild leopard (known to have a penchant for eating dogs), separated by five millimetres of glass.

I have struggled with that scenario since it happened, and though I would never have risked putting it to the test, I still wonder what would have happened if the glass hadn't been there, and they had been able to smell each other muzzle to muzzle. I believe Shilo's courage came from his territorial imperative, while, like the honey badgers, which had offered no confrontation, the leopards would have used their discretion, realised this territory was occupied and bolted.

As it got darker, the leopards moved to the birdbath, where they had probably heard the water trickling in when I opened the tap. Lapping the now cooler water for what seemed like ages, they slaked their thirst and shortly afterwards moved off into the bush.

Needless to say, big cats own the night, so when these leopards melted out of sight into the darkness, I didn't put them out of mind. We had no idea where they were, which complicated things when it was time for Shilo's pre-bedtime ablutions, which would sometimes take him beyond the periphery of the torchlight into the bush ... for privacy, you understand. So we needed to make some alternative arrangements. Using a powerful torch to make sure the leopards were nowhere near the vehicle park, I went out and manoeuvred the Land Rover close enough to the back door to allow Shilo to simply jump straight in, then I drove out a few hundred metres to a relatively safe 'doggy do' spot. What a schlep, I thought; I hope we don't have to do this too often.

Leopards are one of the enigmas of the bushveld; nobody fully understands what makes them tick. They're unpredictable and highly adaptable; it is what makes them able to thrive where other larger predators have long since been eradicated. However, adolescent leopards go through a developmental phase just before maturity, that I believe is a most dangerous period for them, a point in their lives when curiosity can literally kill the cat. The antithesis of the elusive, nocturnal and stealthy creatures these leopards eventually become, they appear to show relatively little fear of humans at this stage, and will boldly enter villages, camps, and homes in broad daylight.

Returning home the following day I was anxious that the leopards may still be in the vicinity of the house. My suspicions were confirmed when Meagan noticed that our resident, but normally shy, common duiker was brazenly showing herself in the open near the back door. We knew she had a tiny youngster tucked away, not too far away; in fact, the little fawn was tucked away under the bathroom window behind some thorny aloes. The duiker mother knew this was not the best spot under the circumstances, so she was sacrificing her safety for that of her young. Only then did we realise that we were witnessing a brave animal's motherly instinct at its best. Although this little antelope could sense that these young leopards were inexperienced hunters, she couldn't risk them coming across her fawn, so she kept them in sight, in case it became necessary for her to lure them away from where her fawn was hidden. Sure enough, we found one of the leopards on the far side of the house, and the other one lying on the stoep again, much to Shilo's consternation. This time there was no stealthy stalk, Shilo simply rushed up to the cottage-paned door and bumped it with his muzzle, and the uncharacteristic sharp bark that followed startled the leopard, which then slipped over the low wall in a fluid, almost serpentine movement and disappeared from view.

* * *

Back at the Lodge the following morning, one of the guests came down to the breakfast patio, greeting everyone and smiling pleasantly. Without a perceptible change of tone and in a rather casual 'by the way' manner, she reported that she had startled a leopard when she opened her rondavel door to come down for breakfast. I listened with interest. Many tourists have been so spoiled by the visual media and have such high expectations that they often treat an otherwise rare phenomenon, such as a leopard sighting in broad daylight, as an everyday occurrence – which, from our reaction, she could see was not so. So what's the big deal, her puzzled look seemed to say, when I showed a mixture of concern and excitement. She went on to say that it hadn't run far, that it appeared to settle down quickly and the last she'd seen of it was when it headed towards the staff houses on the camp periphery.

Fortunately the rangers were having breakfast at the time, so we all got up and slowly made our way to where the leopard was last seen. We arrived on the scene just in time to see the young male, almost certainly one of the two Meagan and I had seen at our house, walk up to the open front door of receptionist Britt Simpson's cottage without a modicum of caution typical of these cats, and go straight in. Britt was a gap year student from the United States, totally besotted with wildlife, but not altogether aware of the dangers of leaving doors open in the African bush.

'Oh shit!' I said. 'Getting a cornered leopard out your tiny cottage is going to be no mean feat.'

'Don't worry,' Britt said. 'I opened the back door as well to give it a good airing this morning, maybe it will use it to get out.'

Sure enough, a couple of minutes later, the leopard exited from the open back door. We watched as it headed past the washing lines and then disappeared into the thick mopane bush on the edge of the camp.

'I hope it hasn't pee'd in the house,' Britt said.

Knowing what leopard pee smelt like, I nodded sympathetically.

The whole time Shilo had stood beside me, bemused but totally unconcerned. I somehow suspect that as far as he was concerned, this was part of the leopard's turf. Back home it was different; the house and environs were strictly his territory.

*   *   *

All too frequent sightings of the two young leopards were being reported in the camp area, which meant they were getting too familiar and apparently unconcerned about human activity. Understandably there was increasing concern for the safety of the guests and ultimately for the leopards themselves. Nearly full-grown now, these leopards could be extremely dangerous, particularly if they were inadvertently cornered or felt threatened in any way.

I was tasked with finding a passive solution to the problem. I needed to encourage the leopards to move somewhere else, not too far away, but a 'safe' distance from the camp area. There was only one practical solution – baiting them. By placing bait progressively further and further away from camp, I would encourage them to stay out of harm's way until they outgrew the brazenly curious stage of their development, a month or so at the most, I thought.

Ration meat in the form of impala was shot every week for the lodge anyway, so bait supply was no problem. Using the neck and head portion of the carcass to start with, we began by securing it in a large marula tree on the quietest edge of the camp, close to the route I'd seen the leopards use before. The first night came and went and the bait had not been touched, but on the second day as the meat began to 'ripen', the tracks around the tree and the amount of bait consumed revealed that a leopard had been there. Unfortunately, from this evidence alone, it was impossible to know which one.

Late in the afternoon of the following day, a second bait was placed in a leafy weeping boerbean tree that grew on the edge of a small sandy wash some 200 metres from where we'd placed the first. This time, however, I decided to kill two birds with one stone and leave an unoccupied Land Rover near the tree, hoping the leopards would feed with the vehicle in full view. If they did this, I thought, we might be able to habituate these young wild leopards to tolerate game viewing vehicles, something most of the wild leopards seen in our traversing area were averse to. But I was still not sure that the leopards feeding on the bait were the same curious youngsters we had been seeing around my house and the main camp area.

Early the following morning found me studying the 'bait tree'. Peering through my binoculars, I could clearly see that the bait had been fed on; overjoyed I slowly retreated and went back to camp. The following day I renewed the bait, this time parking the vehicle less than ten metres from the tree, again leaving it overnight. Sure enough, the carcass was fed on again. Adult wild leopards that are unaccustomed to people and vehicles are too wily to feed under these circumstances – this confirmed beyond any doubt that it was the same two adolescent leopards!

Within three weeks there was no longer a need to put up any more baits, and the two leopards were getting more adventurous and independent each day. The breakthrough came when the young male killed an impala on the airstrip – although we were able to drive to within a few metres of this magnificent animal while he fed, two hyenas came storming in and simply stole his kill. It was clear the young leopard still had a lot to learn, particularly about hoisting his hard-earned prey up a tree and out of reach of these cunning thieves.

In due course, the leopards went their separate ways, and though we saw less and less of them in the camp, they were seen regularly by the rangers on drives. There were times when conditions were favourable and they could be tracked and located, much as we did with our resident lions. Eighteen months later the young female had three cubs of her own, which simply grew up in the presence of our vehicles from an early age, mimicking their mother's lack of fear and tolerance of game viewing vehicles ... And so it all began; today, twenty years later, the progeny of those same leopards still give thousands of tourists that visit Motswari, as well as the many shareholders of neighbouring Ingwelala, the pleasure of their enigmatic beauty each day and night.

*　*　*

It had been a long day. I'd been out since early that morning with a drilling contractor, clearing the sand out of a collapsed borehole. Getting home I stripped down and jumped straight into the shower. How refreshing it was; I could feel myself getting lighter as the layers of dust and sweat-caked grime washed off my weary body. Then I dried myself off and collapsed on top of the now slightly damp towel on the bed, while Meagan pottered around in the kitchen preparing supper. Shilo, who had been lying next to me, suddenly slid off the bed and walked over to the window, where he stood on his hind legs as he often did, just staring out at the bush. However, this time I heard him utter a low growl, the hair on his back standing up like a ridge. I got up slowly, walked over to the window and looked out to the birdbath. Although the light was fading fast, I could clearly make out the outline of a leopard, its head low as it lapped at the water. The highest points on its lithe, supple body as it lay there were its shoulder blades, then typically cautious, it sensed something, stopped drinking and lifted its head. Now, clearly silhouetted against the setting sun, the small ragged notch in her right ear left me in no doubt ... 'My' leopard was back.

Shilo was still growling softly when I reached over and gently stroked his back. I could now feel the ridge of hair going flat as he slowly relaxed; I suspect his naturally hostile fear and distrust of this big cat was now being replaced by bemused curiosity.

'Thanks, my boy,' I said. 'Let me know every time she comes.'

22

PATERNAL INSTINCT VERSUS PRIMAL INSTINCT

Few stimuli incite a predator's hunting instinct faster than a distress cry from a young animal other than its own. And young children, particularly infants, can and do cry most distressfully.

Predators needn't be habitual man-eaters to respond to the cries of a baby. A human infant sends out a distress call that is as primal as any other prey animal's young in trouble, and is therefore indistinguishable from conventional prey to most large predators. From the smallest mongoose to the largest lion, a distress call triggers an instinctive response. Predators and scavengers alike know that the sound of bleating, crying or squealing will almost always lead them to an easy meal, invariably a prey animal that is defenceless, weak or injured. I have seen lions approach a tape recording of a bleating lost wildebeest calf, salivating at the prospect of food, even though the call was purely mechanical, and there was no bait at all. Their mind/stomach association had been made before the need to confirm with the sight or smell of potential prey. This was proof enough that sound stimuli alone could trigger an attack. In such circumstances predators will act seemingly out of character, particularly at night, when fearless, single-minded determination allows them to approach boldly with one aim ... to locate the source of the distress call.

Motswari and Mbali Game Lodges' policy on the minimum admissible age for children was not much different to others operating in big five country. Most do not permit children under two years of age to go on game drives in open game-viewing vehicles, and some upmarket safari lodges do not allow children under twelve at all. This seemingly draconian measure was established for a number of very important reasons, one of which supersedes all the obvious rationales that come to mind. Besides the obvious effect a crying child would have on other guests trying to enjoy the tranquillity of the bushveld from an open vehicle, there is another very important reason infants and young children are discouraged from going on safari. It has to do with provoking the instinctive predatory response from larger predators, such as lions, which under controlled viewing situations would otherwise normally not think of attacking the occupants of a game viewing vehicle.

* * *

Thinking of the danger and abject fear of just such a situation, I am reminded of the weekend a large company sent a number of their senior personnel on an incentive up to Mbali for a few days in the bush. Although they had been made aware of the 'no babies on game drive' rule, the group manager insisted we allow him and his wife to take their six-month-old baby along for a quick drive – it would only be the four of us. Heeding the subtle reminder that they had block-booked the camp, I reluctantly assented, albeit with their understanding and promise that we would not go into any lion sightings with the baby on board. For extra security the baby was placed on the front seat between me and its father, bundled in so many blankets it looked like a Red Indian papoose.

It had to happen, now of all times … the radio crackled into life and one of the rangers called in to say that he'd picked up a pride of lions. All fourteen lions were on the move, slowly making their way along the access road from Motswari to Mbali, and the famous white lioness was among them. I could picture the scene – besides the white lion, of course, it was always an impressive sight to see so many lions completely fill the road as they ambled along at their typically unhurried pace. We were off-road in some particularly thick mopane woodland watching a herd of about fifty buffalo when the call came through. Although still some way away, I knew the lions were heading along the road towards us. This was my cue: the sun had set and the buffalo began moving off, and soon, all that lingered in their wake was a strong bovine odour as they melted into the bush and disappeared. It was time to move.

As we didn't see lions that often, particularly the white lion's pride, I would have loved to go and have a quick look at them. However, heeding my better judgement, I started the Land Rover and began heading back towards the road and then to camp. As the vehicle rolled forward, I realised something didn't feel right, I suddenly had great difficulty steering. Looking down, I saw that the front tyre was almost flat; there was no way we could drive any further without ruining it. Had I known what lay in store for us, I would have driven out on the flat!

All the tools I needed to change the tyre lay behind the front seat. Being a bench seat, it meant having to move the backrest forward, and in so doing, I inadvertently disturbed the baby. Needless to say, despite every effort from mom to pacify the child, it began to cry, a cry that quickly ascended into a screaming wail that reverberated in the otherwise tranquil late evening air.

Wasting no time, I removed the tools and busied myself with changing the wheel. The baby's crying was beginning to make me rather anxious; I knew the lions were getting closer and that soon they'd be within earshot. In my haste I began to fumble and make the odd mistake, despite which I soon had the vehicle jacked up and the flat wheel off. However, before collecting the spare wheel at the back of the vehicle, I leaned in across the driver's seat to grab the microphone in order to find out the latest position on the lions. Straddled on three wheels, the Land Rover stood precariously perched on the top of the jack, a round piece of metal no bigger than a bottle top. That minute shift of weight as I leaned in on the front seat to speak on the radio was all that was needed; the vehicle teetered once or twice then slipped off the jack and onto the front axle. It wasn't the dramatic sudden jolt one would have expected as two tons of metal hit the dirt;

rather it appeared to happen in slow motion, as if the Land Rover knew there was a baby on board and needed to go down gently.

There was nothing I could do but hiss an expletive; I also recall a brief moment of gratitude that I wasn't under the axle at the time. But thoughts of my safety quickly faded, it was the last thing on my mind. I radioed in again, hoping that the lions had taken a side road and veered off, but as I feared, the answer was that they were getting closer to where we were. Obviously the lions had got wind of the buffalo herd we'd been watching earlier and were moving in on them. This would bring them virtually into our laps, I thought, but worse still, I also knew they could most certainly hear the baby crying now. There would be no time to dig out the jack and start again – in less than a minute the lions would be with us.

Trying to remain positive, I said nothing to the parents of the possible danger, which I was still desperately hoping to avert. I called the ranger who had been following the lions, asking him to overtake the pride, which was still on the road at that stage, and move in next to me as quickly as possible. Despite his grasp of the situation and speedy response, by the time he'd arrived, two young male lions that were ranging slightly ahead of the main pride had already moved off the road towards us and begun to circle our vehicle. At first they did a wide loop, to suss things out I guess, much like a boxer circling his opponent, looking for a weakness. I also suspect that being young lions their instinct didn't match their experience ... but they didn't hesitate for long. Stopping to test the wind a couple of times, they circled ever tighter. Heads up, eyes wide and ears forward, the lions began to close in. They completely ignored every attempt I made to discourage them; hurling my already well-thumbed *Roberts' Birds* book into one of their faces elicited a short sharp grunt, nothing else.

Eventually, out of sheer desperation, I grabbed my rifle and fired two shots over their heads, which made them scurry off a short distance away. This was no more than a momentary distraction – I knew that they would quickly collect themselves and return, but it was just enough time to allow the ranger to move in and park his vehicle right next to my crippled Land Rover. By the time the determined lions had returned, the now screaming baby and its shaken parents were safely transferred to the other vehicle and on their way back to camp.

Without the stimulus of the infant in distress, the lions quickly lost interest and moved off in the direction of the buffalo herd. A short while later one of the trackers brought a spare jack from Mbali. Now that the danger had been averted, I was able to change the wheel at leisure. Even so, we kept a spotlight scanning the periphery until we were rolling again.

This was not the last time I would need to deal with predators threatening an infant in distress. However, this time it involved another equally formidable and determined predator, namely a spotted hyena.

*　*　*

I imagine all parents of newborn children are naturally concerned as to what reaction to expect when introducing their babies to their pet dogs for the first time, and so it should be. It is an unpredictable time, a critically important time: not all dogs react to the usual shift of affection in the same way, particularly dogs that are as close to their masters as Shilo and Squealer were to us. However, our initial apprehension about them feeling that they'd be relegated to sucking the hind teat was unfounded. When we brought Eleana home, we laid her on our bed, then we all climbed on and the five of us lay there together. From the moment we allowed the dogs to sniff and explore her, they treated her as though she were a delicate extension of Meagan and me. We never pushed Shilo away, despite his often overzealous displays of curiosity. Squealer showed as much interest, but was less boisterous; I suspect he believed so implicitly that he was also Meagan's 'baby', that even a new baby wouldn't threaten that special relationship. And it never did, right up until his untimely death from a kidney infection a couple of years later.

Shilo's initial response to Eleana's cries was the picture of bemusement, which quickly changed as his paternal instinct took over and he instinctively began to protect her. At times Shilo would abandon his relatively comfy bed and simply lie next to her cot in the small room we used as a nursery, he never saw Eleana as competition for my affection; I never gave him reason to. Eleana was like his baby sister; he clearly loved her, and his affection would manifest itself in a cold-wet-nosed display of affection that sometimes woke her and made her cry. Her reaction was a little confusing for him and he invariably responded with a puzzled look of concern until she was older and his nuzzling affection would elicit squeals of delight from her.

Eleana cried as all infants do. She was only a couple of weeks old when her cries attracted the attention of a hyena that persistently skirted the periphery of the cleared area around our bush house. Initially I thought that once its natural curiosity was satisfied it would move on. However, judging from the spoor we studied each morning, it came right up to the nursery windows and the kitchen door as we slept, and had done so every night since we'd first seen it. The hyena had been hanging around for a few days now, and for a while we felt what the fabled three little pigs must have felt like in their straw house – but then again, they didn't have the reassurance of Shilo for protection.

The hyena was too close for comfort, however, and Shilo was obviously uneasy; it was as if he knew what it wanted. I'd never seen him so preoccupied about a situation before. When we got home in the afternoon he would check the perimeter a couple of times at least, vigorously marking his territory until he'd completely exhausted the contents of his bladder, and with stiffened legs he would scrape fresh earth at each point. Later, when he went out for his pre-bedtime ablutions, he spent more time than usual checking things out; besides renewing his markings, he repeatedly lifted his nose and tested the wind for scent. He could sense that the hyena wasn't far away.

Shilo's low growls on and off throughout the night told us the hyena was more than curious, it was clearly determined to get to the source of the distress calls, it knew instinctively there would be an easy meal. Though it was a solid stone house, we were naturally protective about our baby girl and had reason to be increasingly apprehensive about the situation.

On the fourth evening the hyena appeared once more. Despite my shouting loudly and clapping my hands, it simply stood there, brazenly defying my attempts to chase it away. Then, when I walked towards it, it ambled slowly away into the bush, both reluctant and clearly unconvinced by my feeble attempts. In a seeming act of sheer defiance, the hyena stopped occasionally to sniff the air – and then, circling back around the side of the house, it reappeared again within minutes. I realised it was time to convince this overgrown mongoose that it was not welcome. A couple of shots over its head might just do the trick, I thought.

Not wanting to risk any confrontation, I'd left Shilo in the house, from where he had been watching me through the kitchen window. Not only could he sense my frustration; more importantly, it was clear from his concern that he perceived the threat in a way I could never understand. Unbeknown to me, he had already calculated his move. Shilo never took his eyes off me as I walked back to the house to collect my rifle, and as I opened the door and stepped inside he did something totally out of character. Slipping past me, Shilo charged out at full speed, this time barking loudly and growling like I hadn't heard him utter before. My desperate 'Uh-uh Shilo!' fell on deaf ears for the first time since he was a puppy.

Catching the hyena completely off-guard, Shilo managed to knock it off balance and onto its side. The hyena's response was incredibly quick; it spun around back onto its feet like a cat and was gone in a flash. Having evolved over millennia competing with larger and more powerful predators for survival, with flight usually better than fight, the hyena ran away into the night. Although Shilo gave chase, he stopped short on the periphery of the yard, where we had cleared most of the smaller bushes and grass out to about 25 metres around the house. Though most of Shilo's marked trees were closer in than that, he understood where his territory ended, beyond which he must have known he'd lose the psychological edge. I suspect he also knew that hyenas were incredibly cunning and powerful predators, and that in a one-on-one confrontation, he would draw the short straw every time. In this instance, however, Shilo had reacted instinctively, protecting a vulnerable member of his pack. No training or level of discipline could supersede this primal paternal reaction: Shilo had reached the point where he needed to do what he had to do.

The hyena never returned to the back yard area. Though we saw the odd one drinking from our bird bath in front of the house from time to time, once they had slaked their thirst, they would slink away, melting into the bush and the night they owned. Many creatures of the bush drank from that water point, which was well within the boundary of Shilo's marked area, but we never allowed him to defend it aggressively and he never tried. Did Shilo perhaps view the little birdbath as neutral, as most wild animals treat larger waterholes in the bush? I don't know.

When our son Dino was born nearly two years later, we half expected the hyena to make an appearance again, but it never did.

23

RETRIEVING – SHILO'S FINEST HOURS

Being a cross-Doberman/Labrador meant that Shilo's coat wasn't the ideal colour or consistency for the hot bushveld environment, and although I reminded myself that African buffalo were black, wildebeest were charcoal grey and zebra were at least half black, I do confess, that at one stage, I considered dyeing his coat a lighter colour for the summer months. Having been born and bred in the bush, Shilo showed a remarkable degree of tolerance for the heat, and I have no doubt that his lean build and fitness also helped him cope with the harsh, dry conditions. Besides his dark-coloured coat, which was perceived as a handicap in the heat, he also had a light layer of under-fur inherited from his Labrador genes, which assists that breed with insulation against sub-zero temperatures. This under-fur also trapped and held water, so once thoroughly wet, it dried slowly, and as long as you had adequate water to soak into that layer, its 'radiator effect' would help keep him a little cooler in the heat. Sometimes, monitored and 'topped up', Shilo could tolerate longer periods in the heat than many other dogs. However, I couldn't help noticing that he appeared to be more comfortable in the freezing wetlands of the southern Drakensberg or eastern Free State; it was when we were in those environments that I discovered this Labrador trait in him.

Besides running, Shilo loved to swim, and thought nothing of swimming in icy cold lakes and ponds, in water so cold that it hurt to touch it. Shilo was a natural, a powerful swimmer, and he loved to retrieve objects from the water. Once I had recognised his potential leaned quite heavily in this direction, I took the opportunity to train him for wildfowling. It soon became apparent that all he needed was a gentle nudge here and there: for the most part his genes had already prepared him for the task.

*   *   *

The Tuli area had no suitably deep water to train Shilo in – that is, nothing deep enough that didn't harbour crocodiles or hippo. We simply had to wait until we could locate a suitable piece of water. In the meantime I had to be content with having him splash around in some of the more remote pools in the Majali River, even the biggest of which was too small for him to stretch his swimming legs. As it turned out, we didn't have too long to wait.

Meagan and I were on a spot of leave and staying with my parents at the time. The venue for Shilo's training was the boat club site at Wemmer Pan, a small lake in the south of Johannesburg about twenty minutes' drive from their home. Although it was chosen for no other reason than convenience, I found that it was ideal: the water was cold, with reed-lined shallows, very similar to the conditions he would most likely be expected to retrieve wildfowl in.

Shilo's first formal training to retrieve wildfowl from water started by using a simple block of 2x4 timber which was cut to size, rounded off and tapered in the shape of a duck's body. Then I nailed a pair of yellow-billed duck wings to the sides of the 'body'. I now had the approximate proportions and weight of a wild duck. Occasionally the decoy prop would fall with the wings sticking out at unnatural angles to the block, emulating the realistic situations he would encounter in the field. Most importantly, using real wings got him used to the feel of feathers in his mouth.

Needless to say, it only took a few days of training to polish Shilo's inbred skill to perfection. However, I believe the rapport we'd built in the bush had more than a little to do with his responsive attitude. Shilo could always read me better than I could him.

Word spread quickly among the local shooting fraternity, many of whom had never seen a retriever at work. They were fascinated: later that season, Shilo had already earned the reputation as being one of the finest retrievers around. He had a slight edge on other retrievers from the city which could only stretch their legs on weekends, in that he had incredible stamina, no doubt from all the running training he'd done in the bush. He had absolutely no qualms about retrieving waterfowl for hours on end, under difficult conditions. Shilo really shone in extremely cold weather, which was important, as most of the time wildfowling took place in the winter months, when temperatures dropped to well below freezing.

Once on a shooting trip in the Underberg area, I remember waking at 3.30 am to prepare for that morning's shoot. As expected, it was still dark and bitterly cold outside, but not quite as dark as it should have been; something wasn't right. Perhaps I had set the alarm clock incorrectly and dawn was already breaking? Wiping the condensation from the window, I looked out onto the dimly lit courtyard below expecting to see a faint pink glow in the east, but instead was greeted by something I'd only ever seen in the movies depicting a typical northern hemisphere Christmas scene. It had snowed all night and the snow lay thick everywhere, everything was covered in white; it was just too beautiful not to share, so as early as it was I woke Meagan. Kissing her ice-cold nose, which was all of her that was sticking out from under the covers, was enough to wake her, but Squealer was going to need more encouragement – I could see by the way he squirmed deeper into the folds that he didn't want to get out from under the warm cosy duvet. Dragging the duvet off the bed over the lump that was Squealer, Meagan wrapped it around her shoulders and came to the window. So taken was she by the splendour outside, she decided to join me and Shilo out in the wetlands that morning.

I must say I felt for her as she sat huddled behind a makeshift duck blind in the snow-covered maize field, but apparently the pain from the cold was worth it. Most South Africans are fascinated by snow. Many never see snow in their lives, others usually only see very small amounts, so in terms of African snow, this was a particularly spectacular fall of deep soft snow. Squealer definitely didn't share our enthusiasm, allowing nothing more than the tip of his nose to stick out of the top of Meagan's parka.

Often the pans and dams in these low-lying wetlands were rimmed by two or three metres of thin sheet ice that formed in the shallows overnight. This proved to be a minor obstacle which Shilo overcame by leaping from the relatively firm ground on the edge, onto this layer, breaking through, and then swimming out in the open water to retrieve the waterfowl. Despite ambient temperatures as low as minus ten centigrade, which caused the steam to rise off his wet body, he would remain completely focused on the horizon and the next flight of duck. The cold never bothered him; Shilo lived for wildfowling, and these were indeed his finest hours.

* * *

Shilo's retrieving skill went beyond the recovery of waterfowl on occasion, and by that I don't mean sticks and Frisbees. One of the most dramatic things I saw Shilo do, and where he demonstrated that he had a calculating mind, was when we were at Motswari camp in the Timbavati. It was the day I witnessed him make an important judgement call of his own, acting without prompt or instruction, on instinct alone. Alerted by a squeal, we saw that Shilo had jumped into the swimming pool, grabbed a terrified young girl by the forearm and pulled her to the safety of the shallow end. Although it wasn't much shallower than the rest of the pool, it did have a set of stainless steel rung-type steps on that side.

Normally Shilo would not go into this pool on his own, because the shallow end was too deep for him to stand. The only way he could get out of the water was if you helped him by grabbing the nape of his neck as he got close to the edge, then he would push himself against the resistance of your hand and clamber out. Once in, a dog could never get out unaided, it would swim until exhausted and then simply sink, which was how ranger Roger Ellis's Staffordshire terrier nearly died one day; fortunately the lucky dog was noticed on the bottom of the pool in time, removed and resuscitated. Since that incident we were extremely circumspect about Shilo using that pool, so we'd never encouraged him, yet that particular day he made a decision responding to stimuli inherent in his bloodline ... no matter the consequences to his own safety (not that he knew of the danger to himself, though).

Worried that he might have hurt the girl, Meagan questioned her friend, who then confirmed that the young girl was having difficulty in the deep water, gasping for air and splashing excessively. This is what I suspect triggered Shilo's instinctive response to retrieve. We had purposely never taught him to grab or retrieve people in water rescue scenarios, even as a game, for fear of him exerting too much holding pressure and puncturing their skin. We could never lose sight of the fact that, while he was able to employ the soft mouth pressure essential for retrieving wildfowl, attributed to the Labrador in him, he was still 50% Doberman.

* * *

Another revelation of Shilo's intelligence, used in combination with his natural predisposition to retrieve, occurred near Underberg one early morning, not far from where Meagan and I had enjoyed that beautiful snow-covered dawn the previous winter. Here again he demonstrated a remarkable ability to read a situation, when he consciously made a deliberate decision under pressure to solve a problem. We were sitting on the edge of an enormous shallow pan, its surface area shrouded in mist, which was as a result of the icy water being warmer than the ambient minus seven degrees Celsius. Except for my dark boot prints and Shilo's paw prints, which had broken through the frost when

235

we'd made our way across the field earlier, the surrounding vegetation in the low-lying areas was completely blanketed in white.

We had settled into the soggy blind long before the faint glimmer in the east signified the onset of dawn, and although Shilo appeared comfortable, I felt as if my toes and fingertips no longer belonged to me. It was still quite dark when I poured a cup of coffee from my flask, and no sooner had I taken the last sip when I heard a flurry of wing beats as a flight of red-billed teal flew overhead ... the birds were beginning to move.

As it began to get lighter, we could hear the cacophony from hundreds of other waterfowl getting restless, readying themselves for the morning flight to feed. That particular morning we were after spurwing geese, the largest waterfowl species in Africa. These enormous birds, weighing up to ten kilograms, would arrive in their thousands to take advantage of the winter grain harvest. By splitting up into flocks numbering around thirty individuals, they were able to make effective use of the many smaller dams in the area. From these wetland refuges they would launch their feeding forays, moving in at first light like squadrons of bombers on a raid; wave after wave would come flying in to feed on the fields of ripe maize. In the few weeks prior to harvesting, each goose would consume at least a cupful of grain twice a day, inflicting huge financial losses on the farmers. Once sated, they would return to the water, where they would spend most of the day preening and resting, in preparation for the second flight to feed again later that afternoon.

Immediately behind us was a low barbed wire fence, and beyond that a large paddock of Midmar ryegrass where a herd of dairy cows were grazing up on the higher slope of the field, approximately 200 metres away. They had no idea we were there until the shooting started. The mist had all but lifted when a soft whimper from Shilo made me look up. Against the sky I could make out the silhouettes of at least a dozen spurwing geese flying in typical 'V' formation, heading straight for our blind. Despite their cumbersome size, they were deceptively fast, and before I knew it the skein was high above us. Right overhead now, I took aim on the lead goose providing an ample lead and pulled the trigger. Its wings folded, it was dead at the shot. However, flying at the height it was, its momentum carried it a further 30 metres into the field of ryegrass behind us, where it fell.

Shilo squeezed through the fence easily and was at the dead goose moments later. At the same time, also making their way to Shilo's position, and bearing down on him across the field at full tilt, was the herd of cows. I saw Shilo let go of the goose momentarily to look up at the approaching stampede, then he glanced back at me, grabbed the goose again and started running with the huge, cumbersome bird between his front legs. Eventually he was dragging it more than carrying it, which slowed him down to the point where the cows were almost on top of him, but he wasn't letting go ... no sir, this was his goose!

When he reached the barbed wire fence he realised without even trying and failing first, that there was no way he was going to get through with the goose in his mouth. Dropping the huge bird on the field side of the fence, Shilo squeezed himself through the barbed wire strands, only just making it onto our side as the whole herd of cows rushed up against the fence. Turning around and staring into the wet muzzles of a dozen cows, he stuck his head through the fence, grabbed the goose by its neck and pulled it through under the lowest strand. Once through he carried it over to me, where he proudly dropped it next to my daypack, then he walked back up to the fence and went nose to nose with the cows, lifting his lip and growling his displeasure at their lack of sportsmanship. The stand-off lasted a minute or two, then one by one the cows lost interest and moved off. Shilo too, had more important things to do.

* * *

Gavin Hulme is the scion of a sugar cane farming family in the Empangeni area. As interesting as farming in rolling green hills of KwaZulu-Natal was, it was in big game country that Gavin's heart lay, so he divided his time between helping out on the family estate and the bushveld, where he went on to become a part-time professional hunter. Although Gavin soon became a reputable big game hunter, when it came to wing shooting, he took a rather unconventional approach to things. Shunning the double-barrelled fowling pieces traditionally used in the field, he preferred to use his FN Browning five-shot automatic shotgun, which he nicknamed 'Van Schalkwyk'. I might add that this was much to the consternation of the traditionalists and local wing shooting fraternity of the Natal Midlands. 'It's just not cricket to shoot birds with such a contraption, old chap,' they would say. But, to Gavin this was water off the proverbial duck's back; he carried on regardless.

So, it is with some trepidation that I admit to relenting when Gavin called and requested Shilo's help to retrieve a few ducks that he'd shot using Van Schalkwyk. From his description of events, he had been hunting on a friend's lake when some of the ducks he'd shot had fallen beyond reach in the reed beds, in fairly deep water.

'I hear Shilo is a good retriever ...' he ventured.

'I certainly think so,' I replied promptly.

'Do you think he'd be able to retrieve ducks that he hadn't seen fall himself?' Gavin asked. 'You know, ducks which lay out of view in amongst the reeds.'

Shilo's brown eyes looked straight into mine. Putting my hand on his head, I smiled – he knew we were talking about him. Turning back to Gavin and still smiling confidently, I said, 'Well, Gavin, if Shilo can't, I doubt we'll find another dog around here that will.'

Although Shilo had never before retrieved birds on the water that he hadn't marked, and I was sure that he relied more on sight than scent in these situations, I was sure enough of his ability to have him give it a go. Also, I have an aversion to wasting downed birds, and for that reason, if nothing else, I agreed to try and find the ducks.

We duly arrived at the water's edge to find that besides the reeds and weed beds there was little to see. A number of red-knobbed coots were eating waterweed in the shallows, and a dabchick out in the deeper water dived under at our approach, leaving a swirl not unlike a huge trout breaking the surface. Gavin pointed out the general area in the expanse of reeds where the ducks had fallen. I picked up a lump of dried mud and drew Shilo's attention to it, then threw it into the middle of the reed bed where it landed with an audible splashy plop.

'Teksit!' I said.

Shilo jumped in and swam straight across the open water towards the reed bed. He reached the thick stand quickly and entered it without hesitation. Within seconds he had disappeared from view as the reeds popped back up and closed ranks behind him. We could hear him swimming around searching for the ducks. The tops of the reeds bent over and quivered as his powerful body scythed through the maze of small channels; it was the only indication we had of where he was. Moments later he emerged into the open water, his broad chest pushing a wake that streamed out behind him as he swam towards us, a sodden yellow-billed duck firmly clamped in his mouth. He did that again another four times, while Gavin stared open-mouthed as the pile of dead ducks at his feet grew.

'How many did you drop in the reeds?' I asked.

Gavin closed his mouth briefly and opened it again to answer: 'Five, I think.'

Shilo's empty return this time confirmed that there were no more birds to retrieve.

Clearly in awe of Shilo and what he'd seen him do, Gavin was now all ears to my proud babble. I took this opportunity to explain to him that there is so much more to wing shooting than simply blasting birds out of the sky. Watching a retriever like Shilo working his magic, or a pointer go stiff on a covey of francolins, is what a lot of the sport is all about. Besides the obvious technique that is the quintessence of wing shooting, its related tradition and etiquette in the field go even further than your attire or what shotgun you use. Besides the harmony of having a trained bird dog to share in the effort of the harvest, it is also what you shoot, when you shoot it and how many you shoot, that are the keys to the conservation aspect of this practice. As the great cyclist Lance Armstrong said, years later, about his life and cycling: 'It's not about the bike,' so too, in regard to wild-fowling, it's not about the gun.

*   *   *

To illustrate the importance of knowing the ecology of your quarry, and how to identify the various birds from their silhouette or their wingbeat pattern, we'll go back to the Natal Midlands, and another beautiful midwinter's morning. A crisp, clear dawn heralded the annual guineafowl shoot in the region, a community event that involved strategic farms opening their properties for that one day of the year, when for twenty-four hours everyone put their differences aside and came together for the occasion, and where, needless to say, most of those differences were amicably settled. These shoots were always well organised and meticulously planned; nobody who was anybody was left out, and even those guns that weren't well placed, or whose shooting was below par, invariably had a brace of birds to take home at the end of the day.

Breaking with tradition this particular year, the local green-grocer, who had expressed a keen interest, was also given the opportunity of participating in the shoot. Not being familiar with his gun manners, the organiser had cautiously placed him in a remote position close to a small dam. Here they reasoned that if he pulled off a wild shot or two by accident, the pellets would fall harmlessly on the water, and not in someone's eye or in the backside of one of the dogs.

Shilo and I would be working the dryer uplands and edges of the harvested fields, not really his forte, which was the low-lying wetlands. Nevertheless, he got on well with the pointers and the other dogs brought in to help locate and retrieve the birds that day. Although there were specific traits required when walking up francolin and guineafowl, for example, this rough shooting suited Shilo's technique. While his nose could not match those of the thoroughbred pointers that ranged ahead, their noses scraping the ground trying to pick up the scent, he impressed many of the seasoned bird dog breeders by keeping the guineafowl moving and retrieving his fair share of downed birds. Shilo's running training was paying off: as the day wore on, he showed that he was fitter than most of their dogs. I was so proud of him, it didn't matter that I was not on form with my gun that day; my dog was.

Once the morning's shoot was over, everyone gravitated towards the rendezvous point; there we would load the birds, pick up the dogs and make our way to the local hotel for lunch. However, as usual when so many individuals are involved, there are always stragglers, and almost on cue, a wayward random shot from way down the valley reminded us that Manuel had not yet been collected from the dam. Barry Victor, a regular at these shoots, knew where he'd been placed and volunteered to go down and collect him. Sure enough, he arrived to find the greengrocer sitting exactly where he had been told to wait for passing shots, and on the rusty barbed wire fence in front of him hung the spoils of that morning's shoot. Barry immediately recognised the two dead birds as white-breasted cormorants. Trying really hard not to say anything derogatory, he politely asked Manuel, in a curious, interested sort of way, as to what he had hanging on the fence.

'Issa ducks,' Manuel said confidently.

Barry managed to retain his composure until Manuel qualified his statement: 'But-a is-a sheet ducks, dem taysta laaika feesh.'

The funny side of this was that by his own admission, Manuel had eaten cormorants before, and yet still had no idea that these disgusting tasting birds, which are often infested with huge tapeworms in their guts, are not ducks. Sadly, he still had no idea how to identify them on the wing ... and then, to crown it all, had made the same mistake twice in one morning! On his return Barry was unable to control himself as he relayed the story to us; we all laughed so much that our stomach muscles ached for days afterwards – and needless to say, Manuel was not on the following year's 'guinea shoot' guest list.

24

TROUT FISHERMEN ARE CONSERVATIONISTS FIRST

Until I took up the long rod and started fly-fishing, I thought there could be no two pursuits more incongruous than big game viewing and trout fishing. Admittedly this was my cloistered view; I know now that the intrinsic mindset and approach to both are interwoven at the very root. Going on safari in the bush or wading in a trout stream – both are so much more fulfilling and rewarding when approached with a broader environmental insight and conservation ethos, attributes I find common to both the bush lovers and the trout fishermen I know.

Modern lifestyles demand we maintain a fast pace, while idle time is viewed disdainfully as wasteful and unproductive. It is also a fact that many modern-day ailments and diseases are stress-related, stress induced from chasing a buck in order to pay the doctors, pharmacists, psychiatrists and personal trainers to remedy the symptoms. I believe we don't take the time to 'whittle' any more, or as the Italians do when they take time out and enjoy *'bel far niente'*, the beauty of doing nothing. You no longer see old-timers sitting around shooting the breeze, a faithful old dog lying at their feet, while they carve a piece of wood with an old Joseph Rogers pocket knife.

Activities that slow our hectic pace of life down needn't be that mundane or filled with 'sweet Fanny Adams'. For example, the therapeutic benefits to be had from engaging in the gentle art of trout fishing are well known, and apparently far-reaching as well – as Shilo and I discovered.

I knew that, although Shilo's passion for wildfowling never diminished, it was very physically demanding, and he risked overtaxing himself as he grew older. Though we would continue to enjoy wildfowling for years to come, I felt the need for another reason to get into the highlands, particularly in the cooler months. But it had to be something that somehow included Shilo, and trout fishing appeared to tick all the right boxes.

*   *   *

Autumn is my favourite time of the year, a time of ripeness, of imminent maturity and harvest. It was also Shilo's time, and even as he grew older, the onset of cooler days invigorated his wildfowling spirit; there was an unmistakable attitude of anticipation, the fervent hope that we'd soon head off to the freezing wetlands. This time it is the Drakensberg, where the elusive grey-winged francolin can be found sharing this high-altitude habitat with the rare bearded vulture, it also happens to be where cool mountain streams still boast wild populations of rainbow trout.

Driving down through the Eastern Free State to the sleepy village of Rhodes in the Cape, we see the characteristic Lombardy poplars standing tall and resolute like golden sentinels over isolated homesteads surrounded by fields where neat rows of stubble lie strewn with tightly bound bales of hay. Often, to complete the scene, a wisp of smoke rises straight up through the trees in an unwavering plume as the wind drops and the late afternoon chill sets in. You can almost feel the warmth of burning logs crackling and spitting in the cosy hearth, where the promise of a warm welcome is always guaranteed.

Returning home through the highveld, we follow roads lined with another welcome and non-invasive alien. Belying their true identity as Mexican weeds, cosmos flowers erupt in varying shades of cerise and white, with an occasional rare splash of yellow or orange, a sea of colour dancing in the wind along the highways and fallow fields of the South African highveld. Like the Italian poplar trees, they add richness to the multifarious tapestry that is South Africa ... welcome immigrants, in my view.

Autumn also happens to be the finest time to be on a trout stream.

* * *

Hunting 'wild' trout in the crystal-clear mountain streams of the Eastern Cape, back in April 1989, changed my outdoor recreational pursuits for ever. From the very first little fish I caught in the Bell River, I knew there was no turning back. The only regret I have about taking up fly fishing is not having discovered it earlier in life. Pretty soon, as if on a quest to make up for lost time, I became so wrapped up in it that it must have appeared to those close to me, including Shilo, that I was terminally besotted with the gentle art.

Soon the freezing wetlands began to take a back seat to this new-found pursuit of mine, and Shilo's mature years would see him spending more time with me in the highlands, probing the still waters and mountain streams of South Africa for trout. Since wildfowl and trout are often found in the same habitat, we saw many ducks on these outings. However, despite the occasional sigh and whimper from Shilo in the beginning, he quickly learned that when I had the fly rod in hand, we didn't hunt ducks.

Besides pursuing trout on a fly, I immersed myself in another integral facet of this delightful sport; I discovered the fascinating world of fly tying. So when I couldn't fish, for whatever reason, I concocted trout flies that vaguely resembled the pattern of choice, and which even the most fastidious trout would oblige me by taking on occasion. Some of the patterns called for very specific feathers and fur; however, most of the flies I tied called for English partridge, pheasant, mallard or turkey feathers in their patterns. Though most of this stuff had a strong whiff of mothballs about it, I'm convinced Shilo could smell beyond the naphthalene and identify the scent of the game birds and mammals that originally wore these materials. Fly tying is a messy business, so when he investigated the cornucopia of excess feathers and fur that fell to the floor I'd sometimes look down from my tying vice to find one or two feathers or bits of fur comically attached to his wet nose, or sticking out of the side of his mouth.

Initially Shilo didn't enjoy it when I took him trout fishing, for reasons I'm ashamed of, and which became painfully obvious later when I eventually took off my blinkers and began to make him part of this fascinating art. Although he loved to come along with me wherever I went, particularly anywhere outdoors, when I was fly fishing he couldn't participate in the activity as much as he would have liked to. It was also the only outdoor activity where he would be reprimanded for going into the water uninvited. At first he didn't understand what it was that he was doing wrong, and what on earth all the stealth was for. What was I stalking? It must have been so confusing for him. Without the advantage of Polaroid glasses, which most fly fishermen wear to cut through the surface glare, he couldn't see underwater. He had no idea that when he disturbed a pool, the trout would dash for cover, and of course this in turn made me mumble and grumble.

I don't know what got into me, but in my single-minded focus I neglected to notice Shilo's feelings, and inexcusably began to take my faithful friend for granted. I was expecting an old dog to learn and become part of something new overnight. At times he held his head cocked to one side, with a bemused look on his face that said it all; he was confused, he didn't understand what the fuss was about ... and I was a little slow to notice.

Shilo disliked the noise the trout reel's ratchet made when I peeled line off the spool to cast, which was invariably accompanied by an instruction to sit still quietly while I cast the line. He quickly learned to associate the ratchet with exclusion, and would lie quietly watching me with his head on his paws. Needless to say it got to the point where no instruction was necessary – as soon as the ratchet ran he hung back, looking dejected, as if he didn't belong. The realisation of what was happening suddenly dawned on me one day; it was the last thing I ever wanted, I never wanted him to feel left out ... never ever! Shilo meant so much to me, I loved him and wanted him with me all the time, it didn't matter what it was going to take.

Starting with the noisy reel, I began by ordering a specially designed reel from Hardy Brothers in England, the Hardy Marquis 'silent ratchet'. Success! Then I made a point of inviting Shilo into the water and occasionally letting him nose the fish I'd caught. I'd encourage him to try and bite at them underwater in the shallows; though the fish were still on the end of my line, he was never able to grab them as one sees those grizzly bears do with salmon, but he never gave up trying, sometimes ducking his whole head under water. Most importantly, however, Shilo began to feel part of the activity without having to put too much strain on his ageing body. These were moments of revelation and of truth, of how much Shilo meant to me. I now realised it wasn't about the fishing; it was about best friends sharing each other's company in the beautiful environs in which trout are invariably found. Something vital would have been amiss if we couldn't share this – and if it had ever got down to making a choice, I know I would have put my fly rod back into its tube in an instant. Thankfully, however, it never came to that.

* * *

Back in 1991, Dr Willie van Niekerk, then chairman of the President's Council of South Africa, invited me to his home in Stellenbosch. He was keen for me to try my luck on some fastidious little 'wild' trout in the Eerste River, which happened to glide past his house less than 15 metres from his doorstep. The river was more like a fast-flowing stream, winding through the wooded suburbs in a delightful series of boulder-strewn riffles and runs, in most places as wide as a double bed and just about as deep.

Anyone watching us cross Thibault Street on tiptoe and stalk the river bank in a half-crouch would have been forgiven for thinking we were trying to imitate a couple of rather large praying mantises. Willie motioned for me to walk behind him until we got to the lip of the pavement from where we were able to use our Polaroids to cut the surface glare and peer into the crystal-clear water some three metres below.

'There's one,' Willie whispered, pointing to a trout no bigger than a pilchard holding station in the lee of a boulder right under the bubble line, where much of what they ate would come floating downstream. I noticed how, like a leopard in the dappled shadows of the bushveld, this trout merged perfectly with its environment.

'And another,' he said, pointing excitedly; this time his exuberant gesticulation was too much for the trout, and both fish vanished. Later that afternoon, on the evening rise, I managed to catch and release four small trout on the dry fly. I suspect they obliged the clumsy presentations of a guest in town by rising to my flies in a sporting gesture of hospitability.

Being a trout fisherman himself, Willie took a personal interest in their conservation; he was also proud of the fact that this stream running through the town was clean enough to support healthy numbers of these fish. To the layman, there was no need for test samples to be analysed by bespectacled technicians in well-equipped laboratories to gauge water quality. Trout and the invertebrates they feed on are the miner's canary of water quality. (As an aside, in the early 1900s, trout were caught in fishermen's nets in the Eerste River estuary, the only record of 'sea-run' rainbow trout in Africa. This was indeed a significant indication of the river's health from source to sea.)

When my daughter Eleana began attending Stellenbosch University, nearly eighteen years after I had first made my acquaintance with Willie's trout, Meagan and I went down to visit her. We also took some time out to walk along the banks of this delightful little stream again. Of course I'd packed my tiny four-piece trout rod, just in case this very opportunity should present itself in between parental duties. I was eager to show Meagan the descendants of Willie's trout, but my anticipation was for naught; the soapy coloured water and faint scum line in the slower eddies indicated all was not well in paradise.

Despite diligent exploration with both fly rod and Polaroids, we didn't see a single trout. Later that month, on Carte Blanche's actuality programme, we saw why. Due mainly to changes in the conservation status of trout, injudicious municipal management and the subsequent lack of maintenance of the Eerste River, raw sewage and other contaminants were able to enter the system unchecked. The pollution of what was once a beautiful healthy stream effectively destroyed all the trout downstream of the town, and turned the water into a health hazard. Thank goodness I was fishing the 'dry' fly, and not 'wet' flies, which I always wet prior to casting, usually by placing them in my mouth and soaking them with my saliva! However, although the underlying long-term prognosis of the Eerste River worried me more, I know rivers are forgiving and pollution can be tackled.

* * *

I believe trout in South Africa are getting a raw deal! You may have good reason to question why, as a conservationist, I support the propagation of these exotic fish; I also hear you say that I should know better than to support an alien species. Well, I believe I do, and in spite of this, my stance remains resolute. I like to think of myself as a conservationist, and one who has done and tries to do more than just talk about it. It remains my intention to do as much as I can to help the environment, to make a positive contribution and hopefully leave the planet one day in better shape than I found it. Getting to understand the threats to the ecosystem became an integral part of my life's work, so it goes without saying that the fundamentals of ecology are familiar to me, not the least being the effects of alien species on an ecosystem. Before passing judgement and burning me at the stake as a conservation heretic, please put on your pragmatic hat for a moment, pour yourself a glass of wine and allow me to elucidate.

Thanks to careful management, trout have been able to survive in small pockets of favourable habitat in this country since their introduction in 1890 – that's more than 120 years! This is much longer than many breeds of livestock and agricultural plants imported and grown for our benefit, so it can be argued that they have more rights than most to be here. Trout which have taken out 'permanent residence' in select areas of the country have become fully functional, integrated 'citizens' of the ecosystem. In many ways these immigrants have inadvertently contributed to the conservation of areas that were agriculturally unviable and otherwise doomed to economic desolation. By way of but one example, the environs of Dullstroom, known primarily for its trout fishing, would be nothing but an overgrazed wasteland of bankrupt sheep farms were it not for the huge economic spin-off from the activities related to the pursuit of these excellent sporting fish.

Unlike the majority of exotic plant and animal species brought into this country, trout are not aggressive or invasive aliens – in fact, quite the contrary; they are fastidious animals which need nurturing, and will only thrive in South Africa if cared for and actively encouraged to propagate in healthy environments. In natural systems trout will only breed in cool, well-oxygenated, unpolluted streams, unlike other exotic fish species such as the Malaysian grass carp, Florida bass, or Chinese carp, all of which have a much wider tolerance of adverse conditions.

I believe that trout are much like oak trees – aliens, yes, but very different from wattle, blue gum and pine trees, which spread like a green cancer. Oak trees need nurturing to grow, don't multiply uncontrollably, and invariably grow only where you plant them, and then only if the soil and climate conditions are right. Witness the magnificent specimens in the Western Cape still providing shade and fruit from where the individual acorns were hand-planted over three hundred years ago! Incidentally, the breathtakingly beautiful camphor trees at Vergelegen Estate are also non-invasive exotics – thankfully, however, intelligence has prevailed and they have been declared national monuments.

Trout cannot tolerate a wide range of environmental factors. This makes them predictable, easy to monitor and therefore infinitely more manageable ... and vulnerable. In an ironic twist of disparity, indigenous saw-toothed catfish which were introduced into some rivers and streams of the Western Cape, where they were naturally absent, have done substantially more damage to the local fish and amphibian populations than trout are claimed to have. Fact! Worse still, the type of fishermen I know who fish for them cannot protect and conserve catfish waters, nor will they employ someone to manage the fishery and its environs – they simply don't have the same conservation ethos or the financial means to do so. Subsequently, lack of interest will lead the river or dam down the inevitable road of degradation. On the other hand, trout fishermen are motivated and usually have the means to conserve the environs of a system that contains trout. The fact is, trout require this degree of commitment and support in order to thrive in South Africa.

*　*　*

It was indeed a sad day on the aptly named Treur River in the highlands of Mpumalanga when narrow-minded 'Salmophobes' began their campaign of extermination of the wild trout in the 'Sad' River. This programme was undertaken to save a tiny threatened fish species local to that system known as the Treur River barb, oblivious to the fact that the trout with which they had lived cheek by jowl for over a hundred years were in a similar state of decline, and prior to their extermination, were barely eking out an existence in this river anyway, due mainly to diminished water quantity and quality.

Water extraction by the biggest consumers and polluters – namely the paper pulp industry – has drastically reduced water flow in the Treur River, particularly in winter when it drops to dangerously low levels. Ironically, the extraction of water by the exotic plantations that supply the timber for the pulp that was processed to make up the paper on which the reports condemning the trout were written, does more long-term damage to the environment – in particular, rivers and associated wetland habitats – than any number of trout could ever do. If you knew the quantity of water these trees 'drank', the tannins that leached into the system from their rotting leaves, or if you have ever had the misfortune of smelling the filth that belches from the chimney stacks, or seeing the slurry of chemicals that is piped out into the environment from the mills themselves, you will begin to grasp how insignificant the environmental impact of a few trout in a stream is. It's a no-brainer, but please do continue, I'm not finished yet ...

The sanctimonious xenophobes who murdered those trout will probably never visit the scene of the crime again. Instead they now gaze out of their departmental office windows across beautifully tended beds of exotic flowers and shrubs that fringe imported lawns, no doubt planning the next attack. To the unknowing eye, the scene is apparently peaceful and normal, complete with alien invaders in the shape of Indian mynahs hopping around, their arrogant chests pouted out after having successfully displaced the resident robins and thrushes. They now compete aggressively with the European house sparrows, another exotic, albeit non-invasive species, which have been here from the time of the first European settlers in the Cape ... (don't worry, I'm not going there). The crumbs that the one-sided squabble is over are the remnants of food that was grown from imported exotic wheat and maize cultivars. A while later, sated and nourished by the products of alien – and dare I say it, genetically modified – vegetation, the mynahs fly up into the branches of the surrounding pine, cypress, blue gum, poplar or wattle trees and preen their exotic feathers. But this matters not one whit to the eradication squad; the residual flack from the bombardment of trout has conveniently clouded the skies of reality, and their focus remains firmly fixed on the 'elitist' fish. Will they have the guts and conservation conviction to challenge the pulp giants, and 'exterminate' the real threat ... or are they going to find some more defenceless trout in some pristine stream to pick on in order to distract attention from the real, more challenging concerns? My money's on the latter.

Meanwhile, as energy and resources are inappropriately spent plotting against trout, no one bothers to look up as a flock of Indian mynahs sneaks over the cool highlands, dropping down under the radar into the lowveld. Their destination? That bastion of our country's national wildlife pride, the Kruger National Park, where in a couple of days they will reach Skukuza, the Park's main camp, their invasion complete.

* * *

Given the limited resources available for the conservation of our country's environment, I believe the focus on the eradication of trout to be a completely inappropriate and misguided waste of scarce resources. There are so many bigger threats to our country's waterways, wetland habitats and associated wildlife that need immediate attention ... and guess what? The trout that survive the environmental degradation that is happening as we speak, will wait for their execution day if need be. Where can they go and what harm can they possibly do that they haven't (allegedly) already done in the last hundred and twenty years?

Trout are declared exotic aliens to be destroyed wherever they are found – right, so what would it matter if now, due to the demise of their sport, the 'elitist' trout fishermen – along with their money and support – leave these wetlands and river environments unmanaged and uncared for? I believe a more intelligent and objective study should have found an appropriate solution to accommodate both fish species in a well-managed system, because, given the status quo and developing circumstances, eventually neither will prevail. It is the river that needs saving first, not the little barb swimming in it. You can breed a barb easier than you can a river.

... And who really cares? Well, trout fishermen most certainly do, whether there are trout in the stream or not – after all, we are conservationists first.

25

OLIFANTS RIVER GAME RESERVE

Changing from commercial ecotourism to game reserve ecology management was a pivotal and necessary turning point in my career. Meagan had recently given birth to our son Dino, and Eleana was just two years old, when we moved from the Timbavati to Olifants River, which lies approximately 30 kilometres due north. South Africa was undergoing considerable change, and the prevailing uncertain political situation did very little for the international tourist market on which we depended. It was becoming increasingly difficult to operate an up-market game lodge profitably, and the immediate future prospects looked bleak. So with our heads ruling our hearts, we reluctantly sold up and applied to work where we'd be less dependent on the fickle overseas tourist market for our livelihood. Thinking ahead, we also needed to be close to schools ...

Among the various other reserves and posts we applied for, general manager of Olifants River Game Reserve seemed to tick all the boxes for us. Importantly, they were also among the first to respond, informing us that we'd been short-listed from hundreds of applicants. We were duly invited to be interviewed in Johannesburg at our earliest convenience, so we put in for a couple of days' leave, packed an overnight bag, fuelled our double cab and hit the road.

Shilo and Squealer came along as well, of course. Being able to curl up at Meagan's feet or on her lap made accommodating Squealer so much easier. So the back of my truck was customised mainly for Shilo's comfort while travelling and for those times he had to spend the night in the vehicle – when, for example, a B&B didn't allow dogs. In these instances I would leave a Fisher-Price baby monitor in the back with him. On the rare occasion when I needed to leave Shilo outside a restaurant, or if we needed to enter any other 'no dogs allowed' zone, I'd simply leave an old sweater or windbreaker outside for him to lie on. Though I suspect that for the most part he was more comfortable being left in the back of my vehicle at these times, invariably, I would try and get a window table, just to keep an eye on him.

The first time I had to resort to leaving Shilo alone was outside Phalaborwa airport's waiting lounge. It was too hot to leave him in the truck, and I quickly realised I was totally unprepared, so I resorted to using the only thing at hand, which was a nylon ski rope. Tying a bowline knot, also known to fly fishermen as a perfection loop, to serve as a collar, I tethered him to an outside table situated under a huge tree. Then I gave him my smelly old bush jacket to lie on, and promised him I'd return shortly. About twenty minutes later I returned to find him fast asleep on my jacket, but the nylon rope I'd tethered him with lay severed from the 'collar' section. Closer inspection revealed it had been cut cleanly, as if with a knife; he had simply chewed through the rope using his carnassial teeth. It was the first and last time I ever tethered Shilo.

Years later Piet Lombaard, who was the warden of the Timbavati Nature Reserve at the time, used a similar rope to tie his beloved Staffordshire terrier in the back of his open Land Cruiser. Somehow the rope got tangled and shortened, to the point where it prevented the dog from reaching the ground when it jumped out to follow him a little later. Tragically it hung itself. Piet was devastated, and I was shocked when he broke the terrible news to me. In an instant my mind flashed back to that day I tethered Shilo at the airport, and I realised that his intelligent objection to being tethered was not shared by all dogs.

* * *

Unbeknown to us, before we entered the building to interview for the position at Olifants, Shilo's entire toilet routine and the preparations we made for his comfort had been observed from one of the upper floors. Those watching us knew who we were; it didn't take rocket science to work out that the young couple clad in khaki parking their dusty 4x4 in between the plethora of spotlessly valet-serviced Mercedes and BMWs were from out of town. Having driven straight through from the Timbavati that morning, we may have looked slightly dishevelled. Knowing that the interview could last for an indeterminate length of time, I needed to make Shilo as comfy as possible. So, in the courtyard-cum-parking lot of Dimension Data, I found a shady spot to park, and then let him out to do his ablutions on a nearby patch of lawn studded with lovely trees. Once this function was complete, it was back into the truck and onto his mattress. Sliding both the side windows of the canopy open, I then filled his water bowl, turned the 12 V Hella turbo fan on to medium, and closed the door. I never locked the canopy door when Shilo was in the back.

On termination of the formal part of the interview, the board then moved the discussion on to the previous management. It was immediately apparent that the most contentious issue leading to their demise had been their dogs! Apparently the previous manager's dogs had been uncontrolled and undisciplined; they would go off on forays into the bush on their own, chasing game and barking incessantly. The board was reluctant to have a repetition of this. Dr Melvyn Greenberg, aka 'Dr Platzhund' on his radio show, got up and slowly walked over to the window, where he stood looking out onto the parking lot below, his hands clasped behind his back. This was obviously a calculated move, a subtle strategy to let us know that they knew about the dog. Turning his head slowly, then lifting his eyebrows like Hercule Poirot in an Agatha Christie plot, he asked a question to confirm what he already suspected: 'What about your dog?'

Although Melvyn had no choice but to bring Shilo up in order to clear the dog issue with the rest of the board, he was quick in support and vouched for Shilo without hesitation. Melvyn knew our history; he had met Shilo a couple of years previously when visiting Motswari as a guest. Shilo had also been around when we'd rushed Lex Lawrie, a neighbouring landowner, off to the doctor with a Mozambique cobra bite. Now, years later, his son Richard, himself a landowner in the Klaserie as well as a shareholder of Olifants, was one of the committee members conducting the interview ... It is a indeed a small world.

Despite Melvyn's comments I felt the need to elucidate, to address the board's obvious trepidation. I wasn't there to sell myself and brush over my relationship with Shilo. My answer was as simple as it was sincere: I told the committee that Shilo was eleven years old, bush-wise and well-trained, and if I went to Olifants, there could be no question about it, so would he.

* * *

Prior to our arrival at Olifants, the lowveld had suffered two years of severe drought, which had only recently broken. We arrived on the reserve to begin work in February, the middle of the rainy season and arguably the hottest time of the year in the lowveld. The sweltering conditions were exacerbated by recent rains, which raised humidity levels and made the conditions uncomfortably muggy for our children. Ordinarily this was not a problem for Shilo, but without a pool nearby, it was particularly challenging. In conditions like this he would usually look for the nearest water and immerse himself in it as and when he needed to cool off, so what could be more convenient than a huge river no more than 30 metres from the office? But, as inviting as it was, swimming in it was just not an option. The Olifants Game Reserve straddles some 12 kilometres of the Olifants River, and like the Limpopo where Shilo was born, its cool murky pools are home to huge crocodiles. There is evidence enough to show that some of the reptilian monsters found in this area are over five metres in length. So, as inviting as it looked, this was one stretch of water Shilo was not allowed ever to go near, and for reasons that were painfully obvious.

As if to entrench our concerns, in the same week we started

working on Olifants, two large dogs were taken by crocodiles on the northern bank, directly opposite our office. Both dogs belonged to one of the landowners across the river. They were bush dogs that had grown up on this river, and knew these reptiles well; they'd seen what crocodiles were capable of and were naturally wary of them. I have no doubt that they had also been witness to some desperate struggles, particularly in the winter months when crocodiles fought to drown animals as large as zebra when they came down to drink. However, despite some of these scenarios playing out on the riverside in front of them, these visual lessons didn't help prevent the inevitable. You cannot teach a dog how to avoid crocodiles; in fact there is only one lesson a dog has to learn in an environment where crocodiles are known to occur, and that is to never go near the water's edge. And contrary to popular belief, even the waterbuck, a relatively large antelope which lives practically cheek by jowl with crocodiles, never quite gets their measure either.

Crocodiles are the epitome of stealth and cunning – even highly intelligent and extremely wary baboons are on the menu of these primitive reptiles. To watch a troop of baboons cross a narrow section of river, which they know to contain crocodiles, gives a measure of credibility to the walking on water story – well, they don't really walk on it; rather, it can be described as a meniscus-skimming, mad dash of abject fear, invariably accompanied by ear-piercing screams. So it never fails to astonish me when a crocodile manages to take a baboon ... and they do, regularly.

* * *

Shilo began to mellow with age; no longer did he whine impatiently when I spent too much time tying trout flies. He was content just to be with me; it was enough for him simply to be where he could see me, or to ride with me in the vehicle when I drove around in the course of my routine work. Whenever I took a walk in the bush he would accompany me, something we both really enjoyed, and as will be shown later, these walks were not without excitement and adventure. The fact that he went where I did also meant that I needn't worry about him wandering down to the river as much as I would have had he been younger and more active.

As parents of young children, Meagan and I had other fears to contend with, and there were certain precautions we needed to take to minimise the risks to our young children as well. There are good reasons to rope a kid. As a child Dino should have worn a long rope permanently tied around his waist, and the other end to either Meagan or myself. As he grew older and became more mobile we actually employed this practical measure when we went on hikes in the Mpumalanga highlands, otherwise his determination to venture perilously close to cliff edges would have resulted in him falling and injuring himself, or worse.

Toddlers are like tortoises, slow moving and easy to see; take your eye off them for a second, however, and they have the knack of quickly disappearing. At two years old, Dino was already dubbed the 'happy wanderer': his penchant to simply take off and head for destinations unknown was a constant nightmare for Meagan and me.

It was a Saturday and I'd decided to stay home and catch up with some chores that needed doing around the house. But things don't stop while I take a morning or day off; if I'm on the reserve there will invariably be something or someone that requires my attention. Distracted by a lengthy radio call, I'd left Dino and Shilo alone in the sandpit at the back of the house. The 'happy wanderer' seized the moment and decided to walk down the pathway from our house to the office, a distance of about 200 metres through the bush. This was a safe trip 99% of the time, but today just happened to be a '1%' situation, and the same day he chose to sneak off and visit mom. That alone would have been cause enough for panic, but compounding the peril was that during the early hours of that morning, a pride of lions had killed a young giraffe some 20 metres to the left of the pathway, and were still feeding on the kill!

Needless to say, Meagan had driven rather than walked down to the office that morning. So when Dino arrived in the doorway of the office clad in his Spiderman suit with Shilo at his heels, the blood drained from her face. Though only a toddler at the time, he must have registered some of the danger he had been exposed to when he saw the look of abject horror on his mother's face, confirmed by her high-pitched voice as she told him about the lions.

Dino responded by lisping the few words he knew, trying to reassure Meagan that he wasn't scared of the lions. 'I got this,' he declared, waving his plastic sword around menacingly. However, seeing that this allayed none of Meagan's anguish, he added: 'And Shilo was with me the whole way, mom.'

I suspect the lions were so engrossed with feeding they didn't notice as Dino and Shilo quietly walked down the pathway, a mere 20 metres away from them. To this day I remain convinced that Shilo must have known the lions were there, and having no way of restraining Dino without making him cry, which would no doubt have switched the lions' focus in an instant, he did the next best thing and went along with him, sticking as closely to his side as possible, protecting him the only way he knew how.

Admittedly it took a while, but eventually Meagan got over blaming men for being useless baby minders. In time I was allowed back into the pack as a responsible father, albeit with strict conditions, the details of which I won't go into here.

* * *

Olifants was a welcome change from commercial lodges. I was more involved with wildlife management than ever before, working for a group of like-minded shareholders whose prime focus was the ecological welfare of their game reserve. Before the fences between ourselves and the Klaserie Game Reserve came down we were a closed ecological system, which meant we needed to manage our game numbers more intensively, so we adopted a more hands-on approach than we do now. Monitoring the herbivore biomass in relation to the available vegetation and making the necessary adjustments was challenging and rewarding; I was making important decisions. Although I missed the Timbavati, I felt that at Olifants I was making a positive contribution to the reserve itself, and in turn to nature conservation in a broader sense. This was something I'd hankered for all my life.

There was an added challenge in the shape of the Richard's Bay via Hoedspruit railway line running through the reserve. Having trains hurtling through a big five game reserve meant that inevitably there were going to be collisions between trains and animals, and as might be expected, my life became inescapably influenced by this nemesis.

Minimising its negative effect on the reserve and its wildlife became a priority, but I soon learned that I needed to face reality and understand that – never mind the precautions taken, driver awareness campaigns, speed limits and speed monitoring devices – animals would get killed or injured by trains from time to time.

As frustrating as this is to accept at times, I'm reminded of a poster I once saw of a proud Sioux Indian warrior mounted on an Appaloosa pony. On his bronzed body he wore only a loinskin, a pair of buckskin moccasins and a full feathered headdress. In his hand was a spear, also decorated with the plumage of some huge beautiful bird. Dominating the foreground, stretching almost to the horizon, were thousands of American bison, grazing peacefully on the prairie. In the distant background was an 'iron horse', pulling dozens of carriages, belching plumes of smoke as it rolled across the landscape on steel rails that glinted in the sun. I have no idea what the Sioux word for 'Shit!' is, but I'm sure that it is exactly what that bemused Indian warrior was thinking as he gazed upon the train. Looking at this from another slant, there are those with as much passion for preserving the old steam trains as there is among those who wish to see bison back on the prairie in their thousands. Hopefully, some important lessons have been learned since then ... In the meantime, the options remain – to live with and around progress, or put on your war paint and fight ... unfortunately, except for the battle of the Little Big Horn, we all know what happened when the Sioux opted for the latter.

It is not always the big and the cumbersome that fall victim to the train, the small and precious do as well, as happened recently when three lion cubs were killed by the train on the Palm Loop section of the line. The news filled me with an overwhelming sadness, that helpless kind of sorrow, the kind where tears no longer give comfort. Reluctantly I turned to my son and asked him to come along in case I needed a hand. Dino is a tall, broad-shouldered lad, and though an aggressively competitive swimmer, he has a gentle nature, particularly when it comes to animals. If I could have spared him that morning's tragic scene, I would have. But all our field staff were out in the bush at the time. So without having to waste time looking for anyone else, he and I drove straight out and arrived on the scene within fifteen minutes of receiving the call.

It is ironic that this notoriously sharp bend in the line is located in the heart of the reserve's most popular lion nursery area. Nearly every lion born on the reserve takes its first breath within a few hundred metres of this 'death bend', which has also accounted for a number of other species over the years.

Dino helped me remove the carcasses from the tracks and then load them into the vehicle – although the cubs were only six months old, they were well nourished and surprisingly heavy. I looked at my son as he helped me that day, and although he put on a brave face, the emotion in his eyes was hard to conceal. It was clear to me that within his powerful chest beat a heart of compassion; I also knew Dino would never harden to this.

Then there was the scourge of poaching, and again we were to rely on our own devices, vigilance and persistence. Poaching and illegal hunting by some unscrupulous service personnel maintaining the railway line, as well as rapacious neighbours, posed its own fair share of misery. We realised there would be no help forthcoming from the authorities and that we were on our own: this resulted in our anti-poaching rangers taking on much of what used to be the provincial authorities' responsibility. Soon our rangers had become a force to be reckoned with.

Not only did we have our own poaching problems to contend with, but there is a piece of state-owned land across the

Olifants River, which, although not officially part of the reserve, is inescapably bound to Olifants, Balule and the Greater Kruger National Park ecologically. Unfortunately, it also happens to be a cesspit of escalating illegal hunting and poaching activity, and has steadily become the bane of our lives, and those of countless wild animals. More recently this area has been used as a springboard for rhino horn poachers' incursions into our reserve.

Due to apathy and a climate of lawlessness, South Africa has become a soft target for rhino poachers, illegal hunting and fishing, and the unlawful capture and export of rare and endangered species. Everything from abalone to rhino horn is up for grabs. At R35 000 per kilogram obtained by the poachers for rhino horn, it offers an irresistible reward for the risk and makes for dangerous and determined killers with whom we now have to contend.

Our anti-poaching efforts and surveillance equipment have resulted in a poacher being shot and killed and another wounded. Despite this, they will keep coming ... we may have kept the wolf from the door, but it's bumping and scratching with relentless determination.

26

WALKING IN THE BUSH

Walking with a dog in big game country is not unlike taking a dog for a stroll in New York's Central Park or down a country lane. That is, the enjoyment of the outing is what it's all about. So too in the African bushveld, except that there are a few more critters that can bite you, stomp on you or poke holes in you. Although the excitement and pleasure of being able to share your life walking with a well-trained dog is universal, it is in 'big five' country that the better disciplined dog comes into its own.

One of the most rewarding aspects of walking in the bush is being able to study nature up close. Animal sounds, particularly bird calls, are infinitely more audible – especially the more delicate notes which are so much clearer than when you hurtle around in a 4x4. I guess this is as nature intended – our sensory organs not having been designed to pick up nature's stimuli at 40 kilometres per hour. Despite our relatively useless noses, smells are more noticeable; even the most delicate scents tend to linger. Watching a dog's superior hearing and sense of smell put to use in the bush never ceases to fill me with admiration. How I envied the way Shilo's nose could suck up a stream of scent with billions of molecules of information, and in a single whiff disseminate the data around his brain and process what he needed in an instant. Sometimes repeated rapid sniffs would be necessary to confirm direction and source ... and danger.

I have always been intrigued with tracks and the art of tracking, and this is not limited to following the spoor of the larger animals. Knowing how to glean the subtle signs that leave clues to the intricate lives of the smaller, relatively unknown nocturnal creatures holds a deep fascination for me – and there's no better way to get acquainted with these lesser observed features than on foot. At times, the combination of my eyes on the spoor and Shilo's extraordinary senses and natural instinct produced great results.

Shilo was naturally wary when we walked in the bush together. Cautious to a fault, he would always stick really close to me, at times so close that his body would brush against my lower legs, like a zebra foal sticks to its mother, except that in this instance, I suspect it was for my protection and not the other way around. It didn't matter to him whether I carried a rifle or not; Shilo never let his guard down. Knowing he was there, and feeling him there, was always reassuring; it also allowed me to relax a little and take in the beauty of our surrounds, or focus on tracking.

I often wondered if this demeanour was an instinctive response when we entered primal territory, or was it due to an accumulation of knowledge of the dangers that lurked in the bush, from the experience gained over the years since he was a puppy? I couldn't say for sure. However, what I do know is that Shilo was a different dog when we were outside big game country. His attitude would change completely, especially when we were at the seaside, where he always appeared to be more relaxed. Here he'd scamper ahead of me on scouting forays, usually at a frenetic pace, then come rushing back to me, only to repeat this antic over and over again. It was clear from this that Shilo could differentiate between high-risk and low-risk situations.

Like Shilo, I have always found it very difficult to sit still or lie roasting my skin on a beach. I much prefer to get about and explore the shoreline, or spend hours fascinated with the myriad forms of life found in rock pools and shallow lagoons. I think I prefer fly fishing to sitting and waiting patiently for a bite on a baited hook because prospecting with a fly is far more exploratory and dynamic. When we head up into the high country, climbing in the Drakensberg, I love to explore, poking around in holes, rock overhangs and shallow caves. I am fascinated by the

Bushman rock art on the walls and ceilings of the many sand-stone shelters, and can't resist tentatively scratching around in the substrate of these dwelling places, hoping to find a little piece of ancient evidence, trying to imagine what life must have been like for these early hunter-gatherers.

Developing an interest in archaeology has opened my eyes and stretched my horizons: seeing my surroundings from a different perspective, I have come to know that there is more to be found in many of Africa's game reserves than big game animals. Knowing that mankind originated in Africa – more specifically, South Africa – makes it especially intriguing.

* * *

Winter in the arid bushveld of South Africa invariably signals the onset of resource scarcity. Rain-filled shallow pans and mud wallows are now all but dry, and the greener forage is confined mostly to riverine and drainage lines. The Olifants River's shallow winter flow provides the only drinking water for miles, and the associated vegetation on the floodplain remains greener for quite some time into the dry season. Essentially this is where the plains game now congregates in larger numbers, and this doesn't go unnoticed. Predators are quick to pick up on these concentrations, and this is where the 'action' often takes place.

In early autumn, although we hadn't yet cut into the teeth of winter, herds of elephant had already started to move onto the floodplain to feed. Usually by this time of the day, they would have started feeling the heat and could be found cooling off in the Olifants River drinking and bathing, or resting in the shade of the huge riverine trees. Buffalo that had rested up in the broken hills during the heat of the day would begin stirring, and making their way down to drink in the river, where they'd feed on the tender young reeds and the grass that sprouted as the water receded. There were still a few hours before the rowdy hippo would move out of the river's shrinking pools, and head inland to feed at night.

There's good reason why people in warmer climates take a

couple of hours off after lunch, usually until about four, to have a 'siesta' Nothing much happens at this time of the day anyway, they argue, so why not take a nap? Despite my Latin heritage I have never been big on snoozing the afternoon away, and had no inclination to take it easy after lunch this particular Sunday either. Instead I shouldered the .416 Rigby, put on my hat, and filled a three-litre hydration back pack with water. There was no need to call Shilo; he was up in an instant and at the door before I could reach the handle. He knew the big rifle usually meant walking in the bush, which he loved; besides that, I suspect that walking with me made him feel important. Shilo knew I relied on his keen senses and alertness in this environment – here, where animals had a decided edge, and modern man was apt to flounder.

Despite the lack of game movement at that time of the day, it was a little cooler than anticipated, so we made steady progress along the well-worn game paths. These animal highways are usually covered in tracks and signs of game, and knowing how to interpret the clues can provide you with a wealth of information. But sometimes you need to rely on more than your eyesight to read what is at your feet, as happened this day. Suddenly Shilo stopped, put his nose to the ground and moved off the path for a couple of metres, then quickly resumed his position close to me. I bent over to see what he'd been sniffing, and saw a faint drag mark that ran across the path; then on a sandy section of a small drainage line close by, where the tracks were easier to see, I was now also able to make out leopard pug marks – those of a big tom, by the size – on either side of the scrape. This was no elephant trunk scrape or python track, it was clear that this leopard had killed something that morning and dragged it across the game path.

Intrigued, I began to follow the faint drag mark, which was relatively easy to see, until the tracks began heading up into the hills away from the river. Although the rocky terrain made tracking difficult, the kill was being dragged over rocks, where friction removed enough hairs for me to follow. Were it not for this, firstly we would not have known it was an impala that had been killed, and secondly, what route the leopard had taken.

Shilo could have followed the trail on scent alone, but that would have been very dangerous. I didn't want to send him on ahead and have him bump into the leopard by himself. Seeing Shilo alone could very well trigger a defensive response by the leopard, and I wouldn't risk that. I was curious to see the kill, though. I knew it was highly likely that the leopard would sense our approach, particularly mine, and move off, only to return later when we'd moved on. Contrary to popular belief, not all leopard kills are placed in trees, in fact in the thick bushveld woodland of Olifants Game Reserve, some kills have been known to be stashed in thick bush. I suspect that relatively low hyena numbers and the abundance of thick cover may be contributing factors for this adaptive behaviour.

* * *

Having eaten contentedly on the impala it had killed on the floodplain early that morning, the leopard now lay panting in the shade of a milkberry tree that grew between the huge boul-ders of an enormous soapstone outcrop. Protected from the ravages of elephant, its waxy, evergreen leaves provided a protective shroud from the sun, where this shaded patch remained relatively cool for most of the day. The old tom had used this spot for many years; he felt safe and secure here. From this vantage point he had a commanding 360-degree view of the bush below, while remaining practically invisible in the dappled shadows. Uncomfortably full and needing a drink of water to help digest his bellyful of fresh meat, he lay there guarding his kill against the ravages of vultures. Though it was hidden from their incredible eyesight, it would be the short-tailed eagle, a specialist at locating difficult-to-see carrion at close range, which would give the game away if the kill was left unguarded. Vultures have voracious appetites, and would consume an impala in less time than it would take to slake his thirst. The leopard had endured thirst before, he'd waited before, so he would wait again, and then sneak off under the cover of darkness, rather than leave his kill unguarded.

267

The warm air began to lift, drifting upslope as the day cooled down. A gentle shift in the breeze was all it took for the leopard to get a whiff of that most dreaded sour odour, a smell unique in the animal kingdom, the unmistakable scent of man. It entered his nose and filled his heart with fear; today, the invasion of his privacy wasn't going to come from up above, but from down below. He stopped panting, his eyes widened and his ears flattened; he had survived to a ripe old age by being discreet and avoiding confrontation, and today would be no exception.

The leopard could see us approaching; there was simply no time to hoist his impala up into the tree now. Turning his powerful head to have one more look at his prize, he was unable to control the low growl that seemed to start at the very root of his tail. Reluctantly he slipped off the rock where he'd left the remains of the kill, and with only a fleeting, irritated flash of a white-tipped tail, disappeared into the bush, his spotted coat becoming one with the shadows.

In the grass below the outcrop, where a huge slab of rock tapered down into the soil, we came across the sun-bleached skull and pelvis bone of a small antelope, probably an impala ewe. Holes in the delicate skull appeared to have been made by the canines of a leopard, and the back of the skull hadn't been crushed as is typical of a hyena's feeding pattern on a scavenged carcass. This was further evidence to indicate that the prey had been kept out of reach, probably wedged high in the branches of the milkberry tree. As leopards are the only predators on earth capable of hoisting a 70 kilogram antelope into a tree, there was no doubt as to the culprit. Here I imagined the remains would have completely desiccated over time and then fallen to the ground as they were pushed out of the way when a fresh kill was placed in the branches. A few other nondescript animal remains, including a small warthog tusk that had also slipped down the rock slope, confirmed my suspicion that the old tom had been using this spot for a long time.

* * *

The leopard's lair ceased to be a secret the moment Shilo's nose cut his trail, but we would never have found the soapstone cave had we not followed the drag mark left by the impala carcass as it was dragged through the bush from the distant Olifants River floodplain to this spot.

Confident that the leopard was not hanging around, I allowed Shilo to sniff at the remains of the impala. Although this was the same kill that his nose had picked up nearly a kilometre away, now the smell of the leopard was overpowering, so he cautiously craned his neck towards the carcass, his body quivering slightly from the tension. As I watched his reaction, I just couldn't resist coming up quietly from behind and grabbing his back leg, growling as I did. He yelped with fright and back-pedalled so fast that his ears slapped against his jowls. In hindsight, perhaps that scare took a couple of years off his life. Fortunately, within a second or two, he realised it was just a bad joke on my part, then broke into a smile and sneezed a few times, not that he thought it was funny, but because he'd been embarrassed. After all, he wasn't a youngster any more.

Moving around to what I presumed was the front of the out-crop, I noticed a deep recess tapering into the back of the lean-to. It was not very deep, but it had a high ceiling, and was large enough to have sheltered human beings at some stage. A few porcupine quills on the floor were the only evidence of the most recent occupants.

The leopard and its impala carcass now all but forgotten, Shilo and I went in and began rummaging around. Startled by a few tomb bats that flew out of the cave inches above my head, which automatically made me look up at the rock ceiling, I noticed immediately that it was blacker than the sides of the cave; clearly fires had been made there at some stage. Now my imagination was fired up: who made the fires, when and what did they cook? I wondered. On one side of the wide entrance were the remains of a small dry stone wall about 40 centimetres high; most of the stones had been toppled by baboons, presumably foraging for scorpions and other insects. I suspect this wall had originally been used to protect the inhabitants against large predators, hostile fellow humans or bad weather – my thoughts were exploring all the possible scenarios when Shilo suddenly sneezed again. I turned around to see his normally black muzzle was now light grey, giving him a bear-like appearance. Although it looked comical, I didn't laugh; I knew immediately what it was – he had dug up an ash pit under the soil near the cave entrance. I could hardly contain my excitement. I had read that old ash pits were the daily diaries of the primitive people that made them, and much could be learned about their way of life by studying the contents of the ash. Needless to say, it didn't take too much scratching to reveal evidence that the cave had been used by relatively modern humans.

I only found small shards of pottery, nothing bigger than a match box. The one side of most of the pieces was blackened, indicating that they'd been fired, possibly, and/or that the pots were used to cook in. A few blackened bones of a larger ungulate of wildebeest or kudu proportions appeared among many smaller bones. I knew porcupines bring bones back to their burrows to gnaw on, but most of the bones I had unearthed had been burned at some stage, and none of them bore the unmistakable tooth marks of these huge adze-toothed rodents. The light was beginning to fade, and I was not equipped to excavate properly, Shilo lay there watching me with bemused boredom. I just knew he'd be covered in fleas.

Goodness knows what else lurked in the mixture of bat guano and powdery soil that made up the floor of the cave, but I also knew that there would be time enough to sort that out. I couldn't wait to get back and tell Meagan of our discovery; I knew she was as keen as I was about these things, and that she'd want to see the cave.

The three of us returned to the cave the next weekend, equipped with a few plastic bags, some small digging tools and a coarse sieve. Shilo, who was not much interested in archaeology, immediately went to where the leopard kill had been stashed the week before, only to find that the enigmatic spotted phantom had returned to claim his kill. To satisfy my curiosity, I left Meagan at the cave while Shilo and I followed the now barely perceptible drag mark, only to find that the leopard had moved its kill further up the hill to another smaller outcrop of boulders. This time he had taken the remains up into a boer bean tree, where he had apparently finished his meal in peace. All we found was the head of the impala, and a few bones still attached to some skin dangling from one of the branches.

*   *   *

Women can find things men can't. I believe they have a better eye for foraging, they always seem to find those socks or shirts you could swear have been mislaid or stolen, and they tend to be more systematic and patient. I guess that's why so many women make excellent archaeologists and pathologists. I suspect it has more than a little to do with the fact that they have spent a lifetime learning how to find things in their handbags, where in amongst the plethora of paraphernalia they carry, they can sometimes locate stuff by feel alone!

Meagan is no different; by the time Shilo and I returned she had unearthed some more pieces of pottery and bones, but the smirk on her face told me she'd found something else far more interesting. Dipping into her back pack, which she'd propped up against the crumbling wall, she pulled out a flattish stone, not just any stone, but a stone that had been clearly shaped by man; in her hand she held a stone hand-axe which she then gave me to look at – although slightly big for her hand, it fitted mine perfectly. The bottom edge of the tool was worn, showing that it had seen some use in its time, which was probably why it had been discarded. Later we uncovered a hollow grinding stone and two stone scrapers. By midday we had uncovered enough pieces of pottery to piece a pot together, which revealed its shape and design. Later we found some primitive art on a flat piece of soapstone – it could also have been the idle doodling of a caveman, but the fact that it was unmistakably man-made was what made it so fascinating.

Intrigued, I began to research the history of the inhabitants of the area. What I found was that although we had uncovered stone tools, they may have been used as recently as a few hundred years ago. In fact, some of the locals still use crude pointed stones, not unlike the ancient hand axe Meagan found, to crush marula nuts in order to extract the oil-rich kernels. The pottery we found indicates that the last time people occupied the cave was around the 1800s, and though not as old as I would have liked them to be, the relics were poignant evidence of a lifestyle from the past.

Fifteen years later, compelled to defend our rhino against the increased onslaught by rhino poachers, we concentrated our patrols in the extreme northeast of our reserve. Until a few months before, it had been our quietest region, rarely frequented by either our field rangers or poachers. Focusing on locating possible poacher's camp sites, rather than snare sweeping, the rangers came across more evidence of primitive smelting ovens and the crude temporary bases these early miners built. The pieces of pottery and the hand axe they found were very similar to those Shilo had helped Meagan and me find at the soapstone cave; this time the concave receptacle in which nuts were placed was also located.

* * *

The Kruger National Park's first warden, James Stevenson Hamilton, took a special interest in the history of the region. His *The Lowveld – its Wildlife and its People* describes how the nineteenth century was fraught with faction fights. One of the most significant of these occurred when a Zulu general by the name of Manukosi deserted the Zulu king Shaka, taking with him nearly five thousand warriors and other loyal followers. Manukosi fled northwards until he reached the Limpopo River, wreaking havoc in the lowveld. Shaka then sent a regiment under General Nxaba to destroy Manukosi, but many starved to death while others fell victim to Africa's biggest killer, malaria. The survivors managed to get as far as the Olifants River but, unable to continue, were forced to return to Zululand, needlessly fearing death from Shaka, as in their absence, Dingaan had come to power. In Stevenson Hamilton's words, 'with the enemy (Nxaba) gone, Manukosi assumed the name Sotshangane. Clans who had submitted to Manukosi were now called Ba-Tshangane, while the Zulu overlords were known as the Ngoni. To be um-Tshangane was considered an honour. Accordingly, it gradually became the ambition of every Tsonga to be considered a Tshangane.'

In a more recent history, the late Carl Weavind, a former landowner in the Klaserie Nature Reserve, discovered that a Pedi clan known as the Sekhororo moved from the Lydenburg/Orighstad area into the area where our reserve stands today. Their northern boundary was the Olifants River, which they called the Lepelle River. An offshoot of this tribe settled in the area where the Klaserie Private Nature Reserve is now situated. The main kraal of the Sekhororo tribe is thought to have been located on present-day Dundee. This farm straddles the Balule/Klaserie nature reserves on our north-eastern boundary, which formed part of the area they called Makhutsi (place of peace or tranquillity). From the description of the surrounding area, I imagine that the Dundee Trigonometric Beacon, situated at the northeastern end of Olifants River Game Reserve, would have been roughly the centre of the area they occupied at the time.

Depending mainly on hunting and whatever the bush had to offer for their living had honed the Sekhororo people into undisputed bush experts. To this day, their descendants are still some of the finest trackers in Africa, and in my opinion, their bush knowledge and hunting skills surpass those of the Zulu. They needed the skills, too, as cattle could not survive here in viable numbers, apparently because of the tsetse fly. It is strange, by the way, that the historical records and observations make no mention of predators in this context.

An interesting development then occurred, involving the absorption of the Karanga people, skilled miners and metalworkers who had moved down from Southern Zimbabwe. Their knowledge was passed on to the Sekhororo, which greatly improved their primitive metalworking skills, so much so, that the weapons and hunting tools they now manufactured became sought-after and coveted. A number of their very primitive smelting ovens and some of their iron slag deposits can still be seen today on Olifants River Game Reserve, not too far from where the soapstone cave is situated. They're not much to look at, and unless you really know what you're looking for, you would walk right past one without noticing it.

The furnace area is approximately a metre in diameter, with blow ports situated at three evenly spaced points. It appears the walls may have been about 20 centimetres high when they were in production, but I'm not sure about this, as they are now badly eroded and damaged, and barely five centimetres high. Besides the odd slag heap, some old pottery shards and a few purposefully piled stones indicating some rudimentary shelter, there is no evidence to suggest that these metalworkers lived there in formal communities for any meaningful period of time. They were probably transient miners, trading the raw minerals they mined for supplies to supplement the wild animals they hunted for food. I like to imagine them overnighting in our cave, cracking their store of marula nuts and gazing over the smoke of their fire to the unchanging bushveld below.

The Voortrekker Louis Trichardt recorded his arrival on the banks of the Olifants River on 2 October 1837 – and by all accounts, it wasn't the big picnic then that it is today. These early pioneers were beset by the tsetse fly, which wiped out their cattle, and malaria indiscriminately accounted for numerous lives. According to Trichardt's diary, the Sekhororo had heard that they would be put to work by the Boers, and fled this threat by crossing the Olifants River and moving to the area where Phalaborwa, which means 'better than the South', stands today. This may have been partially true, though it is more likely their motivation for moving to the area north of the river was the relative abundance of metals there.

The area formerly inhabited by the Sekhororo was quickly filled by the Shangaans of Mozambique, and it is the descendants of this tribe who are still predominantly found in the lowveld region, particularly the area in which the Kruger National Park and the adjacent private nature reserves are located. Like the Sekhororo, they are excellent hunters and trackers. Today, they are sought after for their dying and disappearing skills and many are found employed in the hunting, safari and eco-tourism industry.

* * *

There's a lot to be said for developing a passion for exploration in both man and dog – and for following your nose along curious pathways! Be soft on impatience and don't haul back on the lead or with your command too often. Allowing your dog his head will not only enrich his walking experience, but who knows, yours as well. Had we not been on foot, Shilo would not have picked up the scent of the leopard kill, and had our curiosity to follow the drag not led us to its lair, we might never have discovered the soapstone cave. And had Shilo's sense of smell and innate spirit of adventure not remained as acute as ever despite his increasing age, he might never have sniffed out the old ash heap, and its secret history might still lie buried ... and our lives the poorer, but for that knowledge.

The hidden dimension of the world that would have been lost to me had I not walked with Shilo and master trackers in the bush has often left me awestruck. I can imagine a time when an expert tracker employed for forensic tracking will command a higher fee than any other profession you can name! It is a dying art for which there is a rapidly growing need, and no university on earth can train you for the job. Technology will replace most of our abilities in the foreseeable future, but it will never replace the combination of an intelligent dog's nose and the reckoning eye of a skilled tracker, particularly in field conditions.

27

THE BUFFALO WE DIDN'T BALANCE

I remember that morning like it was yesterday. The sun was just breaking through the uppermost branches of the trees on the eastern horizon as I drove up to the slatted fence that screened the guest cottage complex. The Olifants Game Reserve annual audit was in progress, and auditor Hennie Nel and those of his juniors who had drawn the prized straws to spend a few days in the bush had been hard at work since the day before. I could see Hennie standing on the lawn in his pyjama shorts and a pair of running shoes, gazing out on the languid Olifants River, which hadn't received much spate water and was beginning to fine off. In one hand he held a dripping rusk, and in the other what appeared to be a mug of strong coffee.

'Morning, Hennie, did you sleep well?' I called.

'Very well, thanks, Mario, but you should have warned me about Ron – man, can he party!'

Ron Hopkins, our company accountant, had already been crunching numbers since 7am. Ron was notoriously difficult to keep up with, pint for pint that is, and apparently Hennie had found out the hard way.

'I'm sure you'll survive,' I said unsympathetically. 'But you've always said you wanted to come along with me on duty in big five country, and today I've got a job for you.'

Hennie couldn't hide his yearning to be in big five country. He was a man torn, and would often say that if ever there was anything he could help me with while he was here, I was not to hesitate to ask him. He told me he'd love to go into the veld with me just to be among the big five, in particular the notorious buffalo for which he had a special respect and admiration. Unfortunately nothing ever cropped up that warranted me calling him out. Also the financial year end dates meant that Hennie was never around when the more dramatic aspects of game management took place. The annual game census, micro-chipping of our rhino, game capture or culling operations were invariably confined to the cooler winter months, so for years his audits coincided with nothing much more than the day-to-day running of the reserve. Although he had made it clear that it needn't be to do something special or out of the ordinary, I could not justify taking him away from the audit for hours on end while we drove around the reserve on a routine patrol, for example, or when I needed to repair a pump, supervise veld management teams or road labour gangs, on the off chance that something out of the ordinary would crop up.

Hennie's eyebrows shot up and his eyes narrowed as he squinted into the rising sun behind me. 'What do you mean?' he said.

'Hennie, I know you can use a scoped hunting rifle, but are you comfortable using a big bore with iron sights?'

'Yes, I have an open-sighted .375 magnum of my own. *Jy weet mos*, Afrikaners are experts in the use of open sights; after all, during the Boer War we gave the British a musketry lesson they have never forgotten, and all we had were our Mauser rifles with iron sights ... but why do you ask?'

'Bloody train ploughed into a herd of seven buffalo bulls early this morning and we have a wounded buffalo on our hands,' I said. 'I need to follow up on him to ascertain the extent of his injuries, and need a back-up gun in case things get nasty. I was thinking that if you could carry the company's .375 magnum, which is identical to the one you have at home, I'll use my .416 Rigby. Are you ok with that?'

'Of course,' Hennie replied without hesitation. 'Just let me put some clothes on and get my hat.'

* * *

Had this incident occurred a couple of years previously, Shilo would have been part of the team enlisted to track the buffalo. However, he was now twelve, and stiffening up a little, and to ask my ageing dog to help track one of the most dangerous animals on earth at this stage of his life was something I would not even consider. We were going to be on our own on this one; Shilo would be staying home today.

Leaving Hennie to get prepared, I drove up to the house to drop Shilo off and to pick up a few essentials I needed. When we pulled up under the carport a few minutes later, I got out to help him off the vehicle. Shilo was not as nimble as he used to be, and the tailgate of the Land Cruiser was high off the ground, so occasionally he'd stumble when jumping off too quickly. By letting him clamber down from the vehicle aided by my hand supporting his chest, I'd soften his landing and spare him the indignity of falling on his nose. Once on the ground, Shilo turned around and looked straight up at me, his tail wagging; he had sensed some urgency in my tone when I'd spoken to Hennie about the buffalo. There was that unmistakably serious look in Shilo's loyal brown eyes which always sparkled with enthusiasm, they never seemed to age or grow weary, and they always said so much. I was sure he wanted me to know that he was there for me if I needed him.

I knelt down, and now on the same level, grasped his silky soft head in my hands. Pressing my lips firmly against his now greying muzzle, I could feel his canines under the relatively soft skin of his jowl as I kissed him. Then I pulled away at arm's length to focus, holding his head cupped in my hands, and looked into his eyes.

'I know how you feel, my boy, but today I need you to stay home and hold the fort for me,' I lied.

But Shilo saw through the white lie; it hurt me to see the dejection and reluctant resignation in his body language. His tail stopped wagging and he dropped his head as he turned away and slowly made his way to the door. Shilo was starting to get used to these excuses, and he knew I wouldn't relent to his enthusiastic insistence ... he'd tried that a few times before, and to no avail.

* * *

Having packed the rifles and ammunition, water and a spare portable two-way radio into the vehicle, I drove down to pick up Hennie, who was eager as a new recruit waiting for a lift to take him on his first pass. We then went around to the staff village and collected the two game scouts. One of them, a man named Timane, was known to be an excellent tracker, so I was relieved to see him standing there as we drove up. Somewhat handicapped without Shilo, I had a feeling we were going to need Timane that day. The other man, Johann, was not in the same league, and at that point in his career would have had difficulty tracking an elephant through a mud wallow. To date he hadn't done much to impress either me or his anti-poaching team mates with his bush skills, but he was physically strong, a good back-up man, which is a great help when poachers try to resist arrest. Although Johann did not show much promise as a tracker, he was young and I hoped that with time and experience, he would develop the necessary skills. At this point however, I reasoned that if Timane concentrated on the tracking, Johann could give him moral support by keeping an eye on the bush ahead.

We made our way across the Palm Loop's sandy river bed, crossed over the train lines that ran parallel with the servitude road, and were on the scene in less than fifteen minutes. The bloody curled end of the buffalo bull's horn was still lying in the middle of the road next to the railway tracks, the 'Spoornet yellow' paint smear on it identifying the culprit beyond any doubt. It had been broken off at the point where the classic curl of the buffalo's horn joins the formidable amour-plate-like frontal section known as the 'boss'. Apparently he was the luckier of the two buffalo which the train had collided with that morning. Another old bull, which I'd had to shoot earlier because of a broken back leg, lay in the grass about 30 metres from the tracks. The other five had apparently escaped unscathed.

Within a few minutes of us arriving, a team of labourers who had been following behind on the tractor and trailer duly arrived to load the carcass. While they busied themselves squabbling like a pack of hyenas over the mountain of fresh meat, Timane called me over to a patch of bush not too far from the railroad tracks.

Under the protective overhang of a velvet corkwood a pool of blood and trampled grass indicated that the wounded buffalo had spent quite some time mulling things over before collecting himself and heading off into the bush. Having a horn smashed off was obviously a shocking experience even for this extremely tough animal. Knowing what force it had been subjected to, there was also the real possibility that he had suffered more than only the injury to his horn. We needed to find this buffalo as soon as possible and check him out before the trail went cold.

Incredibly, the broken-horned bull's tracks indicated that he'd crossed back over the railway, a clear indication that he made no association between his recent traumatic ordeal and the steel lines that carried the train. The droplets of blood were getting more difficult to find, and although this made tracking more difficult, at least it confirmed that the wound's clotting process was beginning to stem the blood flow. Only now and then when he brushed past a branch would a small fresh blood smear confirm we were still with the right buffalo. Although he was covering a lot of ground steadily, we were able to keep up easily. Following a single animal is less complicated than when the spoor is mingled with others of a similar size, especially now that the blood spoor had all but dried up, leaving us with little else to go on but the tracks.

It is always humbling to watch a good tracker at work; I envy them, and am ceaselessly fascinated by their timeless skill. For me, as a white man born and raised in a city, I feel handicapped; it always seems as if this was the one 'bush exam' I only just managed to scrape through. As the terrain got rockier, Timane really began to show his mettle under some trying conditions. We had covered about three kilometres and the sun was climbing; the cicadas now intensified their piercing metallic 'zizz' which began to ring in our ears. Irritating minute black flies sought the perspiration on our foreheads and around our eyes and occasionally one would get stuck in the moisture on our eyeballs. Any attempt to remove these delicate insects from your eye would cause them to excrete their acidic body fluids, not the most pleasant sensation. It was time to take a break, so we stopped for a drink of water. I passed some energy bars around which we chewed on while slowly cooling down in the shade of a huge marula tree. The smell of its ripe fruit hung in the warm, still air, which made us quite hungry – besides the rusks and coffee early that morning, we'd eaten nothing all day.

Baboons had evidently eaten most of the fruit that had fallen on the ground earlier that morning. Empty skins lay strewn about, discarded when they had popped the whole pip and surrounding flesh into their mouths. Here and there a few fruits that had been overlooked lay ripening in the sun; these we picked up. Choosing the riper yellow ones, we sucked on the tart/sweet Vitamin C-laden juice until our teeth squeaked.

Hennie didn't appear to be as preoccupied with baboon leftovers as the rest of us. The toffee-like consistency of the energy slab he'd bitten into required rather deliberate jaw movements. Thankfully Hennie had a good set of teeth, as chewing these bars didn't appear to be something you could rush. It was obvious he had other thoughts he was chewing over in his mind.

'This must be what it is like to hunt buffalo,' he said eventually, taking his gaze off the bush and looking down at the rifle he was holding. 'You're right Mario, this rifle is exactly like the one I have, except that mine hasn't done a day's work since I bought it, so it doesn't have as many dings and scratches on its stock as this old veteran has.'

'Yes, in essence we are hunting this buffalo, but not to kill him,' I said. 'Keep your voice to a low whisper and use hand signals whenever possible – you know sound travels surprisingly far in the bush.'

Hennie nodded. Shouldering my backpack, I grabbed my rifle and motioned to the scouts that we needed to get going. '*Andiamo*' (let's go), I whispered in my late father's mother tongue, which I disgracefully admit I'm unable to speak fluently. Timane needed no urging: since he was fluent in Portuguese and Tsonga, perhaps a familiar Latin bell had rung.

A fuller answer to Hennie's rhetorical question would have been that an exploratory follow-up on an injured buffalo poses a greater danger to the hunter than a straightforward hunt.

Furthermore, as in this situation, it is always more complicated when discretion is required. If there is no intention of killing an animal unless it is absolutely necessary, it means extra care and more time is required before a decision is made. This time delay is a huge handicap to the person holding the rifle, and equates to a massive increase in the risk when hunting down a wounded member of the big five, particularly buffalo. When a buffalo decides to charge, invariably there is only one thing that will stop him, his death or yours! This could be why the phrase 'He who hesitates is lost' was coined – but not 'lost' as in the Hansel and Gretel sense, rather with the deceased connotation.

Moving quietly through the dense raisin bush and commiphora woodland, we stopped every now and again to scan the bush ahead, even though this tactic hampered our progress. We needed to anticipate where the buffalo would be lying up, and if possible get a good look at him without him being aware of our presence, even if only for a few seconds. However, this buffalo hadn't stopped once since we had been on his tracks, and there was no sign that he was slowing down, nor had there been any visual contact for nearly four hours. Usually when buffalo get an inkling that you're on their trail, they will turn around at some point and wait, sometimes doubling back to watch the trail. Concealing their immense bulk in the shadows of the thickest bush they can find, they will stand motionless, listening and waiting to see what is following them, or to try and pick up the scent of their pursuers, often moving on long before you see or hear them. The spoor confirmed that he did neither, so I was reasonably sure that up to that point the old bull had no idea he was being followed.

Suddenly Timane stopped and bent down to feel a splattered dung pat with the back of his finger. His eyes widened: '*Lo Nyati, yena hai kashane, yena duza,*' he whispered. (The buffalo is not far away, he is close by.)

Hennie needed no translation; I saw him clutch the rifle as if it were about to fall out of his hands, and thought what a good decision it had been to invite him along. Not that his insurance company would have approved – auditors don't usually chase after wounded buffalo while on company audits. He had proved to be no burden that morning. In fact, having hunted since a young boy Hennie knew how to walk quietly in the bush. It was comforting to have someone behind me who knew how to use a rifle (although very few Afrikaans farmers don't). I also noted with approval that there were no apparent ill-effects from the previous evening he'd spent celebrating with Ron – in fact he appeared remarkably fit and alert. Not once did he think about the audit or the office. Hennie understood what was required of him, and was totally focused on the task at hand, as one has to be in these dangerous situations.

* * *

Crossing our southern cutline, we moved into an area of undulating terrain characterised by small sandy drainage lines and washes with thick overgrown verges. The spoor led straight into this area, it appeared from where our buffalo was headed that he was looking for somewhere shady to lie up for the day. Following his tracks on a well-worn game trail, we approached a small dry stream bed. The pathway was relatively well defined and continued down a slope through the sandy wash and up the other side. However, the bush on either side of it formed a wall of dense foliage, a natural hedge. Effectively the only open area was the passage going through it, and the dry stream bed itself, and even though the buffalo's tracks had now left the path, we had no choice but to continue on it. We followed Timane and Johann cautiously, making our way down the sloping bank, unavoidably crunching the loose quartz gravel underfoot as we went. This did not help matters in the stealthy approach department at all. We had now effectively lost the advantage; we had announced ourselves.

Something made the hair on the back of my neck rise through the cool sweat. Suddenly, from deep within the tangle of a downed velvet corkwood tree, branches snapped and cracked like rifle shots going off, as the buffalo bull burst out of his cocoon and confronted us. The bush-wise Timane dropped to his knees in case I needed to take a shot at the buffalo from behind him, but in his haste to get away, Johann back-pedalled so quickly that he fell backwards onto his backside. Now unable to get a solid foothold and stand up, he resorted to running on all fours as fast as his hands and legs would take him, almost knocking Timane over in the process. Thankfully the buffalo was just as surprised as we were, and possibly Johann and his crab-walk-cum-break-dancing routine may have averted its attention from us momentarily.

All the while Hennie stood at my left shoulder, ready to back me in case the buffalo decided to charge, and although he hadn't uttered a sound, I knew he was there. A second or twenty-two ticked by as the buffalo stood in front of us, his one-horned head – no less formidable or dangerous – held high, his glistening broad black nostrils thrust out towards us, fully flared, attempting to inhale every molecule of our scent. Still the charge didn't come. Instead, after what seemed an eternity, the buffalo snorted loudly and shook his head in a low sweeping motion that almost banged his chin against his knee, then turning nearly a ton of body weight around in an instant, ran up the pathway on the opposite bank. I couldn't see much of him as the springy foliage closed behind his broad rump, so wasn't able to monitor how his limbs were functioning as he ran off; instead, I relied more on how he sounded. The even, drumming gallop of the buffalo's heavy hoof beats on the hard ground had me reasonably sure he was moving well.

Turning to Hennie, I said that I thought the buffalo appeared to be okay, and judging from how quickly it had turned, and from what I could hear as it moved off, it seemed to be moving well. Nevertheless I suggested that while there was sufficient light left, we should try to locate him once more and take another look at him, just to be absolutely sure. Trying to lighten things up a little and hoping to elicit a smile, I added: 'This unfortunate buffalo only has one horn now, so he's never going to be able to balance his looks.'

Hennie wasn't listening to my feeble attempt at humour; his

eyes had narrowed to mere slits as he looked straight ahead, staring intently into the bush from where, who knows, the buffalo might have charged us at any second. Without turning or shifting focus, he said, 'Mario, I think we should rather give him the benefit of the doubt.'

It was apparent that Hennie had had enough for one day ... come to think of it, so had the buffalo. Timani was smiling now ... we'd all had enough.

'Okay, let's go home,' I said.

* * *

That evening, instead of the usual banter from Hennie, Shilo and I were greeted by a rather pensive man sitting around a blazing log fire on the banks of the Olifants River. Sipping his beer straight from the bottle while staring fixedly at the flames in mesmerised contemplation, he gave the appearance of a man at peace with himself. Reflecting on the day, he told me that since the exhilarating close-range face-to-face encounter with the one-horned bull that morning, his respect and admiration for buffalo had grown considerably. To have experienced at first-hand how these formidable animals had earned their legendary reputation was indeed a rare privilege, he said.

Shilo stared up at us, listening intently; he could tell by the tone of our voices that something special had happened in the bush that day. The flickering firelight reflecting in his eyes said it as clearly as if he'd mouthed the words ... he wished he'd been along.

Hennie had probably been as close as one can get to the most challenging confrontation in the world of dangerous game, and he had faced up to those inner demons that lesser men have been known to give in to. He had been on a buffalo 'hunt' in every sense of the word, an experience that he will never forget in his life. Most importantly, this showdown was achieved without it having to culminate in the animal's death ... or worse. Who could possibly ask for more? Above all, he had exercised a restraint and calculating cool-headedness truly worthy of an auditor. I didn't envy him having to face the auditing version of the 'grindstone' the following morning, though: how was any day at the office ever going to match that day in the bush?

Shilo and I went home early, leaving Hennie relaying the events of the day to his two drop-jawed juniors. I had something on my mind that I needed to talk to Gerrit about. Despite his tough constitution, I knew this buffalo's injury was extensive and the more I thought about the old bull, the more concerned I was about him pulling through. I also wanted to know the rough time frame for recovery, as while he was licking his wounds, so to speak, this kind of injury may well cause him to become cantankerous, making him a potential danger to the lives of my field rangers.

A buffalo's horn covers a matrix of honeycomb-like bone. These passages open to the sinus cavities and in turn to the brain: this latter aspect of the physiology was worrying me. Gerrit told me to monitor the old bull as often as possible and look for signs of head shaking, sneezing and excessive nasal discharge. Any or a combination of these could indicate blowfly maggot infestation, a sad prognosis indeed, and one with only one solution.

At four every morning for a week, Shilo and I would climb into the Land Cruiser and head out to the general area we knew the buffalo to be sulking in. Fortunately, there was only one waterhole in the vicinity, known as Lion Pan. Although it was actually a small circular cement trough, and not a pan at all, I'd established by the tracks in the mud around the base that he drank there every evening. However, to determine what time he came to drink was difficult and for the first few days the buffalo proved elusive. Shilo would circle the rim of the trough, and using his nose would show me exactly where the buffalo had lowered his head to drink each time. If there had been any maggots or mucus present, evidence would have been left behind on the screed clear to see, or for Shilo to sniff out.

Early on the fifth morning, I assisted Shilo out of the cruiser as I always did, but this time he didn't run to the trough as he had done each time; instead he stood stock-still, staring into the half-light and the dark shadows of the pre-dawn bush surrounding the trough. One spot in particular appeared darker than the rest. As my eyes slowly grew accustomed to the light, the unmistakable silhouette of the one-horned buffalo came into focus. It was the first time we'd seen him since the encounter with Hennie nearly a week before. Proudly he held his one horned head high ... and more importantly, he held it still.

* * *

The one- horned buffalo lived for another nine years, eventually dying of old age. Three days before his carcass was found by our game guards, I saw him on the floodplain in front of the Dinidza Lodge, about three kilometres downriver of my office. At that stage, he had also lost an eye; nevertheless, I'm sure I saw a glint of recognition in the remaining one as he looked at me, then slowly turned away and crossed the river.

28

SHILO'S TWILIGHT YEARS

Time passed and Shilo's age was catching up with him. I could see his waterfowl retrieving days were numbered. And though we were spending a lot of time together while I fished for trout, I knew he still hankered to hunt wildfowl. I searched for the best possible venues, places that didn't involve fourteen-hour marathon road trips and having to break through ice to retrieve birds. But duck hunting is hard work, and the wetlands of the Drakensberg and Free State are far from home. So when 'Zulu' du Toit and his sons Gerrie and Dawie invited me to a social shoot on one of their huge highveld farms near Middleburg, I immediately thought of Shilo and jumped at the opportunity.

Zulu and I first met when he stayed at Motswari for a few days. Using the lodge as a base, he had booked the exclusive use of one of our vehicles, with yours truly as his guide. He was looking to purchase property in the Timbavati, and needed to tap into my knowledge of the area and its wildlife. In the days that followed I drove him around for hours on end; needless to say we became well acquainted. It was also then that he and his two young sons first met Shilo, who after the first morning was invited with us on every drive. Being farmers, they had grown up with dogs; even so, they were intrigued by the close relationship between Shilo and me. When I told them of his penchant for waterfowling, they insisted I bring him along when I went to visit them on their farm that coming season. The Du Toits held one shoot a year, strictly by invitation, and to close family and friends only.

Zulu explained that the occasion was used more as an excuse for those near and dear to get together, than to shoot a few ducks. So for Shilo and me this was a rare privilege indeed; most importantly it meant only three hours of driving, and beautiful highveld winter weather. No pressure ... it was perfect.

* * *

Wildfowling means getting cold, wet, muddy and messy, so minimising any or all of those certainties to a level where they become tolerable, or dare I say it, enjoyable, is what it's all about. Meticulous preparation is all-important, and were one to do this for any other reason, or as the Fenland duck hunters in England used to do, to make a living, it could be described as an onerous, tedious chore. As usual it involved packing so much kit that there was no way I could keep the secret from Shilo, particularly when the odd feather or old cartridge case from a previous trip was unearthed. These insignificant reminders, however subtle, still reeked of memories which he was able to relive in an instant. Shilo whined with excitement and anticipation as I unpacked, checked and repacked the pile of crusty old hunting gear.

Early the next morning I loaded the truck and helped Shilo into the back. With his head out of the canopy window and his ears flapping in the dry bushveld air, we drove out leaving a trailing dust cloud as we set off for the wetlands.

Heading west, the morning sun shining on the Drakensberg at Mariepskop filled my windscreen with a spectacular sight. This vista accompanied us until we drove up from the Lowveld and through the Strydom Tunnel, where suddenly we emerged completely surrounded by sheer rock-faced cliffs, home to the beautiful taita falcon right in the heart of the mountain. From there we made our way past the tufa waterfalls, and eventually climbed out twisting and turning through the orange-studded foothills where a million mountain syringa trees herald the onset of winter. The acacia thornveld around Lydenberg would be the last reminder of bushveld, before we finally reached the relatively treeless highveld.

Climbing to 2 000 metres above sea level the air began to cool noticeably as we headed through Dullstroom and on to Middelburg. Maize fields that seemed to stretch all the way to the horizon dominated the landscape; those lands that hadn't been reaped extended out in neat rows on either side of the road, a calm sea of khaki, standing tall and ready, ripe for harvest. Long before the town itself we turned left off the highway and onto a gravel road that led us through some lower-lying wetland areas. The water in the shallow pans blinked through the hazy, late afternoon sunlight, a promising sight. The moment the tyres began to rumble on the gravel, Shilo leapt off his mattress as though he'd been poked with a cattle prodder. Crossing from one side of the canopy to the other and sticking his head out of alternate windows, he appeared to savour the air until we finally reached our destination, a sprawling ranch-style homestead, at the end of a tree-lined driveway so long it should have been named. Off to the left of the house, in the distance, I could make out horses in what appeared to be paddocks with a row of stables behind that. Moments later I pulled up in front of the house where a meticulously laid out garden created an impression of permanence and pride. The brown winter lawn spread out beneath an almost leafless canopy of pin oaks and poplars; their rust and golden leaves lay strewn about like a loose shaggy carpet ... a most welcoming sight. As if to complete the scene, a smiling Gerrie was there to meet us as we pulled up; I suspect he also needed to control the half a dozen barking dogs that had now surrounded my vehicle. If my memory serves me correctly, among the dogs making up the pack were a couple of Rottweilers, one or two large ridgeback cross boerboels and an English pointer. I had no idea how these dogs would react to Shilo, and he was too excited to feel threatened, so despite his wagging tail giving his mood away, I didn't let him out of the vehicle until later.

'I'm so glad you could make it,' Gerrie said, still beaming from ear to ear. Seeing Shilo in the back, he immediately went over to the canopy window, slid it wider open and made a big fuss of him. Then he turned to me. 'You two settle in and get yourself organised; we're all meeting down there at four,' he said, pointing to a large body of water in the distance.

'Thanks Gerrie,' I said. 'We'll see you there later.'

Later on that afternoon we found Gerrie at the rendezvous point, not too far from the edge of the huge shallow lake. I must admit that I was somewhat relieved to see the farm dogs had been left at home.

'We're just waiting for one more chap to arrive,' Gerrie said, 'then we can move into our positions.'

Looking up from giving Shilo a quick pep talk, I saw the man we had been waiting for walking down the grassy track towards us. He didn't appear to be in any hurry, and there was something vaguely familiar about him. Then, as he got closer, I stood up and looked into his eyes. The mutual recognition was electric: even behind the huge beard, which was longer than I remembered, there was no mistaking who it was; it was my old neighbour from Botswana! The same detestable man who had unjustly accused Shilo of being a 'killer dog' – the dog he had never actually met ... until now, this afternoon.

The conservation circle in South Africa is a small one, and for the most part, everyone knows each other, if not personally then by name at least; nevertheless it was a huge surprise for me to meet 'big beard' again after so long, in the most unlikely of venues. The cold wetlands and maize fields of the highveld were the antithesis of the hot, arid bushveld where our 'battles' had been waged.

What was he doing here on the highveld hunting waterfowl? I asked myself, but as desperately curious as I was to find out, I had no desire to conduct a lengthy conversation with him at this stage. It had been nearly twelve years since he and I had spoken war talk, and although many of the cutting remarks which initially sliced deeply had since been dulled with time, they'd not lost their sting. Understandably, given the circumstances, we were only barely able to shake hands and exchange perfunctory greetings. Putting on my biggest Colgate smile, I maintained my composure, and nobody present appeared to suspect there was bad blood between us. The only one not fooled was 'big beard' himself. In any event, this was neither the venue nor the occasion to defend Shilo's reputation ... Or was it?

Nothing was going to upset Shilo's time, and I made sure he remained unconcerned by the human feud. Shilo didn't pick up any undercurrent, and wagged his tail at 'big beard' in a friendly greeting, as he would with any fellow duck hunter, and who could blame him. There were thousands of ducks out there and Shilo had one thing on his mind, this was his time, these were his finest hours.

To add to my discomfort, everyone was paired off. Obviously the greeting and acknowledgement between 'big beard' and myself was convincing enough, so, no prizes for guessing who Gerrie paired Shilo and me with. Needless to say, I went along with the plans for that afternoon and didn't let on, and to 'big beard's' credit, neither did he.

Shilo was the only dog out in the field that afternoon. As Zulu had explained earlier, this was essentially a social get-together, and it soon became clear that we were among fun shooters and not dedicated wing shooters. Nevertheless, judging by the myriad wildfowl that inhabited the numerous dams and wetlands, I was confident that later that afternoon, there would be at least a few ducks for Shilo to retrieve.

* * *

I stood a good distance away from my 'partner', far enough to avoid any small talk; I also needed to leave enough shooting space between us to ensure we wouldn't be targeting each other's birds. I didn't have too much time to dwell on my misfortune, as it wasn't long before the first wildfowl began to move. Heralded by a number of missed shots from the guns Gerrie had placed on the opposite side of the lake, it was clear that the evening flight had begun. Looking up, I saw hundreds of yellow-billed duck and red-billed teal flying across the huge expanse of water to feed in the ripe maize fields in the surrounding area. A few yellow-bills broke away from the main flight and came towards us, but veered closer to 'big beard', who killed one with his second shot. It fell far into the icy lake, and I could see his hesitation when he realised how deep the water was … he wasn't going to wade into chest-high freezing water for a dead duck. Shilo had seen the bird fall; he sat quivering until I placed my hand on his rump, giving him a gentle shove and the magic word he was waiting for … 'Teksit!' I hissed.

Shilo exploded from my hastily built blind and swam out strongly to retrieve the duck. Clamping it firmly in his mouth, he turned and began swimming straight back towards me. Realising what was happening, I quickly stood up and gesticulated that he was to take the duck to the man who had shot it. Being branded a 'killer' was bad enough, I thought – Shilo didn't need the label 'duck thief' on his rap sheet as well.

Shilo immediately changed direction to the bank close to 'big beard'; there he climbed out of the water, and wasting no time, unceremoniously deposited the duck at the man's feet. Then he turned around, shook himself off and ran straight back to me, there was no time for hanging about, there was work to do … and he knew it.

'Good boy,' I said, swelling with pride as I patted his wet head.

For some reason my shooting was not up to scratch that day. I suspect my mind was focused on this sudden intrusion from the past, which I have to admit was haunting me to distraction. That afternoon I missed a few 'sitters' and all told, Shilo retrieved eight ducks for 'big beard' and six for me. Worse than missing some easy shots was the look I got from my dog each time I did, a sort of confused 'what's wrong with you, mate?' look, the look that no loving dog owner deserves. On the other hand, 'big beard' hadn't fared too badly, and every time Shilo retrieved a duck and deposited it at his feet, I saw him lean forward and pat my 'killer dog'. I also noticed that with each successful retrieve that Shilo made for him, 'big beard's' affectionate demonstration of his gratitude seemed to linger a little longer than the time before.

Typically for that time of the year, the breeze that had persisted for most of the day abated quite suddenly. Blacksmith plovers, greenshanks and avocets took advantage of the lull as they scurried along the edge of relatively calm water hoping for a last tit-bit in the foam on the muddy verge. Looking westward now, I watched as the sun sank below the horizon, bringing another beautiful highveld winter's day to a close in a spectacular display of warm colours that belied the sudden onset of cold. The sky mellowed as streaks of yellow and orange gave way to darkening shades of mauve. A light pinkish hue lingered just long enough to silhouette the skeins of ducks flying high overhead as they returned from feeding to settle in for the night.

I unloaded my gun, preparing to move out of the soggy wet-land before it got too dark, when suddenly I became conscious of Shilo's shivering wet body up against my leg. Reaching down I cupped his head in my hands, but even as I kissed him, his eyes remained firmly fixed on the ducks in the sky behind me. I smiled: 'Tomorrow's birds,' I promised.

It was almost dark now, and I could see the lights of Gerrie's vehicle approaching in the distance. Gathering my ducks, I began to move out of the marsh. 'I'd kill for a cup of coffee,' I remember thinking, as I sloshed my way out of the mud and onto the path that led up to the rendezvous point. Then, as my eyes adjusted to the darkness, I made out a stationary figure up ahead and recognised the familiar outline immediately. It was 'big beard' – and he was waiting for me. As I neared him on the narrow path he stepped forward and extended his hand.

'Mario, I just want you to know I had completely misjudged your dog,' he said. 'I hope you will accept my apology, and that we can bury the hatchet.'

Caught completely off guard, I paused for a moment. It was the last thing I expected from this man, and I found I was ambivalent. Nevertheless, I reached out and shook his hand.

'Sure,' I said.

I couldn't help feeling a little awkward as we turned and walked up the path together, like a couple of old shooting pals who had known each other for ever. There wasn't much to say as we made our way to where the other guys were waiting for us. Looking back over my shoulder, I noticed Shilo was lagging behind a little. He was obviously exhausted. I realised then that despite his enthusiasm there was no hiding the fact that he needed to take things a little easier, I also knew that he wouldn't do it voluntarily; it was going to be up to me to moderate his retrieving tomorrow.

Unbeknown to me, Gerrie had been watching the action through his binoculars that afternoon and witnessed Shilo, in defiance of his age, retrieving for two guns. He was clearly impressed with what he had seen, and although at the time I never fully appreciated the impact Shilo had on him, many years later I would find out just how much.

That evening after supper as I put Shilo to bed, covering him with his cheesy-smelling old blanket, I told him that the weatherman had predicted a bitterly cold night. Then I closed the back of the truck and went through to the lounge where I found everyone huddled around a cozy log fire. Most were sipping some strong stuff, making excuses for missed shots that afternoon, and discussing strategy for the final shoot the following morning. Excusing myself, I went to bed early, and not surprisingly fell asleep easily and slept soundly.

*   *   *

Waking early, as I usually do, it was still dark when I went to let Shilo out of the truck. Opening the back I was pleasantly surprised to find him well rested and raring to go as usual. I was beginning to fold his bedding when I heard the frost on the grass crunching behind me. Someone else had also got up early. Shilo's tail wagged hard against my leg as I turned around to see Gerrie approaching us out of the darkness.

'Morning, Mario, may I join you?' he asked. Then, detecting a modicum of hesitancy in my reply, he added, 'As an observer, just to watch your dog do his thing.'

Of course I was happy and proud to oblige him, but explained that I needed to slow Shilo down, so would be limiting him to no more than half a dozen birds that morning. Needless to say Shilo didn't disappoint – but then, I can't recall that he ever did.

*   *   *

A mixed feeling of contentment qualified with an almost imperceptible twinge of sadness came over me as I drove back to the bush later that day. Instead of lying in the back of the truck on his mattress or staring out of the window, Shilo curled on the front bench seat next to me, his weary but happy head in my lap, while my left hand rested softly on his chest as he slept. It had been a wonderful trip; Shilo had had a great time, we had collected a few ducks for the freezer, and as an unexpected bonus, his reputation had been vindicated by 'big beard' himself. However, this trip had also confirmed something I had been dreading for a while now, something I was reluctant to accept. Inescapably persistent, like that slight ache in your tooth which keeps getting worse, deep down I knew that ignoring it would merely be delaying the inevitable.

As much I would like to have believed otherwise, deep down in my heart I knew that Shilo's swan song had played out on that icy cold morning in the wetlands he loved so much. Reluctantly I began to accept that this episode of his life was over now, and that possibly, even a day boulder-hopping with me on a trout stream could prove to be too much for him.

Living as close to Shilo as I did, I couldn't help but notice the small, barely discernible changes, those subtle indications that his quality of life was slowly deteriorating. It reached a point when, in his fourteenth year, these symptoms were blatantly obvious. He could no longer run more than a few metres before slowing to a trot; even then he was only able to do a few hundred metres before the level of discomfort compelled him to stop and rest a while. He would whimper with frustration whenever he watched me leave the house, and although I hated leaving him behind, he was no longer able to get in and out of the vehicle unaided. I guess he never lost the desire, but the reality was that everything he lived for was becoming difficult to do.

Truth be told, for several years now I had taken Shilo duck hunting because he lived for it, and I just knew it would never be the same without him. Delicious as roast duck with orange sauce is, if Shilo wasn't able to join me in the wetlands, I no longer had any desire to hunt waterfowl. I knew his time and abilities were limited, so the last couple of seasons were all about fulfilling his needs. Essentially I'd kept his love alive as long as it was physically possible for him to enjoy the outing. When Shilo could no longer hunt, I packed up my hand-made decoys, locked my shotgun away and stopped wildfowling altogether.

*   *   *

'Tumour' and 'malignant' – what dreadful words, and never mind how one says them, individually they're bad enough, but the combination conjures up a fear that can instantly dry the saliva in your mouth. If you're fortunate you may hear the word 'benign' instead of 'malignant' attached to 'tumour', an addendum that knocks most of the shock effect out of your worst thoughts. Thankfully Shilo's growths were benign. However, having being active and superbly fit all his life, the effect of these growths on his mobility really began getting to him. As Shilo got older, the lumps grew larger, restricting his movement and causing him increasing discomfort. I suspect that this began to affect him more and more each day, and if dogs could feel depressed as we know it, then that would have been the symptom that best described his demeanour.

Shilo's deterioration was gradual and relatively painless, but the increasing discomfort and frustration was slowly whittling away at his quality of life. When he reached the point where simply getting up to walk around the garden with me became an effort, I knew the day I had dreaded all these years had dawned. I phoned Gerrit, who needed no detailed explanation; he knew from the tone of my voice that it was time. Primarily a wildlife vet at heart, Gerrit never allows himself to get too close to his client's pets on an emotional level, something which I suspect has stemmed from having to do too much of what I was asking of him now. However, Gerrit and I are close friends and Shilo was the one dog that he had a special place in his heart for, so this day especially wasn't simply another day at the office for him. He must have dropped everything and climbed straight into the plane, because a little more than thirty minutes later his little Cessna 182 touched down on Olifants' bush airstrip. We exchanged a solemn greeting and without elaboration drove in virtual silence to the house, and though Gerrit tried hard to take the edge off the vibe, this wasn't the time for small talk and both of us knew that.

As usual, Shilo had heard my vehicle long before we arrived and was waiting for me at the door, smiling so hard he sneezed repeatedly. His tail wagged with increased vigour when he saw Gerrit – he may have thought we were going wildfowling together again, something we hadn't done for a long time. His mind was now occupied with excited anticipation of what he lived for. When Gerrit affectionately ruffled the skin on the back of Shilo's neck, as he usually did when they met, he didn't notice that this time, a pre-prepared tranquilliser was gently injected into the loose folds by those same hands; nor had he noticed that a tearful Meagan had taken Eleana and Dino for a walk up the road past the water tanks – both were too young then to comprehend what was happening, but a concerned, if not confused glance thrown back at me by Eleana told me she could see her father was not himself.

Knowing how sensitive Shilo was, I had agonised over how to go about this; given his incredible perceptive ability, I was mortified that he may suspect something was going to happen. The thought of him feeling the slightest hint of betrayal was almost more than I could bear. But I should have known better, my paranoia was for naught, his mind was not human, it couldn't conceptualise disloyalty, suspicion, lies and premeditation. Shilo trusted me and loved me more than anything, and deep down I knew he'd trust me to the end, which made it all the more difficult to do what I had to.

I tried hard to retain composure, but my legs turned to jelly as I moved through to my bedroom with Shilo following closely behind, his tail still wagging and bumping against the door. A minute or so later Gerrit came up to us and knelt down on the rug next to me. Soon after, in the basket next to my side of the bed, where he always slept, Shilo lay down and got comfortable, then I held his head in my lap while the final 'sleeping' drug was administered. Moments later, the canine love of my life for so many years slipped quietly away in my arms.

* * *

Shilo lies buried under a shady knobthorn tree at the bottom of our garden on Olifants. Here his spirit will live on while his body rests for ever, becoming one with the bush that was his life. There could never be enough space on a headstone for a fitting epitaph to his memory; instead I found a sliver of granite which I cold-chiselled to clearly mark his grave. It reads, simply, 'Shilo'.

* * *

When you are sorrowful, look again in your heart,
and you shall see that in truth you are weeping
for that which has been your delight ...
                                        KAHLIL GIBRAN

Fourteen years later found me in the wetlands of Mpumalanga again, on a farm between the towns of Middelburg and Belfast. This time I was standing alone in the shallows of a small gin-clear lake holding a fly rod in my hand. It had been a typical winter's day on the highveld, and as expected, the icy breeze against my back had dropped slightly as the shadows lengthened. I cast my line in a gentle open loop, then lowered the tip of my rod as if in salute to the setting winter sun, which quickly sank to the horizon. Telltale swirls meant the trout were rising, moving ever closer into the margins as they began feeding on hatching mayflies. Perfect conditions for the dry fly, I thought, as I quickly tied on a size 16 Adams, because I knew as the light faded, I'd no longer be able to see the eye of the tiny hook to thread the line through.

The smooth rumble of a vehicle approaching from behind drew my attention from the water. A luxury 4x4 station wagon was slowly making its way down towards me. I remember thinking that it couldn't be Oom Awie, the owner of the property; he drove a beat-up old Isuzu bakkie, and, although not a fly fisherman, at least he knew it just wasn't cricket to disturb a trout angler fishing the evening rise. The vehicle stopped a discreet distance away; a man climbed out, closed the door quietly, and walked over to me. As he got closer I recognised Gerrie du Toit.

Ever the gentleman, he apologised for the intrusion, explaining that he'd been doing some wildfowling in the area, and Oom Awie had told him I was here. It was really good to see Gerrie after all these years. I put my rod down and we shook hands. This was one time the trout could take a back seat. Hardly had our amicable greeting been dispensed with than he asked after Shilo – I couldn't believe it, he'd remembered my dog's name after fourteen years. When I told him that in fact he'd been witness to Shilo's last retrieve all those years ago, he was visibly moved, and despite the passage of time, offered his sincere condolences. I could see he meant it. A moment later, he looked away from the water and broke the melancholy mood with a huge grin.

'Wait here, Mario,' Gerrie said. Now I could clearly see a glint in his eyes. 'I would like you to meet a couple of my best friends.'

Then he turned and walked back to his vehicle, went around to the back and opened the door. In the fading light I saw two dogs jump out and run towards me, I felt a lump rise in my throat … they were two of the most beautiful black Labrador retrievers I'd ever seen, and for a moment in the fading light they reminded me so much of my beloved Shilo. Though my eyes began to water from the sudden cold as the sun set, the now blurred, but proudly beaming face of Gerrie said it all; he didn't have to say a word. There was no doubt in my mind that Shilo had left a huge impression on him that weekend in the wetlands of his farm, all those years ago. It was obvious that these two magnificent dogs were a manifestation of that: his pride and love for them spoke volumes.

Finally, as he called them away from disturbing the water, he turned to me: 'These are just two of many I've bred,' Gerrie said, making his way back to the vehicle. 'Will you join us later for dinner?'

'I'd love that,' I said, watching as the dogs followed him obediently.

Opening the back door, Gerrie clicked his fingers once, and the dogs leaped into the vehicle. He closed the big tailgate, turned to me and waved goodbye before climbing in. I was sure he was far enough away not to see my face as the memories came flooding back … I lifted my hand in response.

It was calm and still now, the wind had dropped completely, yet my eyes blurred again as I turned back to face the water. Not a ripple creased the lake's oily smooth surface, nor was there a sound, as I wound in the line on my old silent reel.

ACKNOWLEDGEMENTS

This special being came into my life in the form of a beautiful dog, an unexpected and unintentional, but most welcome intrusion. Shilo was the primary inspiration among the other myriad influences that cultivated the fertile field I grew up and matured in. Unknowingly, he contributed to the quality of my life, helped shape the person I am, the way I think, and the way I perceive what is around me. Shilo was the most loyal companion anybody could wish for; he also gave me invaluable insight into many aspects of the bush, lessons that no book could ever have taught me, some of which I owe my life to. In response, I feel gratitude alone falls frustratingly short of what I'm able to express here except to say that I can only hope that this book helps to keep his memory alive – he deserves nothing less ... Thank you, Shilo.

Unavoidably I also happened to bump into a number of beautiful people along the way, in fact, many more than I will be mentioning here. To those who have touched my life but appear forgotten, please know you are indeed remembered, and you live through my words somewhere in the pages of this book.

Thanks first to Meagan, my loving wife and companion, a colleague, a shoulder to cry on and on occasion, the voice of reason in a cacophony of chaos, and yes, we can confirm that even in the bush, life can get quite hectic. Thanks for being the best mother in the world to our children and for 'falling for Shilo' ... Yeah right! I am also deeply indebted to her understanding of the more 'delicate' moments to which I have referred in this book, from a time before she met Shilo and me. Her capacity for patience, her keen eye for detail and her support have contributed in no small measure to this publication. I am especially grateful to my children, who have patiently supported me and understood that there were times when I needed to focus on the memories of somebody else equally close to my heart for a while. What can I say? I am truly proud of them. To my beautiful daughter Eleana, a published poet in her own right, your thoughts on this aspect of the book were invaluable. To my son Dino, whose youthful opinion and insight I often sought and took into account. Thank you both.

Thank you to all my family who have never seen much of me since I left for the bush nearly thirty-five years ago, but were always there when I needed them. Also, to my close friends who, since our childhood, have always had been happy to take second place to the bush – André van Vollenstee, Tyrone Stevenson, Barry Ryan and William Watson. To Howard Walker for his loyal friendship and for introducing me to this country's fly fishing doyen, Tom Sutcliffe, who unwittingly, along with the late Steve Kruger and Rob Mann, were in many ways my mentors, as was Desmond Prout Jones, who never doubted I would make conservation my life. A special word of thanks to my aunt Joan, who wrote my first bush job application to Mala Mala, and to Arlene Fortune who against all odds put her faith in my ability to manage Bushfillan Safaris in Botswana; to David and Willem van den Berg, thank you for a lifetime's access to what I believe to be one of the finest waterfowl habitats in South Africa, and where no doubt part of Shilo's soul will linger forever. Thanks to Paul and Mechtild Geiger, who took a chance on Meagan and me by giving us the opportunity to prove that our dogs were a valuable contribution to the package when they employed us in the Timbavati. To Neil and Morag Hulett, now shareholders of Olifants River Game Reserve, who didn't know me at the time of Shilo, but who, through mutual friends and colleagues, knew of me. Thank you for your sincere friendship and support over the years.

I count myself privileged to know Mark Jevon, fellow dog

lover and bushman, whose respect for the environment and ethics afield with rod or rifle is enviable. Thanks also to Irving Stevenson for introducing me to the Timbavati, and the finer points of wing shooting, both of which became turning points in my life. My special thanks to the late Edward Engela, 'Uncle Ed', who unselfishly took me in as one of the family, and was like a second father to me, an avid outdoorsman with a remarkable fondness and understanding of dogs. To his daughter Bernice, once my fiancée, who was an important part of my life before Shilo, and for whom I shall always reserve a special place in my heart. To Ockert Brits, 'Ockie', for his support and help, which went beyond his normal duty, and without whose persistence Shilo may never have come into my life.

My appreciation, in poignant reflection, goes to Vee Thompson, née Mascall, for dumping me with 'the baby'. In a twist of irony you left behind a bundle of unconditional love that never left me. Undoubtedly this was a pivotal point, the beginning of my life with Shilo, an odyssey indelibly etched in my memory, and without which, the inspiration for this book may never have culminated in its manifestation.

To the veterinarians in Shilo's life – in particular, my eternal gratitude and respect to my good friend Gerrit Scheepers, who has also proved to be a wildlife vet of distinction. To Drs RJ Leadsome, Duncan McWherter and Melvyn Greenberg, though the part you played in Shilo's life may have been relatively small, you have nonetheless been remembered and appreciated.

Thanks also to the unsung heroes of the bush; in particular, to the finest trackers I've known, notably, the late Phinias Sibuyi, who left an indelible mark on our lives. To the many other brave and dedicated anti-poaching rangers and trackers, among whom Jabulaan Makhubedu, Joachim Ntimane, Jose Ngoveni, Paolo Makhuvela, and Januarie Mahlula, as well as John Sibuyi and Kimbian, who showed me the ways of the bush that only a few are privy to. I only wish there were more men like them out in the field today practising the art of tracking, and passing their knowledge on to the next generation.

My apologies go to the family heirs of Carl Weavind, whom,

despite diligent search, I was unable to locate. I wish to thank them for his account of the history of the early inhabitants of Klaserie area and surrounds, to which I refer in Chapter 25.

As the Dog Whisperer Cesar Millan said: 'It takes a pack to raise a dog and a village to raise a child.' So too do story tellers mature by surrounding themselves with the knowledge and experience of professional publishing people. To this end my sincere gratitude goes to the team at Jonathan Ball Publishers. In particular, my grateful thanks go to publishing director Jeremy Boraine, who gave this publication a high degree of latitude and personal commitment. To production manager Francine Blum whose experience, genuine warmth and bubbly personality helped round off the edges and maintain the right perspective throughout. And though some may say I am good story teller, it has taken Frances Perryer, using her extraordinary skill in editing and her deep empathy for animals, to polish my manuscript, which has culminated in a book that has been lovingly crafted, and of which I am very proud. Thank you, Frances. To Valda Strauss, your control of the proofreading is a little like the trust I put in pilots when I nod off to asleep on an aircraft; you elicit that same comfortable 'I feel safe in your hands' feeling. The cover design screams *pick me up!* But marketing aside, it has an extremely poignant feel for me personally, and once read, I suspect many readers will feel the same way each time they close the book and look at it. Thank you Michiel Botha and Kevin Shenton for the book's layout and design – using Jeremy's words now … 'It's a winner!'

And last of all, but by no means least, my sincerest gratitude goes out to all those dogs that have given, and those that continue to give, unconditional loyalty to their owners, love and companionship to the lonely, sight to the blind, protection to the vulnerable, and hope to those who would otherwise never be found. You are all an inspiration to mankind, not the least being me. Thank you.